British Writing from to Brexit

Writing, Identity, and Nation

Robert Spencer, Howard J. Booth, and Anastasia Valassopoulos

LONDON AND NEW YORK

Designed cover image: JohnatAPW, Getty

First published 2025
by Routledge
4 Park Square, Milton Park, Abingdon, Oxon OX14 4RN

and by Routledge
605 Third Avenue, New York, NY 10158

Routledge is an imprint of the Taylor & Francis Group, an informa business

© 2025 Robert Spencer, Howard J. Booth, and Anastasia Valassopoulos

The right of Robert Spencer, Howard J. Booth, and Anastasia Valassopoulos to be identified as authors of this work has been asserted in accordance with sections 77 and 78 of the Copyright, Designs and Patents Act 1988.

All rights reserved. No part of this book may be reprinted or reproduced or utilised in any form or by any electronic, mechanical, or other means, now known or hereafter invented, including photocopying and recording, or in any information storage or retrieval system, without permission in writing from the publishers.

Trademark notice: Product or corporate names may be trademarks or registered trademarks, and are used only for identification and explanation without intent to infringe.

British Library Cataloguing-in-Publication Data
A catalogue record for this book is available from the British Library

Library of Congress Cataloging-in-Publication Data
Names: Spencer, Robert, 1977– author. | Booth, Howard J. (Howard John), 1969– author. | Valassopoulos, Anastasia, 1973– author.
Title: British writing from empire to Brexit : writing, identity and nation / Robert Spencer, Howard J. Booth and Anastasia Valassopoulos.
Description: London ; New York : Routledge, 2025. | Includes bibliographical references and index.
Identifiers: LCCN 2024042000 (print) | LCCN 2024042001 (ebook) | ISBN 9781032137889 (hardback) | ISBN 9781032137865 (paperback) | ISBN 9781003230816 (ebook)
Subjects: LCSH: National characteristics, British, in literature. | European Union—Great Britain. | Great Britain—In literature. | Literature and society—England—History—19th century. | Literature and society—England—History—20th century. | English literature—19th century—History and criticism. | English literature—20th century—History and criticism.
Classification: LCC PR468.N293 S64 2025 (print) | LCC PR468.N293 (ebook) | DDC 820.9/358—dc23/eng/20241021
LC record available at https://lccn.loc.gov/2024042000
LC ebook record available at https://lccn.loc.gov/2024042001

ISBN: 978-1-032-13788-9 (hbk)
ISBN: 978-1-032-13786-5 (pbk)
ISBN: 978-1-003-23081-6 (ebk)

DOI: 10.4324/9781003230816

Typeset in Times New Roman
by Apex CoVantage, LLC

Contents

	Introduction: Breaking Britain	1
1	Nation, Empire, and Identity in Late Colonial British Writing, 1900–1948	24
2	Post-War Unsettlement, 1948–1980	90
3	'We Have Been Made Again', 1980–2016	135
	Conclusion	183
	Index	*193*

Introduction

Breaking Britain

Not only Britain's tortuous departure from the European Union but also the British state's woeful response to the Coronavirus pandemic and the disturbing intensification in recent years of nationalist and racist ideologies all show that the supposedly United Kingdom of Great Britain and Northern Ireland is in a state, if not of decline (for that, as we shall see, is precisely the wrong word for it), then of a kind of terminal debasement and retrogression.[1] The UK, or Britain, and more especially, England, is an unhappy and backward-looking place. Bedevilled by nostalgias and mythologies, profoundly unequal and undemocratic, its elites brazenly unaccountable, its institutions alarmingly dysfunctional, this peculiar entity increasingly resembles a 'banana monarchy', in the historian David Edgerton's scathing description.[2] What it sorely requires is a vision of a future that is characterised by something other than melancholy dreams of empire, obsolete fantasies of unity, impregnable island myths, anti-immigrant demagoguery, and retro visions of whiteness and social order. The sooner we say farewell to this bizarre and redundant entity, the better. We see the twentieth and the twenty-first centuries as staging the all-too-slow 'break-up of Britain' (to invoke, not for the final time, the title of Tom Nairn's important study), the anguished dissolution but also the rearguard reiteration of ideologies of empire, class, gender, race, Crown, and state. This book is a study of how, from empire to Brexit, important canonical and non-canonical literary texts have dramatised a paradoxical process of debasement and dissolution, retrogression, and potential reconstruction.

The nation of Britain effectively came into being in the eighteenth century with the final unification of the island of Britain, followed in 1800 by the temporary absorption of 'John Bull's other island', Ireland. What this process of expansion shows, however, is that, in a sense, Britain is not really a nation at all but an empire, a ruthless, though often prosperous, but also very destructive and increasingly (during the twentieth and the twenty-first centuries) fissiparous vehicle for incorporating very different regions, nations, and social groups. Moreover, looked at slightly differently, the nation state of the UK is more state than nation; it is an entity in which power flows from the top downwards, rather than in the other direction, a territory formed and ruled over by centralised and exclusive institutions (the monarchy, the crown-in-parliament, undemocratic political parties, the City of London, the public schools, etc.) that are piloted by a highly class-conscious elite.

DOI: 10.4324/9781003230816-1

The death of the Queen in 2022 and the coronation of Charles III were extremely instructive moments in contemporary British history, though not so much because of any outpouring of popular royalist sentiments, which were, in truth, no less but also no more than we have learned to expect at these monarchical milestones. The highly choreographed wall-to-wall media coverage of the numerous faux-archaic ceremonial rites, plus the unedifying stampede of emoting loyal politicians, showed the dependence of this largely self-selecting ruling class on the monarchy. Not only does the government exercise extensive powers of patronage on behalf of the monarch (in return for which the Windsors enjoy various legal and fiscal impunities), but the Crown is also, in fact, as Nairn has argued, '*the* ideology of United Kingdom statehood'; it is the 'emotive tissue' that binds the people to the state, whereas republican state formations have ideologies and institutions that work in the other direction, to make the state accountable to the people.[3] That tissue is now rather frayed, to be sure, not to say soiled, given how demoralised this wildly unequal banana monarchy has now become. But what else is there, other than periodic pageantries and callous crackdowns on immigrants and other minorities, to imbue this tenuously multi-national and definitively post-imperial state nation with a sense of itself?

This is one of the first and most important things we wish to note about Britishness: there is no real popular or democratic aspect to it. Other nations have their founding revolutions; the UK does not. Whereas the United States has 1776 and the Revolutionary War, France has 1789, Ghana 1957, Paraguay 1811, Italy 1861 or 1946, and so on, the UK has 1688 (a supposedly glorious supposed revolution that saw the restoration of a Protestant monarchy and an expedient alliance of ruling groups) or, at best, the highly mythologised date of 1940 (which marks a successful resistance to invasion, but not a popular overthrow of an oppressor). Up to now in world history, no better conduit for democratic institutions has been developed than the nation state. This fact is unfortunate in several senses, because nations are usually defined in exclusionary ways. The first thing one notices about them is that they have real as well as imaginative borders and that the distinctions they enforce between citizens and non-citizens are frequently drawn in ways that are explicitly or implicitly racialised. Rights of citizenship are also affected by factors such as culture, gender, sexuality, ethnicity, and religion. But one of the admirable things about nation states is that their legal and political institutions, which were often founded as a result of resistance to some domestic or foreign oppressor, provide opportunities for people to assert their rights and redress their grievances. This is not quite the case with the UK, we shall argue. It is not a nation of this kind but the tattered remnant of an empire, an intensely hierarchical state, albeit a moribund one, an assemblage of disparate nations, regions, and interests forcibly soldered together and now slowly falling apart.

'Britain' is the name given to this now-waning process of territorial incorporation, and 'Britishness' to the forms of undemocratic and chauvinistic identity that underpinned it. When we are talking about Britain and Britishness, then, we are referring to the particularly unpromising ways in which this nation state, or rather state nation, has been constructed and imagined. For a start, Britain is a state and an identity that are highly stratified and class-bound. Britain is presided over by a ruling group that is largely English and largely Southern English and that, these days, makes most of its money in the financial centre of the City of London. That group is allied to various clients, offshoots, and dependent classes in England and the rest of the UK. Britain, which was created from above by the state and not from below by a nation or demos, is inseparable from its unusually powerful and centralised state and from the state's institutions and symbols, including the Crown. Furthermore, Britain is mostly comprised of England, which makes up most of its territory and by far the largest part of Britain's population. *England* used to be employed as a synonym for *Britain*, of course, a usage which reflected the greater presence and priority of England and particularly its ruling bloc in the union, something that nationalist movements in Wales, Scotland, and of course (with most success), Ireland have resisted.

Since Britain and Britishness emerged as part of a process of territorial and colonial expansion, and since the exploitation of people of colour was the route to the island's economic take-off, they have both been defined in racialised terms. Britain, in short, is red, *white*, and blue. This was the case during the age of empire, which, in its simplest terms, meant the violent and lucrative rule by white people over non-white people, particularly via plantation slavery, but also during the period of post-imperial retrenchment after 1945, when 'Britain' was partly redefined as a nation with, as we shall see in detail in Chapter 2, immigration policies designed to keep the nation as white as possible. Even today, Britain remains what the historian Charlotte Lydia Riley calls 'Imperial Island', not only because it has failed to work through the various material, ideological, cultural, and demographic legacies of empire, but also because it has failed to alter the economic shape Britain assumed in the late colonial era; the City of London retains its corrupt relationships with the Gulf monarchies as well as a network of tax havens in miniature protectorates in the Caribbean.[4] Moreover, Atlanticism is the non-negotiable core of British foreign policy, what remains of its world role being to support the United States' endeavours, in major wars, at the United Nations, and at major financial institutions, such as the IMF and the World Bank, to deter rival sources of power and perpetuate imbalances in world trade.

We would add that Britain has frequently been defined in explicitly gendered terms too, partly because of the particular form of imperial masculinity fostered by colonial expansion in the latter half of the nineteenth century, but also because, like other advanced capitalist economies, the British economy has been dependent on a highly gendered division of labour. In *The Postcolonial Body in Queer Space and Time*, Rebecca Fine Romanow refers to the way gender and sexual norms have been policed alongside race and class, in Britain and in Britain's colonies, as 'normative alliances of nationhood'.[5] Anne McClintock's classic *Imperial Leather: Race, Gender, and Sexuality in the Colonial Contest* characterises British imperialism as a patriarchal reproductive order, one of the chief purposes of which was to appropriate 'the sexual and labor power of colonized women'.[6] In short, the imposition of strict hierarchies of class, gender, race, and sexuality was integral to the accumulation strategies of British imperialism. The ways in which texts by women writers, as well as queer and gender-non-conforming writers, disrupt the highly sexist and heteronormative character of Britain and Britishness, its 'normative alliances of nationhood', will be a central part of our narrative.

It is easy to forget, incidentally, how recently the abbreviation 'UK' or the mouthful 'United Kingdom of Great Britain and Northern Ireland' started to be used. The 'UK' designates an entity that only came into being in 1922 with the formation of the Irish Free State and of the six-county statelet in Ulster. The name, Raymond Williams suggests, seeking to defamiliarise this synthetic and esoteric entity, 'should be spelled as it so barbarously sounds – the United Kingdom, the Yookay'.[7] Tom Nairn and Perry Anderson, by the way, both sometimes refer to the UK as 'Ukania' in order to liken the state's absurd flummery to Robert Musil's portrait of the dying Austro-Hungarian Empire as 'Kakania' in *The Man Without Qualities*, a neat, if somewhat niche, gag. Suffice it to say, any nation that has to assert its own unity in its name presumably has something to hide, that is, the intrinsic disunity and the cobbled-together quality of a nation that is, in fact, constantly changing its shape, getting vastly bigger until 1922, and thereafter slowly crumbling to pieces. Norman Davies refers to the place simply as 'The Isles'. 'England', he observes, is typically mistaken for 'Britain', just as 'Britain' or the 'British Isles' are commonly confused with the whole archipelago of Britain, Ireland, the Isle of Man, Shetland, etc. Davies rightly objects to this widespread but totally mistaken belief in the unbroken continuity and unanimity of what is often complacently referred to as 'our island history'.[8] It is striking, for example, how often 'England' itself is represented with markers that are largely derived from the South, and especially the so-called Home Counties around London. The characteristic 'English' landscape is a bucolic and essentially pre-industrial one, the cultivated and orderly scenery of Jane Austen serials on the BBC or pre-war railway posters. Dreaming of the battered landscapes of the industrial North in 'Letter to Lord Byron' (1937), W. H. Auden rebuffed this kind of selective representation:

Tramlines and slagheaps, pieces of machinery,
That was, and still is, my ideal scenery.[9]

In short, a diverse and amorphous archipelago has been rudely soldered together by the assimilatory and effectively colonial ambitions of the class and state that have historically controlled it, that class and state being falsely mistaken for England, England being falsely mistaken for Britain, and then Britain being falsely mistaken for the whole of the isles and for colonial possessions further afield. England and its expansionist alias, 'Britain', are now obsolete as well as insufferable. Britain is no longer what Charles Dilke called it in the nineteenth century: *Greater Britain*. It is an empire without colonies, just as Britain is now a state without a nation. It is a fantastic 'Crown-and-Capital land', 'not really a nation state at all' in Nairn's close-to-the-bone assessment, but 'a Southern-lowland hegemonic bloc uniting an hereditary élite to the central processing unit of commercial and financial capital'.[10]

Britain, we agree, is a largely obsolete construction. Yet particularly since the Brexit vote in 2016, the dark sun or collapsing supernova of this moribund state nation has exerted a baleful pull on the various forces and bodies trying to escape it. The 'break-up of Britain' prophesied by Nairn in the late 1970s has not yet come to pass. The socialist challenge that appeared out of nowhere in 2015 has been put back in its box.[11] The British state is like the Cumaean Sibyl, fated to live forever but destined to wither into ever-greater decrepitude. Perhaps most tellingly and distressingly, this decrepit state's persecution and actual deportation and hounding to their deaths of elderly Black Britons from the Windrush generation led, at best, to a momentary spasm of national introspection; that the perpetrators have not begged for forgiveness or been chased from public life is perhaps the most powerful summation of the national malaise.[12]

This is the first study to read twentieth- and twenty-first-century British writing from the perspective of the Brexit vote and its repercussions. We look, for example, at D. H. Lawrence's *The Rainbow* (1915) as a subtle critique of empire and an exploration of the galvanising effects of immigration, at conflicted perspectives on empire and ideologies of race in post-war plays, such as J. B. Priestley's *Summer Day's Dream* (1949) and John Osborne's *The Entertainer* (1957), and at examinations of the politics of belonging in novels by Sam Selvon and Kamala Markandaya in the 1950s and 1960s. The literature of Britain from empire to Brexit ought to be understood in the light of repeated challenges to the British state nation's colonial and overly centralised as well as highly class-bound and patriarchal structure. But the story of this archipelago really must not be presented as a centrifugal one, in which new forces gradually escape the tractor beam of a strong centre. That process is radically unfinished, according to the literary texts examined in this study, as sobering explorations of the persistent barriers to the break-up of Britain and Britishness show even in the contemporary works that we look at in Chapter 3 and the Conclusion. That strong centre continues to exert a powerful, if hopefully diminishing, gravitational pull.

The twentieth century, it is true, has seen the independence of most of Ireland, the decolonisation of almost all of the rest of the empire, the emergence of separatist movements in Wales and especially Scotland, and the assertion of deeply felt regional identities, as well as the periodic emergence of movements for radical socialist reconstruction. Most of the texts studied in the subsequent chapters amplify the dissentient perspectives of, for example, queer, working-class, immigrant, postcolonial, Black and Asian, and women writers, categories that overlap in pleasing and revealing ways. Many of those texts spurn the dogged hierarchies of a still semi-feudal class structure as well as the complacencies of the dominant xenophobic and melancholically post-imperial forms of English and British national identity. Nevertheless, we think it would be a mistake to see British writing over the last century as only a story of liberation. It is also, alas, the story of 'the persistence of the old regime' (to invoke Arno Mayer's resonant phrase).[13]

This study partly accepts what is rather grandly referred to on the Left as the 'Nairn–Anderson thesis' that Britons failed to renovate their antiquated and unequal society and economy during the twentieth century. Anderson assembled a detailed explanation of the Yookay's sclerotic political and economic structures in more than a score of articles in the pages of *New Left Review* since the mid-1960s, starting with 'Origins of the Present Crisis' in 1964, 'Components of the National Culture' in 1968, and 'The Figures of Descent' in 1987 (collected and slightly amended in Anderson's 1992 book *English Questions*), all the way up to 2020's 'Ukania Perpetua?', a defence, partial modification, and helpful summary of the arguments. Essays over the years by Nairn on the British political elite, Scottish nationalism, patterns of English landownership, the economic and constitutional timidity of the Labour Party, European integration, the monarchy, and so on have been fleshed out in important longer studies, including *The Break-Up of Britain* from 1977 and *The Enchanted Glass: Britain and its Monarchy* in 1994.[14]

In a nutshell, the Nairn–Anderson thesis is that the rumbling crisis of the British state, economy, and society since the 1960s can be traced all the way back to the peculiar class configurations contrived in the seventeenth century. In short, the UK has never had a proper revolution. Furthermore, it is not a democracy. The country has paradoxically been hobbled by the fact that capitalism developed there first and more thoroughly than elsewhere. The dominant aristocratic stratum made itself over into capitalist landlords and later into financial capitalists and imperialists. The bourgeoisie found this group no obstacle to its own emergence and enrichment, so these two groups effectively shared the power of a state that had become increasingly centralised after the Reformation and the Civil War. After the defeat of Chartism in the 1840s, Anderson claims, there has never been a radical trade union movement or mass socialist party or a disenfranchised, and therefore militant, intelligentsia of any significance.[15] We think this narrative is broadly true, though, as we will argue presently, it understates the prevalence of traditions of dissent.

To be clear, we are not saying that there have been no rebellions or upheavals in these islands' histories since the medieval period: there have been major wars, such as the Civil War or Wars of the Three Kingdoms in the 1640s; the Jacobite risings between 1689 and 1745 that pressed the claims of the Stuart pretenders and also contested the Whig settlement of 1689; proto-socialist movements like the Levellers and the Diggers, the Merthyr Rising of 1831, and the Luddite Rebellion of the 1810s; actual socialist movements, such as the militant syndicalism of the early 1910s, Red Clydeside after the First World War, and the New Left of the 1960s; or the Irish Revolution of 1916–1923. But only the last one founded a new state with new institutions. None of the major anti-colonial revolutions that shook the British Empire in the American colonies after 1776 or in Jamaica in the 1830s or in Kenya in the 1950s rebounded on Britain itself the way the Algerian War of Independence precipitated the collapse of the French Fourth Republic in 1958 or military defeat in Portugal's African colonies brought down the Estado Novo regime in 1974. There were no externally imposed dictatorships that produced radical insurgencies in the way the collaborationist Republic of Salò begat the Northern Resistance in Italy after 1943, liberation, a new constitution, and the exile of the House of Savoy.

Nor has Britain been invaded, unless one counts William and Mary's landing at Brixham in 1688 and their bloodless march to London, where they inserted themselves into the existing structures and institutions of power. We think the historian Steven Pincus is wrong to call 1688–1689 'the first modern revolution', because while the overthrow of James II may have enjoyed plenty of popular support and while the joint monarchs may have introduced new policies (such as war with France and a reformed bureaucracy), Britain and, least of all, Ireland, or the rest of the nation's colonies, can be said to have become anything like democracies after 1688.[16] The Glorious Revolution was not a revolution at all but an elite machination, an expedient alliance between the landed aristocracy and the financial aristocracy, which paved the way for the advent of an industrial bourgeoisie a century later. Invasion and liberation founded new states with new constitutions in Germany and Japan at the end of the Second World War, while invasion followed by occupation, resistance, and eventual liberation has birthed new states in far too many postcolonial nations to list. From Napoleon's planned invasion to the German air attacks of 1940, conquests of Britain never got beyond the first hurdle, a good thing, of course, though we are stressing that, whatever its expedient modifications over the centuries, state and class power in Britain have proved strikingly invulnerable to transformative change. As Anderson argues:

> After 1688, the state was never again formally altered, nor was a new Constitution ever proclaimed. Rather, piecemeal reforms of suffrage or administration, in homeopathic doses, slowly modified the structures of traditional power and privilege, without ever radically redrawing them at a stroke.[17]

To be clear, by *revolution* we mean *transformative democratisation*. Virtually all the conspiracies and mutinies in Britain since the seventeenth century have bashed their heads against the basically unchanging nature of class rule. In Britain, revolutions either fail or are not revolutions at all but palace coups. We think it is true that Britain's early economic 'success' in the form of colonial expansion and lopsided domestic development froze the British state 'half-way between feudal and modern forms'.[18] It became adept at economic accumulation, social integration, and political absorption but totally unfitted for any form of substantive democratisation or redistribution.

The nationalism that took hold in Britain had nothing democratic, let alone revolutionary, about it; rather, it was a kind of elite or 'great power' nationalism, as Nairn argues, that 'was innocent of the key, populist notion informing' most nationalisms: 'the idea of the virtuous power of popular protest and action'.[19] As Linda Colley contends in *Britons: Forging the Nation, 1707–1837*, the popular British nationalism that developed during the Napoleonic Wars was fixated on empire, the Crown, Protestantism, war, and social order.[20] But whereas Colley tends to admire this popular nationalism because she thinks that it enabled women and working people generally to play a role in the life of an increasingly prosperous nation and its empire, we see British nationalism as irredeemably hierarchical, undemocratic, and exclusionary. The nationalisms of most other Western European nation states, such as, for example, France and Italy, are also ways of popularising elite priorities in this way, of course, though the main purpose and value of the Nairn–Anderson thesis is to point out that in Britain the state's regressive structures, institutions, and attitudes are not offset or contested to the same degree.

For what it is worth, we think Nairn and Anderson are simply incorrect when they suggest that Britain has almost entirely lacked significant socialist and anti-imperialist political and intellectual traditions.[21] The Marxist historian E. P. Thompson offered an early critique along these lines. Thompson particularly objected to Nairn's crude portrait of 'a dilettante literary culture descended from the aristocracy'.[22] Where does that sweeping judgement leave, say, Romanticism or the nineteenth-century realist novel? 'What the authors overlook is the enormous importance of that part of the revolutionary inheritance which may be described, in a secular sense, as the tradition of *dissent*.'[23] The problem with these dissenting traditions is not that they do not exist but that they have never come close to wielding power.

In a thorough evaluation of the Nairn–Anderson thesis, Ellen Meiksins Wood argues that lopsided modernisation has been the characteristic pattern of British 'development' since at least the seventeenth century, extensive (though violently expansionist and highly uneven) economic development going hand in hand with archaic political structures.[24] The British state has thus been a success rather than a failure, at least in its own terms and from the perspective of its ruling class. Britain turned out the way it did (intensely hierarchical, undemocratic, and unequal) as a result of the way a highly centralised state and a highly class-conscious ruling 'elite' monopolised a political and economic power that depended on the absorption and control of territories and their resources, first Wales in the 1530s, then Scotland in 1707, and Ireland in the nineteenth century, along with an empire of territories, staging posts, and investments in India, Africa, and the Caribbean in the nineteenth century. 'The union' of Great Britain was assembled in order to construct a common internal market and an integrated fiscal system, to ensure the islands' defence from French invasion, and to project their power outwards with the aid of a powerful navy.

From the seventeenth century, England, and later Britain, was able to use its distance from the continent and its maritime power to beat rivals, obtain settlements, open up markets, and control the lucrative slave trade. The enormous wealth drained from India and the proceeds of Caribbean slavery were partly invested in new industrial concerns in Britain in the nineteenth century. Increasingly, this capital was invested in the formal and informal empires and elsewhere; by 1913, 'perhaps half the world's total of foreign investment had been raised in London', according to John Darwin.[25] So British capitalism was more and more divided between its industrial and financial branches. British industry was allowed to atrophy and was eventually overtaken by better-equipped competitors after the First and especially after the Second World War, before wholesale deindustrialisation became effective government policy in the 1980s and after. As Tom Hazeldine argues, there is still a huge divide between the City with its Southern hinterlands and a North that industrialised early but then gradually lost its technological advantages and global competitiveness.[26]

Britain's economy remains dominated by the needs of the City, once the epicentre of colonial expansion and, particularly since the 1980s, a 'service-zone to international capital',[27] in Anderson's phrase, or Wall Street's Guantanamo in Peter

Gowan's.[28] To use one of Anderson's favourite terms for it, the 'Yookay' remains economically 'everted' (turned inside out), with the City of London connected to a network of offshore tax havens in the empire's holdouts in the Caribbean, such as the Cayman Islands and the British Virgin Islands. Britain now focuses almost entirely on dubious 'financial services' in the City, where American-, Japanese-, and European-owned banks take advantage of low taxes and a 'relaxed regulatory environment' to multiply the surplus capital of petro-states and post-Soviet oligarchs. The enormous wealth of the City of London is surrounded by little islands of prosperity and much larger oceans of dilapidation, deprivation, and disgruntlement. Britain, if we are honest, consists of an immensely privileged financial centre, a services sector, and a runaway property market ruled over by a network of unscrupulous people whose goal is simply predation or parasitism.[29] Executives of companies, for examples, are rewarded for increasing share prices and sweating monopolies, not, as the flooding of Britain's rivers and seas with human excrement since 2019 proves, for long-term investments in infrastructure. Politics is concerned with shoring up discredited institutions and redirecting public anger at scapegoats rather than with acknowledging, let alone addressing, the social and other costs of extreme inequality. The aim seems to be to keep the racket going for a few more years while kicking various cans (collapsing public services, decrepit infrastructure, declining biodiversity, energy dependence, pandemic unpreparedness, demographic ageing, regional inequality, low productivity, low wages, high levels of debt, etc.) endlessly down the road.

Still the task remains: How is it possible to break away from the slowly collapsing sun of class and state power in a perennially waning 'Ukania'? In the absence of another party or movement that speaks clearly and consistently to their fears and aspirations, some working-class voters have gone over to the Brexit fantasy and its sponsors, either falling for fraudulent pledges to 'level up' the regions or settling for xenophobia and imperial nostalgia. Brexit's most dedicated supporters, however, remain the asset-rich and, therefore, largely recession-proof denizens of the shires who dream of cultural homogeneity and a bygone *national* capitalism. Brexit feeds off various and often incompatible resentments, some of them real and many of them almost entirely imaginary. It was a kind of blank canvas onto which those grievances could be projected, though by now the projection onto that canvas of so many different urges makes it look more like one of Jackson Pollock's. The 52% is made up of an uneasy coalition of what David Edgerton calls 'inchoate nostalgias', dreams of restoring racial and cultural homogeneity, but also the ambition of the financial oligarchy to free themselves from all obligations and regulations, and among other social groups a vague yearning for the economic sovereignty that has been lost since the 1970s (though not to the EU).[30]

It needs to be stated that, for many Brexit voters, the chance to vote Leave simply represented an opportunity to make foreigners and minorities go away. The Leave.EU wing of the Leave campaign, headed by Nigel Farage, dedicated itself to this kind of anti-immigrant demagoguery. The likes of Farage and Aaron Banks and the self-styled 'Spartans' of the Tory Party's 'European Research Group' dream of an 'Empire 2.0'. Presumably, this empire would commit itself not to the acquisition of actual colonies but to elaborate forms of unregulated financial chicanery. Hence the bizarre Frankenstein's monster-like appearance of the Brexit coalition, part elite power grab on behalf of finance capital and part plebeian insurgency *against* finance capital's manifold depredations. The point is that Brexit is a boon for impractical nostalgists.

Many Britons have embraced a kind of scapegoat nationalism, the main purpose of which is to belittle out-groups: shirking welfare claimants, grasping refugees in dinghies, privileged climate change activists, statue-toppling BLM protesters, 'woke' humanities students, bathroom-visiting trans people, and so on.[31] Indeed, one of the most deplorable political developments of recent years has been the way conservative gender norms have become rallying points for reactionary nationalisms. From Duterte's Philippines to Trump's America and Modi's India to Brexit Britain, as Pankaj Mishra has argued, right-wing insurgencies are being powered by the self-interest of the super-rich allied to the self-pity of the insecurely affluent middle class. Mishra points to 'the incendiary appeal of victimhood in societies built around the pursuit of wealth and power'.[32]

Another of the most disturbing developments in contemporary British life, as Peter Mitchell has shown, is the intensification of imperial nostalgia. Just as the authoritarian British state and its everted colonial economy were shaped by empire, so has empire lastingly shaped British culture, including its fantasies of supremacy and what Mitchell calls 'the deep structure of how we engage with race, class and gender'.[33] When politicians or newspapers or social media provocateurs bewail the removal of the slave trader Edward Colston's statue in Bristol, for example, or the National Trust's investigation of its properties' links with the slave trade or the banning of 'Rule, Britannia!' at the last night of the Proms, they are not so much defending the empire, which they rarely trouble to talk about in any detail. More precisely, these loudly disseminated, misrepresented, and (in the case of the last example) often entirely fabricated talking and rallying points allow for the affirmation of ideas that are tricky to espouse outright but that the empire can be made to implicitly stand in for, especially hierarchical ways of thinking about nation, gender, and especially race. For imperialists, Britain was, quite simply, white, and it had a right, even a duty, to rule over people who were not white. Contemporary nostalgists might not share this confident expansionism, being committed instead to more defensive and paranoid forms of nativism, but whiteness is certainly one of the things that is being implicitly extolled in this now worryingly ubiquitous nostalgia for empire. Imperial nostalgia has become an integral component of a hegemonic form of scapegoat nationalism dedicated to the defence of existing privileges and to the belittlement and persecution of out-groups.

But this study is not a lament for Britain's membership of the European Union. The EU that Remainers were trying to defend has itself failed to overcome the legacies of European colonialism. Italy, France, Spain, Portugal, Germany, Belgium, and even Denmark have their own forms of anguished and incomplete reckoning with empire's legacies. Nor has the EU done much to prevent the grotesque widening of social and economic inequalities across Europe. We should also mention the militarisation of the EU's Southern border as well as the locked-in inequalities of its single currency and the European Commission's deathless commitment to fiscal austerity. The EU has no answers, it seems, to the rise of nationalist authoritarianism in Poland and Hungary and elsewhere, to the permanent indebtedness and protracted social crises of its peripheral member states, let alone to the existential problem of climate change. Remainers have found themselves in the absurd position of defending this status quo, dying in a political ditch in defence of a dysfunctional First World trading bloc.

Britain awaits – still! – what we are tempted to call a cultural revolution that might awaken it from the nightmare of its history. Or rather, since that formulation sounds too much like some myth of national renaissance or the hoary trope of 'Britannia Unchained' (to invoke the title of a book by Brexit ideologues), let us suggest more soberly that what Britons need is liberation from being British. In Scotland, that goal will take the simple form of becoming Scottish, an identity that, as the antithesis of Britishness, will involve equality and democracy as well as liberty, a vision that, by the way, we do not believe the timid Scottish National Party has yet succeeded in articulating.[34] In Britain's former colonies, Britain's incremental break-up has meant the freedom to be Irish or Jamaican or Zambian or whatever instead. When Samuel Beckett was asked by an interviewer, 'Alors Monsieur Beckett, vous êtes anglais?' his celebrated answer was, 'Au contraire'. The character of a once-colonised people should, in fact, be the opposite of the identity of the racialised, assimilationist, hierarchical, and barely democratic power that previously held them down.[35]

In England, the goal of ceasing to be British will mean something more unusual. It might well involve acknowledging, as Alex Niven's *New Model Island: How to Build a Radical Culture Beyond the Idea of England* (2019) does, that England is nothing but a geopolitical void.[36] A country that has not existed since the start of the eighteenth century, one that has no institutions of its own, nor any widely shared culture, except the jingoistic one fostered by colonial expansion, will find it difficult to develop a kind of civic and democratic nationalism. All national communities are imagined, of course, as Perry's brother Benedict Anderson reminds us, but few nations could have been imagined so poorly as England has. The alternative to Britain, we have been arguing, is not a *better* Britain, since Britain is an inherently assimilationist, hierarchical, and racialised construction. It should be broken up. Similarly, our view of Englishness is that the English need to rip it up and start again.

If there must be an England for Scotland and Wales to share an island with, then let it be a little one, a nation among European nations, albeit one with historic links and obligations to the rest of the world. A curse on the Big Englanders, as J. B. Priestley pronounced in his *English Journey* of 1934, the 'red-faced, staring, loud-voiced fellows, wanting to go and boss everybody about all over the world, and being surprised and pained and saying "bad show!" if some blighters refused to fag for them'.[37] Only by overthrowing those fellows will the English make an England worth belonging to. At the end of Alan Bennett's 2018 play *Allelujah!*,

Dr Valentine, an altruistic Indian doctor working in the Dusty Springfield Geriatric Ward in a Yorkshire hospital, resolves, 'I must leave the burden of being English to others'.

> Why, I ask myself, should I still want to join? What is there for me here, where education is a privilege and nationality a boast? Starving the sick and neglecting the old, what makes you special still? There is nobody to touch you, but who wants to any more? Open your arms before it's too late.

'In the meantime', having been denied a visa, '[he] cannot be English'.[38] What would hopefully emerge from the destruction of this England is a radically truncated England, a nation one would want to join, in which care is all-embracing, not selective, and in which *nationality* is just another word for *citizenship*.

Niven's ingenious solution is to split England up into a number of powerful regions. That policy would simultaneously satisfy a desire for collective identity *and* provide a set of manageable institutions to which the power currently monopolised by an unaccountable state and powerful economic interests might be devolved. It might seem inconsistent, if endearingly quixotic, of Niven to question the existence of a distinctive English identity on the grounds that England, as such, has not existed since 1707 while, in the same breath, espousing the revival of the Anglo-Saxon kingdoms of Wessex and Northumbria! But however the cake is sliced, we are convinced that the devolution of political power to smaller units is a feasible proposal. An embryonic sense of regional identity is already emerging in England, several decades after local governments were disempowered in the 1980s. Yorkshire, for example, which has a population roughly the same size as Scotland's or Denmark's, patented its own flag in 2008, the white rose on a fetchingly azure field. Two of the three authors of the present study hail from that diverse county and are anxious to stress the opportunity in Yorkshire for a substantial devolution of power and the elaboration of a new civic form of identity. Presumably, the farming folk of the North and East Ridings and the residents of the affluent villages and suburbs would have a very different idea of what to do with such a democratic body to the residents of post-industrial cities and towns like Bradford and Rotherham (themselves torn currently between Brexit-inspired nationalism, the traditions of municipal socialism, and sheer apathy). But at least devolved bodies might have a better chance of addressing competing social and economic visions on their own terms instead of obfuscating them with jingoistic fantasies and specious 'culture wars', as currently happens at Westminster.

Culturally and economically, Niven argues in his idiosyncratic study of Northern culture *The North Will Rise Again*, Northern cities, such as Manchester, Newcastle, Liverpool, and Sheffield, and smaller cities and towns, such as Halifax, Preston, Bolton, and Hull, were 'the real historical capitals of modernity' in the nineteenth and twentieth centuries.[39] The aristocrats and financial capitalists of the South-East cloaked their class power and colonial reach with a duplicitously nostalgic culture of bucolic landscapes and country houses. In the North, however, a vaguely resentful sense of being exiled from the centres of power often catalysed a 'rebel commitment to modernism and progressive change'.[40] This is the independent and inventive spirit, at once grumpily melancholic and brazenly futuristic, which Niven detects in the Northumbrian late modernism of Basil Bunting's long poem *Briggflatts* (1966), even in the revolutionary posturing of the seminal Manchester band The Stones Roses' first album (1989) and in the weird soundscapes of the pioneering electronic composer Delia Derbyshire, this 'basic, historic northern belief that an energetically reconstituted future for their region is both desirable and plausible'.[41] This sense of a future outside or in opposition to dominant forms of national belonging is what needs to be resuscitated.

Building a radical culture – in short, Nairn's wholesale 'break-up of Britain', and even what Niven calls the 'break-up of England'[42] – is what we think many of the writers whose works are discussed in this study envision. What we are getting at is the long-overdue radical reconstruction of the Yookay's polity, society, economy, and culture, so that all the peoples of this diverse archipelago, even the English, can follow the rest of the empire's excellent example and finally *cease to be British*. This means rethinking and remaking both 'race and class in the ruins of Empire', to invoke the subtitle of the hip-hop artist Akala's exciting memoir-cum-historical-study *Natives*.[43] At the forefront of this slow-burning but now hopefully accelerating revolution since at least the start of the last century have been novelists, playwrights, and poets, the archipelago's unacknowledged legislators.

We take as axiomatic Benedict Anderson's claim in *Imagined Communities* that texts of various kinds actively help produce national identities. 'Nation-ness' for Anderson entails a 'remarkable confidence of community in anonymity'.[44] That is, the modern citizen knows that he or she or they belong to a bordered and sovereign national collective even if – in fact, *because* – that collective is usually experienced not directly but imaginatively, through rituals, cultural practices, and texts of various kinds. The nation, thus, is an imagined community, though certainly not an imaginary one, since it possesses very real borders and bureaucracies in addition to a monopoly on legitimate violence. Anderson's thesis is that since the early nineteenth century, first in Latin America and Europe, and then universally, 'print capitalism' (the mass availability in vernacular languages of texts, especially the novel and the newspaper) was decisive in the development of modern nations and of the accompanying ideologies of nation-ness. Literary texts, though, are not pieces of plasticine on which the shape of a nation's self-image or the forms of its social struggles are simply imprinted. Rather, as Anderson shows, texts help construct and, we maintain, often deconstruct, and even potentially reconstruct, nation states and the dominant forms of identity that underpin them.

What would this study look like if we had chosen to prioritise texts that affirm rather than question dominant definitions of Britishness? Only slightly different to the way it looks now, for we are convinced that literary texts very rarely simply reinforce a given culture's dominant ideologies. This disruptive quality is a product of the way texts dramatise multiple voices and perspectives or else find ways of foregrounding the partial nature of the viewpoints they express, also because of their avowedly fictive and contestable quality in addition to the inescapable fact that literary texts are not necessarily read in the same spirit in which they were written, nor can the intentions of those who wrote them easily be divined. Even patriotic adventure stories like Ian Fleming's enormously popular James Bond series of the 1950s and early 1960s need not be read as patriotic adventure stories. The Bond novels, it is true, are a last-ditch defence of Britain's imperial clout and of male power in the changed conditions of American supremacy, second-wave feminism, and the consumer society. Indeed, their principal appeal is their meticulous enactment of fantasies of male consumption. In his ingenious account of the ideology of the British spy thriller, Michael Denning sees the Bond novels as 'redeeming' and even 'heroizing' the 'activities of consumption'.[45] Bond's foes are rapidly dispatched in wryly absurd set pieces so that readers can mainly enjoy imagining 007 consuming fine wines, toothsome meals, expensive cigarettes, attractive women, stylish clothes, fast cars, exciting journeys, and posh hotels. Bond is a fantastical projection of the sporty post-war suburban hobbyist, skiing to flee an Alpine fastness, shooting a round of golf against a nefarious gold smuggler, or playing bridge against a diehard Nazi industrialist.

Bond and his irascible superior, M., both agonise over social change and Britain's geopolitical decline. 'Balls to you, Tiger! And balls again!' an oddly juvenile Bond tells his Japanese contact in *You Only Live Twice* (1964) after Tiger Tanaka baits him about Britain's 'slide into impotence at Suez'.

> England may have been bled pretty thin by a couple of World Wars, our Welfare State politics may have made us expect too much for free, and the liberation of our Colonies may have gone too fast, but we still climb Everest and beat plenty of the world at plenty of sports and win Nobel Prizes. Our politicians may be a feather-pated bunch, and I expect yours are too. All politicians are. But there's nothing wrong with the British people – although there are only fifty million of them.[46]

What a laughably unimpressive account of the nation's supposedly undiminished greatness! The Bond novels amount to a fantastical, if anxious and, at times, somewhat droll, avowal that 'there's nothing wrong with the British people'. They are a fictional postponement of the overdue supersession of male as well as national and colonial power. The realisation that this fantasy is a lie and a joke is also a productive reading made available, though not exactly encouraged, by Fleming's novels. Works of literature of all kinds, we are suggesting, in different ways and to varying degrees, are sites in which dominant identities are produced and often interrogated. They are virtually never simply wax impressions on which the nation's complacent self-image is passively recorded, which is why it is so important to grapple with the questions about nations and national identities that they pose.

'Literature offers no model for rescuing England from its current crises and anxieties', concludes John Brannigan's study of literature in England since 1945. 'On the other hand, the hope of this book, and one of its enabling assumptions, is that literature is also available as a voice for the silenced, and as an imaginative space for dissidence, critique, and reinvention.'[47] We share this hope, even belief, that twentieth- and twenty-first-century writing *does* offer a model for rescuing England and the other parts of these islands from their current crises and pathologies. Not only do literary texts stage and amplify these various crises; they also indicate potential alternatives. Our thesis is thus slightly closer to that of Graham MacPhee's *Postwar British Literature and Postcolonial Studies*, though we want to ground our literary readings in a more detailed account of the struggles enacted in both British culture and society over the entire period since 1900.[48] Brian W. Shaffer's edited collection *The British and Irish Novel, 1945–2000* examines British (and Irish) novels during that period 'as a battleground on which competing artistic, philosophical, social, and political agendas wage war'.[49] We are looking at how novels, plays, and poems dramatise political struggles specifically within the integument of the British state over a rather longer period, from the apex of nationalism and empire at the turn of the twentieth century through to Britain's zombified reanimation in the form of the Brexit vote. Moreover, we also attend in a politicised register to the emergent possibilities explored by these texts, which we think help open up possibilities for socialist and feminist struggle, queer liberation, and anti-racist, anti-imperialist, and even anti-fascist movements. This study shows how works of drama, poetry, and fiction agitate for the long-overdue break-up of Britain. They open up post-national futures after empire and after Brexit.

Let us look briefly at the work of one important writer on Englishness in order to flesh out our belief that literary texts might do more than simply redefine national identity and might help build radical cultures that move beyond national identity altogether. In 1935, the novelist E. M. Forster told the International Congress of Writers in Paris that he thought any successful struggle *against* fascism and *for* freedom needed to face up to the fact that freedom in England was currently severely race- and class-bound.[50] In other words, the struggle against fascism in Europe required fascism to be crushed at home and in the colonies, that is, in the body and tentacles of the British state itself. Already in 1920, in his 'Notes on the English Character', Forster had argued that 'the English character is incomplete. . . . It is the machinery that is wrong'.[51] It was too repressed and too repress*ive*. Identical with the damaged masculinity of the middle class and the public school system, with thoughtlessness, incuriosity, and colonial hypocrisy, Englishness, Forster prophesied, would be enormously freed up in the next 20 years or so. As indeed it was, though not nearly enough, by the greater informality and egalitarianism of a 'people's war', by relative post-war affluence and full employment, by the greater personal and cultural freedoms associated with the 1960s, and most of all, by the seismic and wholly salutary influence exerted in all areas of British life by immigration from Eastern Europe, the Caribbean, and South Asia. We endorse Forster's appealing declaration in the same essay that 'English literature is a flying fish'.[52] In other words, there are numerous emotional and political complexities and diversities happening beneath the surface of English culture in the way that life forms teem beneath the surface of the sea; in literary texts, they fleetingly emerge into the light.

In his *Identity of England*, the historian Robert Colls espouses what he calls '*oppositional* Englishness'[53], the ways in which national identity can be redefined and made much more complex and potentially inclusive by the articulation of other voices. Forster wanted to open the way to these alternative voices and perspectives that he hoped were starting to emerge. He did not define *Englishness* therefore. Or rather, he pinpointed only what its official definition or mode happened at that distant time, when British prime ministers still mainly went to Eton, to be, that is, repressed, bourgeois, and imperialist. Forster awaited other writers who could articulate new experiences and complexities, though it is worth adding that in much of his own work, *Howards End*, for example, or *Maurice*, Forster's novel about a young gay man's emotional and erotic self-discovery that was unpublished in his own lifetime, there is a deep commitment to radical change *in* England and radical change *of* England. 'England has always been disinclined to accept human nature', the hypnotist Lasker Jones tells Maurice.[54] But Maurice does not abscond to more freethinking climes such as Italy or France. Indeed, he and his lover, Alec Scudder, seek refuge in the highly resonant site of the English greenwood to be 'outlaws' like Robin's merry band. Maurice eventually spurns the inner voice that chides him for being a fool:

'You've done for yourself this time,' it seemed to say, and when he stopped outside the park, because the King and Queen were passing, he despised them at the moment he bared his head. It was as if the barrier that kept him from his fellows had taken another aspect. He was not afraid or ashamed any more. After all, the forests and the night were on his side, not theirs; they, not he, were inside a ring fence.

(*M*, 190)

There is the intransigent England of the Crown and state, and outside it there is another England (or whatever name you choose to give it) in which people and the rest of nature are free from being permanently policed, where you may live 'outside class', though with companionship: this 'England belonged to them' (*M*, 212). *Maurice* would not be published, Forster decreed, 'until [Forster's] death and England's', that is, until the hopeful emergence of a new nation state from the regrettably slow decease of the repressed and repressive one.[55] Forster was, in many ways, part of that dying England, with a largely Victorian intellectual formation, not least because he still used 'England' as a synonym for 'Britain'. The writers studied in this book are the oppositional voices that Forster was waiting for.

This veritable squadron of flying fish, to use Forster's attractive metaphor, explores the shape of cosmopolitan and egalitarian alternatives to the dominant nationalist ideology that currently prevails in these islands. Chapter 1 covers British writing between 1900 and 1948, Chapter 2 the period from 1948 to 1980, and Chapter 3 looks at 1980 to the present. We thus examine British writing from what might broadly be termed the late phase of British imperialism, after 1900, to the complex period of social, economic, and cultural crisis around the Brexit vote of 2016. We certainly do not see Britain as having 'declined' since the end of empire, since this event marked very considerable progress for the empire's subjects, whatever the impediments they have encountered since independence. The twentieth century also represented significant advances for other groups previously excluded from the complex of British state life. 'The British Empire declined; the condition of the people improved', was the historian A. J. P. Taylor's neat summary of British history in the first half of the twentieth century.[56] The story of Britain in the last century or so is of advance in some areas and retrogression or paralysis in others, which is why we are so reluctant to talk about the nation or about national identity as if these things were somehow unitary, whether advancing or declining, rampant or couchant. Our narrative is the questioning and then the dissolution of the empire, followed by the travails of an incompletely postcolonial British nation after 1945 and, eventually, Brexit, but also the constant presence throughout these periods of radical plans to deconstruct Britain and Britishness altogether.

We thus eschew the commonplace but largely arbitrary periodisations based on monarchical reigns and dates of wars and elections. The book's claims to originality are partly methodological, to do with the way we read texts. We have no desire to provide an encyclopaedic survey of figures and trends in British writing during these periods. Rather, we read important and representative texts (both canonical and non-canonical) in order to show how, at the levels of their themes, styles, and forms, they dramatise struggles over national definition. Experiences and understandings of nationality are mediated and, to a degree, actively produced by texts of all kinds. Texts, therefore, help shape and potentially reshape Britishness as well as related identifications centred on gender, sexuality, race, region, religion, rival nationalisms, and so on. We therefore value close rather than distant reading, since it is in the detail where texts both register and help effect these changes in how we think about identity. We think that something like Williams's cultural materialist method is the best way to draw out the dominant and the residual as well as the *emergent* elements of British writing. In Williams's words,

> however dominant a social system may be, the very meaning of its domination involves a limitation or selection of the activities it covers, so that by definition it cannot exhaust all social experience, which therefore always potentially contains space for alternative acts and alternative intentions which are not yet articulated as a social institution or even project.[57]

Our task, then, is to detect, elucidate, and amplify these alternatives. We do not understand British history as a linear tale of liberal progress. It is an arena of competing projects or rival political cultures.

Williams's own book *The English Novel: From Dickens to Lawrence* (1970), a relatively overlooked work in the canon of the man who we think is the most important British critic of the decades after the war, offers some clues about how to trace competing definitions of the nation through detailed readings of literary texts and their forms. Williams's argument is that 'the formal problems of the novel are in the end mainly problems of relationships'.[58] To put it the other way around, dominant as well as emergent definitions of the social and of the national are expressed by novels' forms. Admittedly, Williams's readings are hampered, here at least, by his exclusive attention to the *English* novel. Williams looks at how the category of

Englishness is intriguingly unsettled in the case of Joseph Conrad, though he is not interested in how Englishness is inflected by the particular experiences of women in the nineteenth century in the cases of George Eliot and Charlotte and Emily Brontë. Williams is concerned mostly with how the forms of English novels respond to the greater complexity and scale as well as the far sharper class divisions in English society after the Industrial Revolution. To what extent, Williams asks, can novels assemble examples or images of what he calls a 'knowable community', even in the midst of the profound social dislocations of industrial capitalism? Williams is mainly interested in class and in, say, the difficulty of mapping the inordinately complex social relationships of the modern city even in a voluminous realist novel like Charles Dickens's *Bleak House* or the way that conflicting sympathies and voices in Thomas Hardy's novels express the various borders thrown up between classes and regions during the prolonged agricultural depression in late-Victorian England. Such tensions, for Williams, which he calls 'disturbances of language and form', register the increasing complexity and disconnectedness of English society during the period covered by his study, roughly 1840 to 1930. Often in surreptitious and incomplete ways, however, these texts also express auspicious new forms of human relationship, the way *Bleak House* extols 'heavenly compassion'[59] in the densely interconnected but socially stratified city or Hardy's fiction imagines new forms of marriage and love.

We, too, want to think about how dominant understandings of the nation are negotiated in the styles and forms of literary works, though not just in novels, and certainly not just in English novels. Williams was admirably conscious of D. H. Lawrence's status as one of the very few working-class writers in the canonical tradition of the English novel. He was less attentive to the heterodox perspectives of women writers and not at all to those of queer or gender-non-conforming novelists, and only briefly in his account of Joseph Conrad to the centrality of empire and immigration to British writing. Our aim, then, adapting Williams's method but, at the same time, moving beyond his more restrictive focus, is to think about how texts, often through 'disturbances of language and form', interrogate dominant understandings of the national community from these divergent viewpoints. In so doing, they allow a variety of new identities, relationships, and communities to emerge.

Lastly, then, we view British writing over the last century or so from a postcolonial angle. We are convinced that prevailing definitions of Britishness have been complicit in the colonial project and in other forms of inequality and exclusion. Not only that, but also the turbulent political context of recent years has been, in part, a struggle over whether to address persistent forms of racial and class hierarchy or, as we have already seen, to fall back on nostalgia for both empire and a mythologised sense of national cohesion. These are the topical questions the book seeks to address through the forms of awareness, clarification, and anticipation enabled by the critical engagement with literary texts. We are convinced, as Edward Said was in *Orientalism* and *Culture and Imperialism*, that imperialism (in this case, British imperialism and the vital role played in that nefarious project by the peculiar formation of British nationalism) depended for its force and durability on the production of a certain cultural imagination of empire, a whole paraphernalia of images, narratives, figures, rituals, and so on. Said's *Orientalism*, in his biographer Timothy Brennan's words, was 'a meditation on the degree to which *representation is part of reality*, not just its rendering in words'.[60] The responsibility of the critic, the importance of whose role is stressed time and again in Said's work, is to show how imperialism's crimes were made possible through the production of legitimating representations that put forward iniquitous ideas about, for instance, national missions and racial and civilisational hierarchies. The critic is also charged, we want to stress, with the converse task of elucidating the ways in which texts of different kinds contest those imperialist doctrines and representations and thereby open up alternatives.

We employ Said's method of reading 'contrapuntally': studying the complex overlaps and connections between apparently discrepant worlds in the way that musical counterpoint juxtaposes overlapping voice parts or melodic lines.[61] More recently, Ariella Aïsha Azoulay has theorised the task of 'unlearning imperialism', that is, of showing how forms of knowledge or academic disciplines as well as revered cultural objects and whole social and economic systems cannot be understood without looking carefully at the pervasive influence of empire.[62] This does not at all mean that, for example, as a certain wilfully philistine conservatism fears, university syllabuses must be purged of canonical authors and texts. To the contrary, decolonising the discipline of literary studies means understanding *more* carefully and *more* precisely the connections between empire and the oeuvre of, say, Shakespeare or Austen or, indeed, British writing in the twentieth and twenty-first centuries, since that is what important texts like *The Tempest* and *Mansfield Park* or *The Rainbow* and *The Lonely Londoners* are explicitly about. To pretend otherwise would be to censor and simplify them unforgivably, to demote these texts to the status of cultural capital in the service of the nation's complacent self-image. So the present study is totally committed to the task of decolonising the discipline, which involves both reading familiar works more expansively (or contrapuntally) and augmenting the canon with other texts that demand inclusion on the basis, firstly, of aesthetic merit and, secondly, of their ability to ask pertinent questions.[63] The present study does not examine postcolonial writing as such, but its method is postcolonial. We look at British texts in order to explore critically and to show how the texts themselves explore critically both Britain and Britishness. Those texts also indicate ways of dismantling that nation state and its dominant identities, of decolonising them, if you will, and thereby serving the ends of what Raj Patel and Jason W. Moore call 'recognition, reparation, redistribution, reimagination, and recreation'.[64]

Indeed, our hope is not just that British national identity might be reimagined but that, like Britain itself, it might be laid to rest entirely. Think of the present work as a literary and cultural extension of the Nairn–Anderson thesis. It is a study of how writers and their texts have presaged the overdue break-up of the superannuated British state. Benedict Anderson's memoir *A Life Beyond Boundaries* has no time for forceful assertions of identity, preferring instead to stress Benedict and Perry's cosmopolitan Anglo-Irish background and their itinerant and multi-lingual childhood.

'In growing up, it was understood that we had soul and character, yet we were seldom troubled with identity. Identity was mainly connected with mathematics or the forensic investigation of a corpse.'[65] Identity, in other words, implies sameness, predictability, and stasis. We do not deny or denigrate the desire of most people for forms of connection and solidarity – quite the contrary. In the context with which we are concerned in this study, but of course not only in that context, national identity serves as a diversion from and a compensation for the evacuation of solidarity from other spheres of life over the last 40 years or so, particularly in the context of the increasing enclosure of social and economic life by capital. Here, in Britain, in the words of the Care Collective, 'carelessness reigns'. One of the goals of progressive politics is to recognise the fact of human interdependence (on each other and on the rest of the living world) and to transform it into the value of solidarity and into the achieved forms of collective provision that are essential to communal and individual flourishing. In the next few decades, these forms of collective provision will hopefully take the form of everything from publicly provided hospitals, care homes and other essential services, libraries of things, cooperatives, solidarity economies, public spaces, and green energy infrastructures. Such developments would assume a capacity for care and solidarity that is trans- or simply non-national. Thus the Care Collective talk of 'promiscuous care' and 'caring across difference'. Many forms of care, like sharing economies and public spaces or forms of community wealth-building, are, in fact, *sub*-national.[66] We just think that national identity is a peculiarly abstract and inadequate way of satisfying this vital need for identity and solidarity, particularly in a country as badly and often malignantly imagined as Britain. Benedict Anderson is surely correct that all communities are, to some extent, imagined; only the smallest neighbourhoods and kinship networks are encountered directly, and even our experiences of these are mediated by images, memories, narratives, and so on. Yet we insist that nations and national identities and, above all, this nation and its national identity are *especially* abstract ways of describing and organising human connection. Our utopian hope is that they might be broken up.

Notes

1 The best account so far of the British government's deplorable response to the pandemic is Jonathan Calvert and George Arbuthnot, *Failures of State: The Inside Story of Britain's Battle with Coronavirus*, London: Mudlark, 2021.
2 David Edgerton, 'Brexit is a Necessary Crisis – it Reveals Britain's True Place in the World', *The Guardian*, 9 October 2019.
3 Tom Nairn, *The Enchanted Glass: Britain and its Monarchy*, London: Vintage, 1994, p. xxii.
4 Charlotte Lydia Riley, *Imperial Island: A History of Empire in Modern Britain*, London: The Bodley Head, 2023.
5 Rebecca Fine Romanow, *The Postcolonial Body in Queer Space and Time*, Newcastle: Cambridge Scholars Press, 2006, p. 6.
6 Anne McClintock, *Imperial Leather: Race, Gender, and Sexuality in the Colonial Contest*, London: Routledge, 1995, p. 3.
7 Raymond Williams, *Towards 2000*, London: Chatto & Windus, 1983, p. 182.

8 Norman Davies, *The Isles: A History*, London: Macmillan, 1999, p. xxxvii. Davies lists the many states 'supported' by the Isles over the centuries, including (but by no means limited to) the ancient British tribal principalities; the Anglo-Saxon kingdoms; the independent British/Welsh principalities from the fifth to the thirteenth centuries (such as Cornwall, Cumbria, and Strathclyde); the Kingdom of Ireland until 1800; the Kingdom of the Scots to 1707; the Commonwealth of Great Britain and Ireland, or the First British Republic, in the 1650s; the Kingdom of Great Britain (1707–1800); the United Kingdom of Great Britain and Ireland (1801–1922); the United Kingdom of Great Britain and Northern Ireland (since 1922); plus the Irish Free State, later Eire, and then the Republic of Ireland (also since 1922). Davies, *The Isles*, p. xxxix.
9 W. H. Auden, 'Letter to Lord Byron', in *The English Auden: Poems, Essays and Dramatic Writings, 1927–1939*, ed. Edward Mendelson, London: Faber & Faber, 1986, p. 175.
10 Nairn, *The Enchanted Glass*, p. 243.
11 The best account of the waxing and mostly waning fortunes of the Labour Left, including its detailed critiques of British capitalism and the British state, as well as its alternative strategies for democratisation and international cooperation, is Leo Panitch and Colin Leys, *Searching for Socialism: The Project of the Labour New Left from Benn to Corbyn*, London: Verso, 2020.
12 See Amelia Gentleman, *The Windrush Betrayal: Exposing the Hostile Environment*, London: Guardian Faber, 2019; Maya Goodfellow, *Hostile Environment: How Immigrants Became Scapegoats*, London: Verso, 2019.
13 Arno Mayer, *The Persistence of the Old Regime: Europe to the Great War*, London: Verso, 2010 [1981].
14 Perry Anderson, *English Questions*, London: Verso, 1992; Perry Anderson, 'Ukania Perpetua?', *New Left Review*, 125 (2020), 35–107.
15 The argument here is indebted to Ralph Miliband's account of the three basic ideas of Labour politics: (1) politics is a contest between elites; (2) the extra-parliamentary party is a subordinate adjunct to its MPs; (3) citizens are voters, not participants in democratic self-government. *Parliamentary Socialism: A Study in the Politics of Labour*, London: Allen & Unwin, 1961.
16 Steven Pincus, *1688: The First Modern Revolution*, New Haven: Yale University Press, 2009.
17 Anderson, *English Questions*, pp. 155–6.
18 Anderson, 'Ukania Perpetua?', p. 43.
19 Tom Nairn, *The Break-Up of Britain: Crisis and Neo-Nationalism*, 3rd edition, London: Verso, 2021, p. 32.
20 The Great Britain that emerged in the eighteenth century was a highly centralised and expansionist entity, 'a markedly aggressive and predatory state' (xiv). But Colley is keen to stress that active British patriotism was also a popular movement for the working and middle classes in this period, for both men and women, giving them access to forms of citizenship, social visibility, and commercial opportunities. Linda Colley, *Britons: Forging the Nation, 1707–1837*, 3rd edition, Yale University Press, 2009.
21 To focus only on the neglected tradition of anti-colonial dissent, Priyamvada Gopal's important study *Insurgent Empires* demonstrates the 'significant diversity in attitudes to the Empire within the metropole, but also, at various moments, interrogations of and even opposition to the imperial project itself', particularly among feminist and socialist movements and intellectuals. Gopal stresses that liberation struggles in the colonies often influenced metropolitan dissent rather than, as is usually assumed, the other way around: *Insurgent Empire: Anticolonial Resistance and British Dissent*, London: Verso, 2019, p. 6.
22 Tom Nairn, 'The Nature of the Labour Party – 2', *New Left Review*, 28 (1964), 33–62: 61.

22 *British Writing from Empire to Brexit*

23 E. P. Thompson, 'The Peculiarities of the English', in *The Socialist Register 1965*, eds. Ralph Miliband and John Saville, London: The Merlin Press, 1965, pp. 311–62: 332 (emphasis in the original). To be fair, Anderson acknowledges the force of these criticisms in 1987's 'The Figures of Descent': 'we had failed to register the variations in the political hopes and horizons of the working class and its different institutions over a century and a half, attributing too homogeneous a subordination to it, and too static a hegemony to the exploiting classes over it.' *English Questions*, p. 168.
24 Ellen Meiksins Wood, *The Pristine Culture of Capitalism: A Historical Essay on Old Regimes and Modern States*, London: Verso, 1991, pp. 11–9.
25 John Darwin, *Unfinished Empire: The Global Expansion of Britain*, Harmondsworth: Penguin, 2011, p. 184.
26 Tom Hazeldine, *The Northern Question: A History of a Divided Country*, London: Verso, 2020.
27 Anderson, 'Ukania Perpetua?', p. 45.
28 Peter Gowan, 'Crisis in the Heartland', *New Left Review II*, 55 (2009), 5–29: 16.
29 Aeron Davis, *Reckless Opportunists: Elites at the End of the Establishment*, Manchester: Manchester University Press, 2018. See also Owen Jones, *The Establishment and How They Get Away with it*, Harmondsworth: Penguin, 2015.
30 David Edgerton, *The Rise and Fall of the British Nation: A Twentieth-Century History*, Harmondsworth: Penguin, 2019, p. xxi.
31 Attacks on minority groups are, of course, 'inherently fascist', as Shon Faye has argued. *The Transgender Issue: An Argument for Justice*, London: Allen Lane, 2021, p. 164. Moreover, trans people pose an implicit threat or, as we see it, an auspicious alternative to the authoritarian nation state by virtue of what she calls their 'rejection of dominant, ancient and deep-seated ideas about the connection between biological characteristics and identity'. The obsession with 'gender ideology' shared by authoritarian populists in Hungary, Brazil, Poland, the United States, and now Britain is aimed at upholding the dogma that there are two fixed biological sexes. The war against trans liberation is thus part of concerted conservative efforts to reify unequal gender roles. The ideological fixation with 'gender ideology' is literally reactionary, part of an effort to forestall and push back an array of challenges to the privileges of the wealthy, to whiteness, the heteronormative family, and the professed purity of the nation state.
32 Pankaj Mishra, *Age of Anger: A History of the Present*, Penguin, 2018, p. 112.
33 Peter Mitchell, *Imperial Nostalgia: How the British Conquered Themselves*, Manchester: Manchester University Press, 2021, p. 6.
34 Support for independence seems stuck at around 40% of the Scottish electorate. The problem is how to expand this support, given the ideological diffuseness of the SNP, its platform of tepid social democracy, and its vision of a dependent independence that retains most of the features of the British state, such as sterling, the Bank of England, the monarchy, and even ongoing fiscal austerity. 'The 2014 referendum created a nationalist movement that was deeply committed to the symbolism of a popular vote for independence and saw the transition to Scottish statehood as a decisive rupture from the British model of politics and economics. How can this more muscular nationalist support base be reconciled with the cautious and gradualist outlook of the SNP leadership?' Ben Jackson, *The Case for Scottish Independence: A History of Nationalist Political Thought in Modern Scotland*, Cambridge: Cambridge University Press, 2020, p. 179.
35 For sure, this is an ongoing project in the case of Ireland, for example, where what Fintan O'Toole calls the republican virtue of equality needs to be vigorously reasserted. Fintan O'Toole, *Ship of Fools: How Stupidity and Corruption Sank the Celtic Tiger*, London: Faber & Faber, 2009, p. 94.
36 Alex Niven, *New Model Island: How to Build a Radical Culture Beyond the Idea of England*, London: Repeater, 2019.
37 J. B. Priestley, *English Journey*, London: William Heinemann, 1934, p. 416.

38 Alan Bennett, *Allelujah!* London: Faber & Faber, 2018, pp. 86–7.
39 Alex Niven, *The North Will Rise Again: In Search of the Future in Northern Heartlands*, London: Bloomsbury, 2023, p. 9.
40 Niven, *The North Will Rise Again*, p. 10.
41 Niven, *The North Will Rise Again*, p. 232.
42 Niven, *New Model Island*, p. 123.
43 Akala, *Natives: Race and Class in the Ruins of Empire*, London: Two Roads, 2019.
44 Benedict Anderson, *Imagined Communities: Reflections on the Origin and Spread of Nationalism*, Revised edition, London: Verso, 1991, p. 36.
45 Michael Denning, *Cover Stories: Narrative and Ideology in the British Spy Thriller*, London: Routledge, 1987, p. 104.
46 Ian Fleming, *You Only Live Twice*, London: Vintage, 2012 [1964], p. 109.
47 John Brannigan, *Orwell to the Present: Literature in England, 1945–2000*, Basingstoke: Palgrave, 2002, p. 204.
48 Graham MacPhee, *Postwar British Literature and Postcolonial Studies*, Oxford: Blackwell, 2011.
49 Brian W. Shaffer, 'Preface', in *The British and Irish Novel, 1945–2000*, ed. Brian W. Shaffer, Oxford: Blackwell, 2005, pp. xvi–xix: p. xvii.
50 E. M. Forster, 'Liberty in England', in *Abinger Harvest*, London: Edward Arnold, 1936, pp. 62–8.
51 E. M. Forster, 'Notes on the English Character', in *Abinger Harvest*, London: Edward Arnold, 1936, pp. 3–14: 13.
52 Forster, 'Notes on the English Character', in *Abinger Harvest*, p. 8.
53 Robert Colls, *Identity of England*, Oxford: Oxford University Press, 2002, p. 111.
54 E. M. Forster, *Maurice*, ed. P. N. Furbank, Harmondsworth: Penguin, 2005, p. 188. Subsequent references are given in the main text after *M*.
55 Quoted in David Leavitt, 'Introduction', in E. M. Forster, *Maurice*, ed. P. N. Furbank, Harmondsworth: Penguin, 2005, pp. xi–xxxvi: xxviii.
56 A. J. P. Taylor, *English History, 1914–1945*, Harmondsworth: Penguin, 1970, p. 600.
57 Raymond Williams, *Politics and Letters: Interviews with 'New Left Review'*, London: New Left Books, 1979, p. 252.
58 Raymond Williams, *The English Novel: From Dickens to Lawrence*, London: Chatto & Windus, 1970, p. 188.
59 Charles Dickens, *Bleak House*, ed. Norman Page, Harmondsworth: Penguin, 1976 [1853], p. 705.
60 Timothy Brennan, *Places of Mind: A Life of Edward Said*, London: Bloomsbury, 2021, p. 180 (emphasis in the original).
61 Edward W. Said, *Culture and Imperialism*, London: Vintage, 1994, pp. 59–60.
62 Ariella Aïsha Azoulay, *Potential History: Unlearning Imperialism*, London: Verso, 2019.
63 Gurminder K. Bhambra, Kerem Nişancıoğlu and Dalia Gebrial, eds., *Decolonizing the University*, London: Pluto Press, 2018.
64 Jason W. Moore, *A History of the World in Seven Cheap Things: A Guide to Capitalism, Nature, and the Future of the Planet*, London: Verso, 2018, p. 207.
65 Benedict Anderson, *A Life Beyond Boundaries*, London: Verso, 2018, p. 5.
66 The Care Collective, *The Care Manifesto*, London: Verso, 2020.

1 Nation, Empire, and Identity in Late Colonial British Writing, 1900–1948

If England was what England seems,
An' not the England of our dreams,
But only putty, brass, an' paint,
'Ow quick we'd drop 'er! But she ain't!

These lines are the refrain of Rudyard Kipling's poem 'The Return'. Like his other *Service Songs* it adopts the voice of a British serviceman at the time of the Second South African War (The Boer War) of 1899–1902. In 'The Return' a working-class soldier returns to London ('Thamesfontein'), and specifically Hackney, in the poor east of the city (''Ackneystadt'). While in South Africa he has seen something beyond the everyday world of his fellow Britons. The poem powerfully evokes landscape, war, and death abroad – all of which Kipling had observed first-hand in South Africa – but also the interchange with those from different places:

Also Time runnin' into years –
A thousand Places left be'ind –
An' Men from both two 'emispheres
Discussin' things of every kind;
So much more near than I 'ad known,
So much more great than I 'ad guessed –
An' me, like all the rest, alone –
But reachin' out to all the rest!

It brings about 'The makin's of a bloomin' soul'.

The poem goes on to question whether he will be able to sustain his new maturity when he reaches London – 'But now, discharged, I fall away/To do with little things again . . .'. The poem sees deeper forms of experience in the modern world as happening in the colonies, while lines such as those quoted at the head of this chapter call into doubt a clear, fixed essence of Englishness.[1] A fuller, richer England may well be something one 'dreams', and that is idealised and possibly fabricated. Though the I-voice of the poem returns to England, what he finds there may all be show, a land of false appearances, like the 'putty, brass, an' paint' used in theatrical scenery that only convinces at a distance. The 'But she ain't' at the end

DOI: 10.4324/9781003230816-2

of the refrain seems sure and certain – the print conventions of the time mean that the move from italics back to the ordinary font denotes emphasis – but we might feel that it is over-insistent.

Kipling was an imperialist, though one who harboured few illusions about what gaining and holding an empire involved. His formation in a family of Pre-Raphaelite artists, though, often exerted a counter-pull to these fixed views; there was a loyalty to where his artistic craft led him. Kipling's extraordinary popularity means that we cannot leave him out of the story of these years; he is part of the cultural fabric. 'The Return' seeks both to assert an identity – one that connects nation, empire, gender, and class – and to acknowledge an uncertain modern world. For the I-voice, depth and meaning are found more in the colonies than in London.

A knowledge of identities made and remade, and an awareness of the utility of maintaining that some things are 'essence', is often present in writing from the first half of the twentieth century. Kipling was not averse himself to making claims that fixed definitions of the nation reside in history, in nature, and even in people's bodies. Nature and nurture are both present, and we can see this if 'The Return' is compared with a poem with a similar title, 'The Recall'. The latter addresses Anglo-Saxon affinities and accompanies the short story 'An Habitation Enforced' in Kipling's 1909 collection *Actions and Reactions*. An American couple discovers that they will live most fully in a house in the Sussex landscape of the wife's ancestors. In 'The Recall' we learn that this true homeland will 'order their souls aright'. Short sentences and heavily end-stopped lines convey certainty. The poem begins: 'I am the land of their fathers./In me the virtue stays./I will bring back my children/After certain days'.[2]

The depiction in 'The Return' and 'The Recall' of movement between 'home' and lands currently or once colonised informs much of the historical writing about Englishness in the decades around the turn of the twentieth century. For John Seeley, in his long popular *The Expansion of England* (1883), English identity was enlarged by the empire beyond its island of origin. As Bill Schwarz observes, 'Seeley conceptualized England as constituted by its overseas possessions, and he was prepared to push this hard enough that the very differentiation between England and colony, internal and external, came to be questioned'.[3] As we will see later in this chapter, during the Second World War a different position gained ground, with George Orwell's wartime writing an influential early example. In contrast to writers such as Seeley and Kipling, England had always been distinct and largely untouched by its colonies.

The widely held position in Britain in the second half of the twentieth century was that colonialism was now long in the past and had had little impact at home anyway. That narrative, and the way it recasts the stories told about the first 50 or so years of the twentieth century, is contested in this chapter. Catherine Hall and Sonya Rose argue that 'prior to decolonisation, "being imperial" was simply a part of a whole culture, to be investigated not as separate from but as integral to peoples' lives'. In this period, to quote Hall and Rose again, the 'everyday lives' of Britons would have been 'infused with an imperial presence. Furthermore, important political and cultural processes and institutions were shaped by and within the context of empire'.[4]

Starting in the 1940s, facing up to colonialism and the harm, violence, and racism it involved, was eschewed. Instead a story about the British Empire became dominant and still persists, even among many who at some level know better. In this account, the British Empire is founded in the late nineteenth century, but not long after its terminal decline was acknowledged and it rapidly came to an end. Imperialism is then but a brief episode in the wider history of the Irish and British Isles. Thinking about colonialism as part of the very fabric of national identity and of centuries' duration still produces a reflex of denial, one that, among other consequences, cruelly distorts accounts of post-war migration to Britain. Every subject of the Crown had the same status and the right to live anywhere in the empire until legislation in Britain and the colonies started to change things after the Second World War. Having been told to regard Britain as the 'Mother Country', those coming to Britain from the colonies were undertaking – to pick up Kipling's words – a 'return'. However, once in Britain, they found themselves regarded as different, the object of suspicion and worse. That was even though they were, because of Britain's post-war need for their skills, answering a 'recall' of a kind.

Modernist studies adopted the attitudes of the time of its inception in marginalising issues of colonialism. An account of writing in Britain that largely omits race and colonialism remains in place. Raymond Williams noted of the construction of modernism in a 1987 lecture that 'in that retrospective generalization ideological points have been made but made surreptitiously. [. . .] [T]he appropriation of "modern" for a selection of what have in fact been the modern processes is an act of pure ideology'.[5] A turn to issues of form, and a focus on individual geniuses in metropolitan coteries, allowed the experience of most of the world's population, and indeed of most Britons, to be ignored. Hierarchies founded on race persist in modernist studies even though they are recast in different form. Writers, artists, and musicians from a similar class background as those involved in colonial trade and military leaders, and residing in nearby parts of London, are said to be a new and different elite and to offer a radical alternative. The hierarchy put in place by racial theory does not change but is now described in languages of aesthetic and cultural value and the quality of subjective experience. Those outside the ruling elite, who were often driven by circumstance to address the material conditions of late colonialism in their writing, are seen as inferior artists with less interesting lives. They adopt – with the following seen pejoratively – realist modes, conventional poetic forms, and write allegories.

When called on to address modernism's colonial context, a standard response from modernist studies has been that a vanguard of formally innovative writers were thoroughgoing opponents of empire and racism. This claim is very rarely sustainable. There is often the further ahistorical assumption that high modernist writing strategies are inherently anti-colonial and anti-racist. Pointing to the importance of empire in the modernist period is decades old. The key issue has long been the lack of substantive change. The 'new modernist studies' from the end of the 1990s was supposed to question the founding assumptions of the field. However, that often involved augmentation rather than sustained questioning and reform. Texts that fitted the existing assumptions and narratives were incorporated into the field; modernist studies itself became centrifugal, colonising. As Douglas

Mao and Rebecca L. Walkowitz wrote unironically in their 2008 article 'The New Modernist Studies', '[w]ere one seeking a single word to sum up transformations in modernist literary scholarship one could do worse than light on *expansion*'.[6] It is striking that much of the pioneering work on the anti-colonial networks and writing in the period has come from within historically aware postcolonial literary studies rather than from within modernist studies; the writing of Elleke Boehmer and Priyamvada Gopal provides examples.[7] It is now necessary to take an 'after modernist studies' approach to the writing of the first half of the twentieth century, which I call here late colonial art. (Some historians prefer the word 'imperial' to 'late colonial', but that serves to take the start of the period back to the 1870s.) Modernist studies, emerging after the Second World War as part of a compromise formation that sought to avoid fully working through colonialism and its legacies, has undertaken a form of cultural imperialism that misrepresents and sanitises the period it has purported to research and teach.

In the first half of the twentieth century, a somewhat different set of texts was valued than those seen as important by post–Second World War modernist studies. Those trying to describe and characterise the literature of their own time in the first half of the century also stressed different styles and themes, where one such theme was colonialism. Well known later in the century, perhaps because it stressed a formal characteristic, was *Axel's Castle: A Study in the Imaginative Literature of 1870–1930* (1931) by the American critic Edmund Wilson. Modern literature was seen as an ongoing, developing symbolist movement. As Vincent Sherry notes, in later years Wilson was most unhappy with the way the writing of the first half of the century was now being discussed, responding to someone he heard use the word 'modernist' with 'Never use that filthy disgusting word in my presence!'[8]

T. S. Eliot offers another description of the period from that time. In 1933, he led a course titled 'English Literature from 1890 to the Present Day' at Harvard University, assisted by Theodore Spencer. Eliot's syllabus and lecture notes survive, and they were first published in 2015. The course moves between British and American writing, between high and low moderns, and between a number of genres; it is unaware of walls that would be built subsequently. Eliot's chronological account begins with extended discussions of Kipling and Wells, writers he juxtaposes: 'Kipling imperialist[:] Wells Fabian'.[9] They were in fact not polar opposites, because being a Fabian did not mean believing in racial equality or wanting the empire to end anytime soon. An initial example of this last point is the Fabian Society's manifesto for the General Election of 1900, which was fought during the Second South African War. *Fabianism and the Empire*, edited by George Bernard Shaw, included all policy areas for Britain under that title. On the empire specifically, it offered to help develop colonised peoples, but it also supported the British war effort in South Africa and the maintenance of the empire by force.[10] The document involved compromises, and some members had resigned over its support for colonial violence, including Ramsay MacDonald. Others soon joined, however, including, in 1903, H. G. Wells – though he later left what Duncan Bell has called 'the most proimperial of the British socialist organizations of the time' to call for a single world government.[11]

Contrastingly, the year 1900 saw 33 delegates of African heritage gather in London for the first Pan-African Congress – it is said to be the first use of the term 'Pan-African'. The Congress's final statement, read out at its close by the African American W. E. B. Du Bois, stressed the dignity of human life and opportunities for development in Africa and the Caribbean. The document featured the first outing of Du Bois's claim that '[t]he problem of the Twentieth Century is the problem of the colour-line', with white nations above that line, and those below it denied 'the right of sharing to their utmost ability the opportunities and privileges of modern civilisation'. As well as calling for self-government for the 'Black colonies', the statement also had a spatial dimension. New communications were collapsing distance and issuing a challenge to power and exclusion.[12] The Congress is itself an example of the back-and-forth encounters across the world's nations and regions that Priyamvada Gopal and Elleke Boehmer have seen as characterising anti-colonial efforts. Boehmer, however, notes the paucity in the Britain of these decades of throughgoing anti-racist and anti-colonial positions outside of these interactions.[13] As we will see, changing attitudes in Britain to empire and nation were often led by the Black and Asian writers and thinkers residing there.

The first extended examples in this chapter will, like T. S. Eliot's in his Harvard course, also involve Kipling and Wells. This chapter is also chronological, but it addresses a more diverse set of writers,[14] keeping race, class, gender roles, and sexuality in view in its discussion of nation and empire. As elsewhere in this book, though, there is no claim that we are exhaustive.

Before the First World War: Empires and Nations, Class and Migration

British writing in the years before the First World War responds to tensions within and between empires as other nations industrialised. In Anglophone modernist studies, the Edwardian period has often been seen as a transitional one before first the war, and then fully modernist texts like *Ulysses* and *The Waste Land* after the conflict – thus asserting an unusually late date for the arrival of modernist innovation in comparison with other European literary cultures. An idealised version of the Edwardian period remains pervasive in the wider culture today. Pre–First World War Britain provides a contrast with the horrors of the First World War; it becomes the time 'before'. Though long debunked, for example in Alan Bennett's first play *Forty Years On* (1969), this myth has not died. The summers were not always long and hot, and neither was it a time of social cohesion and plenty. Rather, these were hard times for many economically. Rising class tensions issued in strikes and state violence. The 'labour unrest' of 1910 to 1914 started to forge modern British trade unions.[15] Winston Churchill sent troops into the Rhonda during the miners' strike of 1910 to 1911 – he was never forgiven there, with these events later inspiring Lewis Jones's innovative novel *Cwmardy* (1937) – and he also ordered thousands of troops to be stationed in Liverpool during the Liverpool General Transport Strike of 1911, which was led by Tom Mann. Hundreds were injured in disturbances in both locations; people died, with two men shot dead by soldiers in Liverpool. Among the plays that addressed labour relations and the impact of strikes on the community were John Galsworthy's *Strife* (1909) and D. H. Lawrence's *The Daughter-in-Law*. The latter was written in early 1913, and though it is now recognised as one of most important British plays of the early twentieth century, the middle-class and London-focused structures of British theatre meant that it only received its first performance in 1967. Written before the First World War, Robert Tressell's *The Ragged Trousered Philanthropists* (1914; fuller version 1955) gradually established itself as the most influential British working-class socialist novel with its highly memorable and linguistically lively exposure of exploitation, poor pay, and bodged work.

The resolve of the wider population to maintain nation and empire, and the fitness to fight of the coming generation, was questioned after the Second South African War. The science of that time – now known to be pseudo-science – claimed that cities were allowing people to have children who would not have done so in the past, or the children would not have survived, and that the race was 'degenerating' as a result. Such views were particularly popular on the Left and were enthusiastically adopted by Fabians. There were fears that Anglo-Saxons were losing a supposed advantage over other races, putting the empire in peril.[16] After the Second South African War, Kipling wrote in his poem 'The Lesson', first published in *The Times* on 29 July 1901, 'We have had an Imperial lesson. It may make us an Empire yet!'[17] Immediate action was required, and young people needed to be brought up to be healthy, strong, and able to serve nation and empire. In response to these fears, the Scouts were founded by Robert Baden Powell, who set out his aims for the movement in *Scouting for Boys* (1908).[18] The groups of the Scouts for younger boys, the Cub Scouts, drew on Rudyard Kipling's *Jungle Books* (1894, 1895) for their nomenclature.

Writing for the next generation became a priority. Kipling wrote two short story collections, *Puck of Pook's Hill* (1906) and *Rewards and Fairies* (1910), in which Puck appears to two children, Dan and Una, to tell stories of the land's past and uphold Anglo-Saxon affinities. That means it does not only address those born on the archipelago, also featuring Romans, Danes, and Normans; further, in the later collection a number of the stories are set in eighteenth-century Philadelphia. Efforts were also made in children's writing to resist the loss that attended modernisation. Kenneth Grahame's children's book *The Wind in the Willows* (1908) represents worries about new technology and the harm it brings using Toad and his motor car. As Joseph L. Zornado argues, *The Wind in the Willows* maintains the need for strong parental guidance in the face of the new century's challenges.[19]

C. R. L. Fletcher and Kipling's history book for children, *A History of England* (1911), noted that the Second South African War 'showed us how very badly equipped we were for war upon any serious scale', though it still stresses that 'we won'. Young readers were told that colonialism was a noble project.[20] Another history book for children, H. E. Marshall's *Our Island Story* (1905), took a very different approach. It brought forward the history of ordinary British people, taking its cue from J. R. Green's popular and progressive *A Short History of the English People* (1874). Probably because it did not focus on imperial themes, and misrecognising its political intent, it was republished by the right-wing British 'think tank' Civitas in 2005; they aimed to place a copy in every primary school. In 2010, the new Prime Minister David Cameron declared it to be his favourite children's book, and he returned to *Our Island Story* again when campaigning against Scottish independence in the 2014 referendum campaign.[21]

Migration from outside the empire became a major topic of debate. Competition between empires led to fears of encroachment and counter-invasion. There was violence against migrants in Britain – many Jewish people had fled Russia as a result of Tsarist persecution, the pogroms – and calls for an end to free movement by 'aliens', the word used at that time. The result was the Conservative government's 1905 Aliens Act, which became law shortly before they were ejected from office in the 1906 general election by a Liberal landslide.[22] The debates about the Act were often racialised and seen through overlapping British and empire-wide frames. Those opposing the Act did not see all races and peoples as equal. Why, the Liberal opposition's spokesman Sir Charles Dilke maintained, did the Conservative oppose Jewish migration, given that Jews were assimilable to the British way of life, when the Tories had brought unassimilable Chinese labourers to the Transvaal? Dilke was deploying widespread anti-Chinese tropes of the time, including the view that South-East Asians were biologically disposed to hate Europeans.[23] Published just before the 'Boxer Rebellion' of 1899–1901, M. P. Shiel's novel *The Yellow Danger* (1898) had gained a wide popular readership.[24]

Joseph Conrad's story 'Amy Foster' (1901) addresses migration and Englishness in Edwardian England at the start of the century. It charts the experiences of a shipwrecked man, Yanko, from 'Central Europe', who becomes the title character's husband. Conrad himself was, of course, a migrant from Poland, writing in his third language that he had learned as an adult, becoming a British subject. David Glover's sensitive reading captures the tale's complexities and ambivalence,[25] but the dominant note is that Yanko is an outsider, something he never overcomes. When Amy rejects him, Yanko dies alone.

The context that informed the Aliens Act also brought into being the modern thriller and spy story, with novels including Erskine Childers's *The Riddle of the Sands: A Record of Secret Service* (1903), Violet Guttenberg's *A Modern Exodus* (1904), and Edgar Wallace's early novel *The Four Just Men* (1905). As Glover maintains, '[w]ritten as the new restrictionist legislation was being drafted and debated, each of these novels sought to sensationalise the forms that the law might take in order to draw out its pitfalls and the dangers it posed to the country'.[26] A pervasive sense of the fragility of the modern order fed into anxieties about invasion and panics over violent foreign anarchists and their tactics (exploding bombs as 'propaganda of the deed'). All of these are present in Conrad's *The Secret Agent: A Simple Tale* (1907). John Buchan's *The Thirty-Nine Steps*, published in wartime in 1915, exemplifies the paranoid fear of a nation that believes it is about to be betrayed by and to the 'alien', something that, as Glover argues, both points back to the Edwardian context of the Aliens Act and forward to interwar British fascism.[27]

Younger writers who asserted an image of England rooted in the countryside differed from the older generation of Thomas Hardy and A. E. Housman because they wanted to place the countryside in opposition to the new forms of modernity found in cities. Rupert Brooke's 'The Old Vicarage, Grantchester' was published in first Georgian poetry anthology of 1911–1912. The Georgians aimed to bring more direct forms of expression to English poetry and to revivify the tradition.[28] Brooke's poem is remembered for its evocation of a warm summer's day and its concluding line, 'Is there honey still for tea?' However, that image is contrasted with the backward rural villages outside Cambridge and modern life in imperial capitals. For the I-voice, the Old Vicarage provides an appealing counter-image to what surrounds him as he sits writing the poem in a Berlin café and '*Temperamentvoll* German Jews/Drink beer around'.[29] The class-based image of uniquely English summer days, cultivated leisure, and afternoon tea – hopefully with honey – is opposed to rural backwardness, febrile modern city life, and other races and empires.

Three Condition-of-Empire Novels

Reflecting on the state of society in Britain at the start of the century meant considering the empire. The Condition-of-England question, drawing on the language of Thomas Carlyle's *Chartism* (1839), had spurred debate and fiction in the 1840s and was again at issue around the turn of the twentieth century. The texts from this later period are, though, better seen as Condition-of-Empire novels, and among the most significant examples are H. G. Wells's *Tono-Bungay*, E. M. Forster's *Howards End*, and D. H. Lawrence's *The Rainbow*. These novels also consider how gender identities and relationships were changing, albeit from the perspective of male authors.

H. G. Wells's Tono-Bungay

Tono-Bungay links new scientific discoveries and the birth of consumer capitalism to the early twentieth-century world order. It was to garner responses from musicians, politicians, and fellow writers. Started in 1906,[30] *Tono-Bungay* was serialised from the very first issue of the major English early modernist journal *The English Review* in 1908, edited by Ford Madox Hueffer (later Ford Madox Ford), before being published in book form the following year. *Tono-Bungay* reached for fictional forms to represent and explore a new context.

Wells is known as a prolific writer in multiple genres, including as a pioneer of science fiction, who veered between the extremes of optimism and pessimism. His reputation does not rest on the precision and care of his writing, perhaps because he is considered to have lost his dispute with Henry James on fiction. Wells claimed that the novel should preoccupy itself with life, while Henry James questioned the opposition between art and life this relies on, contending that life at its richest can be located in the processes of creating and engaging with art.[31] In his later reflections on the debate, Wells maintained in his *Experiment in Autobiography* (1934) that his best writing was highly considered and innovative. He argues that around 1900, after the 'social fixity' of the nineteenth century started to break down 'through a new instability, the splintering frame began to get into the picture'. At the time *Tono-Bungay* appeared, he says, 'I was the outstanding instance among writers in English of the frame getting into the picture'.[32] Elsewhere, in Wells's comments on the novel for the 1925 Atlantic Edition of his works, he claimed that he had planned the novel with 'elaborate care' and saw it as his 'finest and most finished novel' (*TB* 3). The tight use of a first-person narration in *Tono-Bungay* is striking, and as David Lodge noted in an insightful essay on *Tono-Bungay* from 1966, 'one might almost say the frame is the picture'.[33] We come to focus precisely on George's limited view of a rapidly changing world, which he is trapped wholly within. *Tono-Bungay* anticipates by more than a decade Georg Lukács's discussion in *History and Class Consciousness* (1923) of how modern capitalism, with its language and value system, was becoming a 'totality' with nothing outside of it.

Older literary forms are no longer fully adequate by themselves, and the novel works by recombining and recasting them. *Tono-Bungay* deploys genres such as the Bildungsroman – though George does not find a place in society at the novel's close – and it utilises many older texts and plots, most importantly another novel that links Kent to London and the colonies, Charles Dickens's *Great Expectations* (1861). George's experiments with airplanes and airships, and the view of the ground he gains from above, not only show a changed relationship to space but also conveys modern disorientation. The French philosopher Henri Lefebvre spoke of how the experience of space changed around 1910 with the advent of new modes of communication and transport.[34] Late in the novel, an airship is used by George to transport his rapidly ailing uncle Edward to the European mainland because, after the collapse of his businesses, criminal proceedings are threatened. As well as being in an airborne nowhere, with George unsure of where he is, the sense of time is also lost.

The marriage plot is central to the history of the novel form, but in *Tono-Bungay* we instead get the end of a marriage that is not among George's most significant relationships. Marion is seen from George's perspective as the narrator, but we can discern that her conventional view of marriage means that she is left baffled and hurt by the way George behaves. The marriage ends when she finds out about his affair with Effie. Working in the typing pool of the Tono-Bungay enterprise, Effie represents the women entering a workplace created by new technology. The topic of single women and sex outside of a framework of moral condemnation was a new one for the novel,[35] and George views his relationship with Effie more positively than he does his marriage. Wells's next novel was to be *Ann Veronica*, also published in 1909, which broke new ground with its generally sympathetic account of an extramarital affair.

George's relationship with his aunt is more significant than his marriage. Though they are not blood relations, it takes a while for both to see its suppressed incestuous aspects, with George the least self-aware. The main love of George's life is Beatrice, whom George first knew as a child. His fantasy construction of her fails to recognise her sadomasochistic desires or, until the novel's end, to acknowledge the evidence of her drug addiction. George idealises Beatrice, as Dante does his Beatrice, but the difference is that in *Tono-Bungay* that image is shown to be false. There are many similarities between Beatrice in *Tono-Bungay* and Estella in *Great Expectations*. For George and Edward, who has a brief and unhappy affair, new forms of masculinity are both helping make capitalism and the world anew and damaging others at an intimate level.

In a new environment of colour posters, department stores, and suburban life, *Tono-Bungay* explores the needs created, and fears preyed upon, by advertising. The novel takes further the exploration of these themes in fiction, inaugurated by such texts as Emile Zola's *Au Bonheur des Dames* (1883) and George Gissing's *In the Year of Jubilee* (1894). *Tono-Bungay* is the story of Edward Pondervero's fake health tonic Tono-Bungay, a product that seems to have been based in part on the early days of Coca-Cola. It is known from the start that it offers no benefit to those who take it; indeed, one of its ingredients is known to damage the kidneys (*TB* 137, 131). At times, though, Edward believes his own marketing. As he works alongside his uncle, George knows it is a swindle, though here, as elsewhere, his self-awareness is partial.

Near the start of his narration, George says, 'And once (though it is the most incidental thing in my life) I murdered a man . . .' (*TB* 10). This encourages the reader to think the very opposite and to ask how it is of a piece with the rest of what we learn about him. It aligns with the way Edward comes to operate as a businessman, seeking to control resources so he can charge prices that are largely profit. As the 'How we Stole the Heaps of Quap from Mordet Island' chapter makes clear, the colonial relationship – the fictional island is off the coast of Africa – is one of theft, resource extraction, and monopoly control. *Tono-Bungay* is aligned with writing that was noting a global economic system and the place of Britain within it, including J. A. Hobson's *Imperialism* (1901). Others demanded that the empire be upheld to protect the economy. The historian George Townsend Warner, father of Sylvia, warned in the 'Trade and the Flag' section of his book *Landmarks in English Industrial History* (1899) that the time was coming when Britain would have to fight competitor empires to maintain its colonies, which he saw as the source of its power and wealth.[36]

As George's ship returns from Mordet Island, the quap shows its destructive force. It emits 'a phosphorescence such as one sees at times on rotting wood' (*TB* 327), and it 'poisoned' those on board (*TB* 320). The damage it does to the ship brings to mind Coleridge's *The Rime of Ancient Mariner* (1798). Though he does not acknowledge it, George's path through life is attended by abandonment, death, and destruction. For Gauri Viswanathan, the novel repeatedly returns to the word 'value' – as when Edward says to George before his African expedition, 'Show value, George. That is where the quap comes in' (*TB* 309). For Viswanathan, this nebulously defined 'value' is something more than pounds sterling on a balance sheet. She sees it as suggesting a spiritual dimension, but in an aside she notes that Theodor W. Adorno preferred to use the term 'occultism' for this 'complement of reification' rather than religious terminology.[37] Staying with Adorno's insight, from our later perspective we might see George's unmoored and violent selfhood, with his yearning for 'value' and fretting over its absence, as showing the connections between colonial and fascist masculinities.[38]

The extraordinary closing chapter of *Tono-Bungay* sees George testing a new kind of destroyer that he has been developing on the Thames. Destroyers were then smaller, fast torpedo boats. (Wells might well have had in mind Kipling's poem 'The Destroyers' (1898), which revels in a destructiveness *'That seeks the single goal;/The line that holds the rending course,/The hate that swings the whole'*.[39]) George's narration regards the new England of his time as 'the last great movement in the London Symphony' (*TB* 385). The conclusion of *Tono-Bungay* informed the extended coda to the original 1913 version of Ralph Vaughan Williams's second symphony, which was, as part of its response to Wells's novel, titled *A London Symphony*.[40] The final pages of the novel suggest the lack of an 'outside' to George's narrative or depth to his subjectivity; he is the pure representative of his time. George says of his narrative, 'I wanted to tell *myself* and the world in which I found myself' (*TB* 381), but he also wonders, 'Perhaps I see wrongly. It maybe I see decay all about me because I am, in a sense, decay' (*TB* 382). George surveys the state of the nation and 'finds no hope in this Empire or any of the great things of [our] time' (*TB* 382). Modern capitalism is bringing a culture to an end: 'It is quaint no doubt, this England. [. . .] The realities are greedy trade, base profit-seeking, bold advertising' (*TB* 384). In this context, the word 'destroyer' takes on a double meaning, signifying both the function of a kind of warship and the modern forces that are consuming everything, including George himself: 'I and my destroyer [. . .] London passes, England passes . . .' (*TB* 387).

Some were unable to fully accept the novel's implications. The New Liberal writer and politician Charles Masterman quotes at length from the final pages of Wells's *Tono-Bungay* in his 1909 book *The Condition of England*.[41] However, Masterman remained committed to the empire, contending that '[n]o nation need be ashamed of Empire on a large scale, or apologise for the overlordship of a Continent'. Disturbed by 'the weakening or vanishing of the qualities by which such conquest was attained,'[42] he asked, '[I]s the future of a colonising people to be jeopardised, not by difficulties of overlordship at the extremities of its dominion, but by obscure changes in the opinion, the religion, and the energies at the heart of the Empire?'[43] *Tono-Bungay* provides a powerful analysis of these 'obscure changes'.

Benita Parry acknowledged *Tono-Bungay*'s powerful depiction of modernisation, space, and place, but she saw it as 'transitional' because of the failure to go beyond the world it depicts. She says that high modernist writing styles would have helped Wells go further. This fails to see that *Tono-Bungay*'s acute intervention is precisely that there is no such readily accessible 'outside' position from which the modern could be understood and changed. Benita Parry's later work was to go beyond definitions of modernism that came from the imperial centre. Questioning criticism on 'peripheral modernisms', she advocated forms of writing that combined material from modern and traditional cultures, utilising voices new and old. Timothy Brennan went further still in his essay 'Against Modernism', proposing that Europe be viewed through writing undertaken elsewhere in the world.[44] It is not, though, necessary to wholly discount European writing from the first half of the twentieth century in Europe. It can be re-examined to see how it explored and to an extent pushed back against late colonial society. *Tono-Bungay* foregrounds multiple forms of boundedness, and, as a result, the reader of the novel might well initially despair, only to feel compelled to try to go beyond its frame.

E. M. Forster's Howards End

Howards End finds ways of exploring how the global imperial context of the turn of the century changed the experience of space and place in Britain. The use of form and style did not, as with *Tono-Bungay*, rely on reworking earlier writing so explicitly. The novel is critical of modernisation, and Forster's writing can be seen as part of what the art historian T. J. Clark has called a 'tremendous reparative countermovement from within modernism itself'.[45] Forster's science fiction story 'The Machine Stops', published in 1909, depicts a giant system that provides for people's physical and psychological needs, and through which they communicate. Vashti lives contentedly within the machine, though she is irritated by any operational problems. Her son, Kuno, is fascinated by the possibility of a life outside of it and the rumours that some still live on the planet's surface, stories widely discounted due to its environmental degradation. Mother and son are briefly reunited when the machine starts to fail due to a lack of maintenance. Though all is lost for Kuno and his mother, he is able to assure her that there will be a future for humankind. He tells his mother that he has now visited the planet's surface, and that the outsiders do exist: 'I have seen them, spoken to them, loved them.' Using a historical allusion often deployed in radical histories, he tells her, 'We die, but we have recaptured life, as it was in Wessex, when Aelfrid overthrew the Danes'.[46] As we noted in the Introduction, outsiders also learn to live afresh in the natural world in Forster's queer novel, *Maurice*, first drafted between 1913 and 1914 and published posthumously in 1971. The two lovers, Maurice and Alec, take to the 'greenwood', living and working beyond the reach of their biological families, social norms, and the law.

Howards End (1910) explores English society at the turn of the century. Critical responses to the novel have shifted markedly in recent decades. Earlier critics viewed as a problem the novel's differences from high modernism and its questioning of narratives of modern progress. That made it a backward-looking and nostalgic text. In recent decades, the class, queer, ecological, and colonial themes of *Howards End* have come to the fore, along with an exploration of its innovative form of realism. An example is the oddity of its third-person narration, something that had long caused puzzlement. Paul B. Armstrong argues that the narrator, in addition to the quirky and questionable interpretation of events, gives the novel a queer, camp quality.[47] A way of performing gender roles and sexuality is present in the novel even though it would have been impossible at this date to include an openly queer character.

Howards End seeks to bring together a divided nation, as its famous epigraph '*Only connect . . .*' suggests. The ellipses here can be taken in multiple ways, including a wistful acknowledgement that connection is hard to sustain. It also alerts us to those points in the text when connection is mentioned, including Margaret Schlegel's 'sermon': 'Only connect! That was the whole of her sermon. Only connect the prose and the passion, and both will be exalted, and human love will be seen at its highest. Live in fragments no longer.'[48] When read allegorically, the novel can be seen as opposing the mercantile Wilcox family and the Schlegels who, with their private income, devote themselves to culture. The novel's closure brings about an incomplete reconciliation, and the fragmentariness in part remains. The children at Howards End, which Ruth Wilcox had brought to her marriage, include the son of Helen Schlegel and Leonard Bast, born outside of marriage, who will inherit Howards End. The novel not only probes conventional gender roles and conceptions of the family, represented in particular by the Wilcoxes, but also queers narrative expectations through exploring, Robert K. Martin has argued, queer families and begetting.[49]

However, the novel has troubling gaps and absences. Leonard is not from the working class, which was then the majority of Britain's population, but the lower middle class. The working class are almost outside the novel's purview, and thus it seems beyond connection. Leonard's class position at this time was a precarious one: 'he stood at the extreme verge of gentility', and '[h]e knew that he was poor'.[50] Working practices in offices were changing, and women were entering the labour market – Effie's job as a typist in *Tono-Bungay* is an example from the fiction of the time. Dress and accessories were the outward signs of Leonard's class, and maintaining them took a sizeable portion of a clerk's salary. This is the context for Leonard wanting his umbrella back and the force of Helen's unthinking comments on its condition. Leonard's struggle leaves him with few ways to access the world of thought, culture, and self-development he craves. He is distracted by his living conditions when he is trying to read Ruskin in the evening, or to attend to the music when he is at the concert in the Queen's Hall and sitting near the Schlegels. Leonard becomes more and more 'unconnected' as the novel progresses. His partner, Jacky – he is too young to marry her when the novel opens – stays with him, but she is seen as a burden and responsibility, something that really stands out in a novel that stresses women's resilience. The novel's main working-class character, she is seen in terms of appetite and vulgarity and is never mentioned again after she reveals at Margaret and Henry's wedding that she had had a sexual relationship with Henry years before, on Cyprus, when he was married to Ruth Wilcox.

Howards End does, as Ruth Wilcox had hoped as her death approached, become Margeret Schlegel's home (though Henry remains the legal owner of the house). It falls on the women in *Howards End* – other than Jacky, anyway – to be the real active agents in this modern world. They not only hold things together but also have to work out how lives can be restored, even if only provisionally. The Wilcox world of 'telegrams and anger' leaves Charles in jail for Leonard's death – though this was hastened by his weakened physical state – and Henry, who ages quickly, leaves himself to Margaret's care and direction after the public disclosure of his affair with Jacky and his son's trial and disgrace. *Howards End* at once analyses male power and its limitations; damage and failure, and the constriction of vision and language, are pervasive. The world of heterosexual male power still dominates, however, across houses, regions, nations, and colonies.

The alignment of women and nature in *Howards End* could well be seen as problematic. It takes the form, as in the case of Ruth and Miss Avery, of care and nurture, something captured when the trees are pollarded near the churchyard during Ruth's internment. (Not seeing it in these terms, the Wilcox children disapprove.) With its stress on a responsiveness to nature, critics have followed in the footsteps of Nicholas

Royle, who, in 1997, called *Howards End* 'the first ecological novel in English'. The novel responds to debates of the time about motor cars and air pollution – the dust they threw up on as yet unsurfaced roads – re-inflecting the pastoral tradition in England, and exploring connections between the environment and colonialism in a global context.[51]

The links between the Wilcoxes and empire run deep. Henry's early career involved colonial Cyprus. Paul, briefly engaged to Helen at the novel's start, goes to work in Nigeria for the family's Imperial and West African Rubber Company. (Rubber enabled modernity, for example, it was used in the tyres of bicycles and motor vehicles and to insulate machines using electricity.) The company owns what the narration describes as 'a helping of West Africa', while a map of Africa in their offices suggests their attitude towards the continent – it is 'like a whale marked out for blubber'.[52] As David Bradshaw explored, the years when the novel was written saw a boom in the price and financial speculation; we are told that Henry doubles his wealth in this period.[53] For Margaret Schlegel, no doubt aware of the association of colonialism and brutality in Africa laid bare in the reporting of atrocities in the Congo, '[I]mperialism [. . .] had always been one of her difficulties'.[54] However, she also feels that the capitalist Wilcox 'spirit life', as it is strikingly called, moved humanity out of the 'protoplasm', made the England of law and order, trains, ships, 'us literary people' – and also, by implication, Howards End.[55]

As the title suggests, places accrue meaning and significance in the novel. However, *Howards End* also foregrounds movement and the spatial. That takes the form of journeys between and across continents – Henry's to Cyprus, Helen's to Germany to hide her pregnancy, Paul's to Africa – as well as within England. Leonard is freest from his worries on his night-time walk from London out into the countryside. It is a novel of movement, though that is not to say that always brings liberty or understanding.

Spatial uncertainty and dislocation can be seen as what drive modernist representation, rather than its innovations originating in the minds of metropolitan artists. Fredric Jameson uses *Howards End* as one of his main examples in his 1989 article 'Modernism and Imperialism'. Jameson starts from economic structures that involved competing empires, a competition that became increasingly tense as the amount of uncolonised land dwindled. There was an increased awareness of an interlinked global system, but one that was located elsewhere and thus could not be comprehended, a 'spatial disjunction'. Jameson explores the relationship 'between the emergence of a properly modernist "style" and the representational dilemmas of the new imperial world system'. Jameson's argument turns the founding positions of modernist studies on their head. Rather than colonialism being some minor theme addressing life far from the important cultural centres, the forms, styles, and content of modernism were made by a world of competing empires. Instead of imperialism being incidental to the writing of that time, then, it is integral. Jameson's close reading in the pamphlet is of Mrs Munt's train journey in *Howards End*. For Jameson, writers of the period were not self-consciously aware of the issue, rather this is something he can discern in retrospect.[56] Jameson's claim on this score is highly questionable, however. Texts such *Tono-Bungay* and *Howards End* reflected on how life in Britain early in the twentieth century was part of a wider, global economic system and represented new forms of spatiality – which is not to claim that they did so in ways that were full and convincing.

The treatment of space and place in one passage from *Howards End* can serve as an example. In what follows, the earlier manuscript version and the final published novel are overlaid; the text in bold is only in the manuscript version:

> And the conversation drifted away and away, and Helen's cigarette turned to a spot in the darkness, and the great flats **over the way** opposite were sown with lighted windows, which vanished and were relit again, and vanished incessantly. Beyond them the thoroughfare roared gently – an **eternal** tide that could never be quiet **and seemed to transcend the motions wishes of the men who set it going. Could anyone, willingly, have created its unlovely channel? While**, while in the east, invisible behind the smokes of Wapping, **rose the gibbous moon** the moon was rising.[57]

In the drafting process, Forster tightens the expression while retaining a sense of something beyond the immediate environs. Some of the suggestiveness is lost in the final version – 'over the way' is replaced by the more literal 'opposite', and the extended image of tides and sea in the manuscript is pruned. The reflection on whether there is any human agency in modernity is excised, but the sound of the traffic still suggests that what is angry and violent now belongs to the machine. In the manuscript, there was more effort to represent the modern city as existing in relationship to what lies beyond it. The final version, though, still sees life in the capital city being lived with an awareness of the world at a distance.

D. H. Lawrence's The Rainbow

D. H. Lawrence believed *Tono-Bungay* to be 'a great book', but it left him feeling that Wells 'is a terrible pessimist'.[58] He saw it as being a writer's role to offer solutions as well as critique. Lawrence's novel *The Rainbow* (1915) offers a different response to the modern world than did Forster's *Howards End*, one that takes the form of a utopian vision of human life transformed. Lawrence's novel explores the emergence of a new order through three generations of the Brangwen family. As so often in Lawrence fiction, wider changes transform all aspects of individual life and relationships. Sexual lives alter, too, though sex, and the natural more generally, is also a site from which new possibilities emerge. The novel has long been heralded as accurate social history – F. R. Leavis held it to be 'unsurpassed' in such terms[59] – but the focus has usually been on the immediate locality of Nottinghamshire, with much less attention given to the regional, European, and colonial contexts. The Lensky and Skrebensky families, who play such an important role in the novel, are in exile in Britain from Poland. Paul Lensky's life is consumed by the Polish nationalist cause after he comes to England with his family after the failed 1863 Polish uprising against Russia. His widow, Lydia, moves to Nottinghamshire with their daughter, Anna, when Lydia finds a post as a housekeeper there. She meets and marries Tom Brangwen, with Tom attracted to her by her difference from what he has known before. Though the marriage is not unhappy, their lack of articulacy about their very different past experiences leaves a distance between them that is never bridged.

While still young, Anna's daughter, Ursula, forms a relationship with Anton Skrebensky. While he is away in the army during the Second South African War, Ursula becomes the first in the family to gain an education and to establish herself, with difficulty and at personal cost, as a teacher in the 'man's world' of work. She also has another relationship, with an older woman, and is alienated from both her past and from her labour, which is expressed in the narration in spatial terms: 'She was isolated now from the life of her childhood, a foreigner in a new life, of work and mechanical consideration.' Like the radical feminists of the time Lawrence was writing the novel, such as Dora Marsden, Ursula regards votes for women as an attempt to gain a role in the nation's existing order – what the narration calls the 'automatic system' – when what is needed is more fundamental change.[60]

In an extraordinary exchange, Ursula tries to get Skrebensky to tell her what it is he sees himself as fighting for:

'I hate houses that never go away, and people just living in the houses. It's all so stiff and stupid. I hate soldiers, they are stiff and wooden. What do you fight for, really?'
'I would fight for the nation.'
'For all that, you aren't the nation. What would you do for yourself?'
'I belong to the nation and must do my duty by the nation.'
'But when it didn't need your services in particular – when there *is* no fighting? What would you do then?'
He was irritated.
'I would do what everybody else does.'
'What?'
'Nothing. I would be in readiness for when I was needed.'
The answer came in exasperation.
'It seems to me,' she answered, 'as if you weren't anybody – as if there weren't anybody there, where you are. Are you anybody, really? You seem like nothing to me.'[61]

The realist mode is stretched with Ursula deploying what we may well feel to be an improbably nuanced spatial language in such circumstances. Ursula tells Anton that he is not there in front of her, not really occupying his own bodily space. The absence and nothingness that characterise Skrebensky's masculinity for Ursula can be compared with the language of hollowness in Joseph Conrad's *Heart of Darkness* (1899), which T. S. Eliot drew upon in his poem 'The Hollow Men' (1925).

Back with Ursula on his return from the war, Skrebensky is offered a posting to India. Their relationship already failing, he proposes marriage, but Ursula refuses to become a colonial wife. A scene involving sex on the beach makes it clear that their relationship is over. Ursula then falls ill – life in this inimical modernity takes a heavy toll – but recovers to have a vision of a very different world at the end of the novel. Ursula sees a future England that is beyond empire and the masculinity it makes – or 'unmakes' as it renders men like Skrebensky nowhere and nothing. The Midlands locality is transformed:

> She saw in the rainbow the earth's new architecture, the old, brittle corruption of houses and factories swept away, the world built up in a living fabric of Truth, fitting to the over-arching heaven.[62]

And what of Skrebensky? Not long after the relationship with Ursula ends, he marries someone else and goes to India. His life and career continue on their course, at least outwardly, with what he represents in the novel retaining its dominance. However, it is the utopian vision of an alternative world with which the novel closes.[63] When *The Rainbow* was published on 30 September 1915, the First World War was into its second year. Thoroughly out of kilter with wartime attitudes, it was soon suppressed.

Primitivisms Near and Far and the Reception of Colonial Writing in Britain

The allure of otherness and difference in *The Rainbow* can be seen as a form of primitivism. Other peoples, places, and cultures offer something different, a new element that might revitalise. The appropriation this involved was often both confident and unthinking; it was a deeply unequal form of cross-cultural contact. The other side of the coin is that there was an implicit acknowledgement that European life and artistic forms needed to be re-energised by otherness and difference. Other cultures were said both to be less developed and inferior, but they also had something that Europe lacked.

Primitivism was often deployed by those who sought to construct an alternative to industrial, modern societies. However, this move often involved recirculating racial hierarchies; D. H. Lawrence's response in writing of the mid-1920s to the Southwest of the United States and Mexico is one of many possible examples. The attraction of the 'primitive' can be linked to the discourses described as operating in the Levant by Edward W. Said in his classic study *Orientalism* (1978), which, when extended to other locations, helped found postcolonial studies. The work that had been undertaken by Orientalists was not, Said demonstrated, disinterested scholarship, rather their writing was moulded by European needs, desires, and anxieties. Other cultures were often described as being exotic and alluring, while also being seen as inferior. The writing from the new discipline of anthropology may have fascinated writers in the late colonial period, but it, too, was mediated through colonial relationships of power.[64]

Older accounts of modernist primitivism see it as part of an artist's style. For example, Picasso's engagement with artefacts from elsewhere in the world in the Trocadéro in Paris informed his practice in his Cubist period. Focusing on artistic style and technique avoids asking questions about how the artefacts came to be in museums. We can look at an example here: the actions of the British expeditionary force in Benin in February 1897. They had a traumatic impact on Edo society and culture. As well as being used for ritual purposes, the objects were used to remind people of the narratives and stories of past times in an oral, rather than a written, culture. Dan Hicks's *Brutish Museums* (2020) addressed how artefacts were given directly by the state to such institutions as the British Museum, while others, kept by servicemen and sold on the private market, took longer to enter museums. The Digital Benin project investigates provenances, identifies current locations, and brings the items back together in a virtual space.[65] The Manchester Museum, part of the university where the authors of this book work, has, at the time of writing, 23 looted objects in its collection. The Manchester Museum is now committed to a policy of 'unconditional repatriation of secret sacred objects to communities of origin'.[66]

Colonial engagement can be seen in the very form and style of many artworks from the late colonial period. Elleke Boehmer has noted that the

> survey, command, and communication which were utilized by Britain and other imperial powers at their height, brought the metropolis into contact with at least the signs of other subjectivities, both recalcitrant and subjugated, which were emerging out of – or out from under – colonial contact with other cultures. [. . . Those processes] resemble in certain respects the layered and multi-voiced style of some of modernism's key canonical works.[67]

Often, in the early decades of postcolonial studies, European and North American engagements with otherness and difference were grouped together and labelled 'primitivist'. The anxieties around being given this label created the conditions for a withdrawal into insularity. Thomas Etherington's reinvestigation *Literary Primitivism* (2017) instead suggests contextualising and evaluating writing about encounters with other cultures and places.

Such contact happens within nations as well as with other nations and continents. A broad definition can also inform the way the past is reworked, as with the Celtic Revival.[68] Britain shared in the Europe-wide trend to map and record cultures that were being supplanted by modernisation. For example, songs from across Britain were collected by the Folk-Song Society, founded in 1898. Ralph Vaughan Williams first noted down 'Bushes and Briars' as sung by a 74-year-old Essex labourer, Charles Potiphar, in 1903; it was to be the first of over 800 such encounters. Vaughan Williams maintained the distinctiveness of the music of different nations, but collecting folk songs also revealed differences between locations and regions within countries in ways that unsettled a one-voiced national discourses.[69]

Writers born elsewhere also turned their gaze on Britain. In the 1930s, Marxist theorist Christopher Caudwell, who died young fighting for the Republic in the Spanish Civil War, argued that British writing of the period was often undertaken by writers from elsewhere. The texts they produced showed an awareness of 'the epistemological problem of the observer' and that was what made these writers 'artistically considerable'.[70] Not only did the writing of the time feature characters who were outsiders, it also paid careful attention to point of view and narration. Kipling famously asked, not long after settling in England from India, 'And what should they know of England who only England know?'[71] Many years after Caudwell developed this argument, the young Terry Eagleton argued that modernism was staffed by 'exiles and émigrés'.[72] Playing with the title of Virginia Woolf's first novel, *The Voyage Out* (1915), this has been termed the 'voyage in'. The list of possible writers under this heading is a long one, including Henry James, Joseph Conrad, and Katherine Mansfield, and it can be extended to include those who were outsiders because, for example, of their class (D. H. Lawrence), gender (Virginia Woolf), or sexuality (E. M. Forster). By this point, it could be said that the majority are being seen as somehow outsiders, but one remembers that this is a nation where power is concentrated in the hands of a few. Those mentioned in accounts of the 'voyage in' from outside Britain are usually white writers, though not always: for example, Anna Snaith explored a number of women of colour in her *Modernist Voyages: Colonial Women Writers in London 1890–1945*.[73]

A writer making the 'voyage in' could use their alternative experiences to view the Irish and British Isles from a different perspective. That could act against the 'sealed subjective worlds' in fictional representations of subjectivity, as Fredric Jameson noted in his essay 'Cognitive Mapping':

> Modern fiction conveys the sense that each consciousness is a closed world, so that a representation of the social totality now must take the (impossible) form of a coexistence of those sealed subjective worlds and their peculiar interaction, which is, in reality, a passage of ships in the night, a centrifugal movement of lines and planes that can never intersect. The literary value that emerges from this new formal practice is called 'irony', and its philosophical ideology often takes the form of a vulgar appropriation of Einstein's theory of relativity. In this context, what I want to suggest is that these forms, whose content is generally that of privatised middle-class life, nonetheless stand as symptoms and distorted expressions of the penetration even of middle-class lived experience by this strange new global relativity of the colonial network.[74]

Again, Jameson believed the importance of the colonial dimension can only be perceived retrospectively. However, as we have seen, writing from the time noted, and responded to, lives lived in the colonial world system; an outsider's perspective aids that attempt.

Writing produced elsewhere was subject to scrutiny and what would now be called gatekeeping. An example comes from the reception in English of the great Bengali polymath Rabindranath Tagore. In March to April 1912, as a prelude to a journey to England, Rabindranath translated poems from his Bengali collection *Gitanjali* ('Song Offering') of 1910 into English. Rather unwisely he used an old-fashioned English poetic idiom. On arrival in Britain, William Rothenstein was excited by when he read the manuscript and arranged publication. The English version of *Gitanjali* had a huge international success and Rabindranath became the first Asian winner of the Nobel Prize in Literature in 1913.

W. B. Yeats's introduction to the English-language version of the collection has been read by Elleke Boehmer in terms of transnational literary contact between the colonies and the centre, and in particular between Bengal and Ireland.[75] However, the publication and reception of the English language *Gitanjali* can also be seen as further embedding in Anglophone cultures a set of Orientalist accounts of South Asia. William Radice's extended introduction to his retranslation of *Gitanjali* tells the story of how, for the English version, Yeats and others reordered and edited Tagore's poems. They took control of how Rabindranath himself was presented; he became an exotic figure and a purveyor of spiritual insights. The manuscript with which Rabindranath stepped off the boat read differently.[76] He was a writer who mounted a remarkable, developing response to a modernising Bengal. Anglophone readers got something different.

The culture of late colonialism did not simply ripple out from the metropolis and imperial centre. The South African writer Olive Schreiner's *The Story of an African Farm* (1883) is now read in terms of its modernist form and style, rather than as an eccentric example of Victorian realism. Schreiner's writing influenced writers in Britain, including D. H. Lawrence and Virginia Woolf, especially her feminist text *Woman and Labour* (1911), which advocated the recognition of unpaid female work in the home and community.[77]

The First World War

The First World War saw individual agency and heroism replaced by impersonal, mechanised conflict. Artillery had a range beyond the horizon and, like the bombs dropped from airships or aircraft, or the torpedoes or mines that could bring death without warning to those on board ships – and that would be a better death than that inflicted by poison gas. To fight a 'total war' involved utilising all the resources the state possessed, taking powers over individual freedom of action. Conscription was introduced in Britain and, by the end of the conflict, the minimum level of medical fitness for military service had been reduced and the age limit raised to 51.

D. H. Lawrence opposed the war, warning readers of the form it would take in an article in the *Manchester Guardian* of 18 August 1914, a fortnight after Britain had entered the war.[78] In the two versions of 'England, my England' (written in 1915 and 1921) and in *Women in Love* (1920), the sequel to *The Rainbow*, he saw the war as the outcome of modernisation's cumulative damage. The character of Gerald in *Women in Love* appears to embody the entrepreneurial and active masculinity Britain needed if it were to gain 'national efficiency'.[79] However, as the novel proceeds Gerald's inner emptiness is revealed. This results in violence towards others, including his partner, Gudrun, until finally it is directed inwards. After achieving some self-knowledge, Gerald walks off to a snowy Alpine death.

Others welcomed and embraced wartime anger and violence against the enemy. Rudyard Kipling had feared after the Second South African War that Britons did not have the resolve needed to fight a European war, but he was pleasantly surprised to be proved wrong. He wrote in his poem 'Sons of the Suburbs': 'If the churchwarden's wife never danced in her life/She'll kick off your hat when she starts.'[80] Kipling's short story collection *A Diversity of Creatures* (1917) ends with the poem 'The Beginnings' with the repeated line 'When the English began to hate'. The story that precedes it, 'Mary Postgate' (1915), sees the title character, a lady's companion, experiencing atavistic pleasure – for some critics even an orgasm – as she thrusts a poker back and forth in a destructor, a small outdoor furnace, while believing that she hears the death agonies of a crashed German airman: 'She thumped like a pavior through the settling ashes at the secret thrill of it.'[81]

The response to the conflict in poetry varied in its response to issues of nationhood and identity. At the start of the conflict, the I-voice of Rupert Brooke's 'Peace' sees the young as 'swimmers into cleanness leaping,/Glad from a world grown old and cold and weary'. 'The Soldier' suggests, though, that this was a doomed generation, with the poem's most famous lines maintaining an eternal colonisation of the space of a decomposing body: 'If I should die, think only this of me:/That there's some corner of a foreign field/That is forever England.'[82] Wilfred Owen's poem 'An Imperial Elegy' writes back to these lines: the grave is 'Not one corner of a foreign field', but rather Europe is one enormous grave 'the length thereof a thousand miles'. Only the ghosts of the past are left upholding 'the Path of Glory'. Going beyond a war poetry of the individual response to conflict, Owen's poem 'Strange Meeting' explores complicity in the violence and death as well as forms of connection that surpass national affiliation: 'I am the enemy you killed, my friend.'[83] The Jewish poet and writer Isaac Rosenberg, who grew up in a Yiddish-speaking family in the East End of London, saw the British Empire, in his 'A worm fed on the heart of Corinth', as like the empires of the past in that it was being eaten away from within. The poem, though, is ambivalent, as it also maintains the majesty, even the beauty, of the empires so corrupted.[84] The most impressive long poem by a combatant is David Jones's *In Parenthesis* (1937), which dazzlingly combines his experiences of the Western Front, modernist poetic strategies, and the Welsh history and myth that he saw, in his autobiography, 'as an *integral* part of our tradition'.[85]

The war did not only happen outside Britain but also it came to the home front with, for example, the Zeppelin raids and with the German submarine blockade that resulted in the introduction of food rationing in 1918. Writers had different perspectives on the impact of the war at home. For Edward Thomas, whose poems were written in the few years before his death at the Second Battle of Arras in 1917, the rhythms of life were being disturbed rather than fully giving way. 'As the Team's Head Brass' (1916) is all about such rhythms, with the conversation between the ploughman and the I-voice happening only in the brief periods when they are within earshot. Preparing the ground for the new crop parallels the lovers who disappear into the wood towards the start of the poem and then re-emerge at its close. All is not unchanged by the conflict, however. The ploughman says that he and is mate, who went to France and was killed, would have removed a storm-blown tree at the field's edge. There is a sense of loss, but also fatalism, when the ploughman compares the real world with the alternative world in which this took place: 'Ay and a better, though/If we could see all all might seem good.'[86] One death here makes some, but not much, difference. The technical control of Thomas's speaking

I-voice and the use of free verse form deeply impress. However, the confidence in rural life as fundamentally unchanging can be questioned. Tractors and other new farm machinery would change the way the land was worked, with implications for the number of rural workers; then came artificial fertilisers and pesticides.

Despite its name, the First World War is not remembered in Britain as a global conflict, something that has long distorted the understanding of writing about the conflict. The Western Front, however significant, was not the sum total of the conflict, and there were other theatres of war beyond Europe. Those from Britain did not make up all those in service of the Crown; according to the *Statistics of the Military Effort of the British Empire During the Great War, 1914–1920* (1922), 37% were from the colonies. Among the most neglected campaigns are those in Africa. Brutally fought, the German colonial forces were in the ascendant before the signing of the armistice in Europe brought the war there to an end.[87]

A wider spread of contexts and experiences of the First World War in Britain's colonies is now being addressed.[88] The consequences for identity have also been considered with more nuance. For example, the historian John Connor notes that for white settler colonies, the Dominions, whose national identity was forged in conflict – the experiences at Gallipoli helped form the national identities of Australia and New Zealand, for example – were not simply becoming distinct from Britain or the empire. The historical record shows, for Connor, the 'problems of applying modern ideas of nationhood to the British Empire in the Great War', because 'the local "national" identity and the broader "imperial" identity were generally – but not always – seen as separate but compatible identities'.[89] Forms of belonging involving regions, nations, and the empire are also seen in Britain at this time.

The war meant that many from the Irish and British Isles engaged with other parts of the world that they would not otherwise have seen. This led them to reflect anew on their own home culture. In her *Conceiving Strangeness in British First World War Writing* (2015), Claire Buck examines writing about a number of such engagements. She has a chapter on E. M. Forster in Egypt where, as well as working for the Red Cross, Forster wrote two books about the country. Befriending C. P. Cavafy, he was to help introduce one of the major poets of the time to the English-speaking world. Forster's Egyptian experience was transformative: he began his sexual life there and met the love of his life, Mohammed el Adl. The Forster who went to India for a second time after the war's end, and then completed *A Passage to India*, was a different person than the one who had begun the novel before the conflict. Forster's friend T. E. Lawrence, 'Lawrence of Arabia', became very well known for his exploits fighting in the Arab Revolt during the war; campaigns in what we now call the Middle East took a more traditional form, and heroic narratives could be crafted. Lawrence's *Seven Pillars of Wisdom* (1926) blurs fact with some fantasy, though its early readers did not know that. The end of the war saw the Ottoman Empire distributed amongst the victorious powers through League of Nations mandates. Borders and areas of British and French control were established by the Sykes–Picot Agreement, roughed out by the two British and French representatives over dinner. There were, though, subsequent tensions, and indeed some fighting, between the two powers.[90]

At the start of the war, the campaign for women's suffrage had secured a promise of the vote at the conflict's end. That was enacted for women over 30 years in 1918, and later, in 1928, it was reduced to 21, the same as for men. (Women's suffrage did not ripple out from an enlightened colonial centre; New Zealand led the way with votes for women in 1893.) With the male workers called up during the war, women undertook labour in previously male occupations, such as in factories and transport, often crossing class barriers to do so. The young Sylvia Townsend Warner produced her first piece of writing about her time working in a munitions factory. D. H. Lawrence, in his story 'Tickets Please' (1918), explored how the gendered roles of the working class were disturbed by the conflict.

During the war women were called upon for emotional labour in the home and undertook caring roles, such as nursing. In Virginia Woolf's *Mrs Dalloway* (1925) the narrator, focalised through Clarissa Dalloway, tells us that during the war Lady Bexborough opened a bazaar having just heard of the death in the conflict of her favourite son, the telegram still in her hand. Rather than simply showing a strong sense of duty, this raises the issue of the personal cost of self-suppression and keeping respectability and the social order in place. Vera Brittain nursed in the Voluntary Aid Detachment (VAD) in Britain, France, and Malta, and the deaths of a number of young men close to her informed her writing and later pacifist campaigning. Her 1923 memoir *Testament of Youth* addressed her loss and its impacts. In Brittain's writing, a general disillusionment with war sits uneasily with the effort to depict the individual deaths of loved ones as meaningful in ways that draw on an older language of service and heroism. She is one of many writers who responded to grief with what Graham Dawson has called structures of 'subjective composure'.[91] *Testament of Youth* was an early example of a text that questioned the war, something that had had begun the year before with C. E. Montague's *Disenchantment* (1922). The 'war books boom' came when the climate for that questioning was more widely established, and had to wait until the end of the 1920s.[92]

There were gaps in writing that represented women's experience, as there also were for life in the colonies. Later writers have used historical fiction to address these absences, with examples including Abdulrazak Gurnah's novels about war and colonialism in Africa in the decades around the turn of the century, *Paradise* (1994) and *Afterlives* (2020), and Pat Barker's novel about a working-class woman in the North-East of England, *Liza's England* (1986). Going beyond literary texts of the time increases the range of texts that can be examined – it is possible to look, for example, at letters, surviving artefacts, and how the war was memorialised. Santanu Das has written impressively and movingly about the South Asians who participated in the conflict. He examines a broad array of sources to capture the range of affective experiences of Indians. Among the literary texts he discusses, Das sees Mulk Raj Anand's novel *Across the Black Waters* (1940) as 'the most sustained and powerful'. *Across the Black Waters* critiques war, empire, and antiquated Indian social hierarchies. (The reference in the title is to the then-prevalent belief among Hindus that they lost caste status when crossing oceans.) Anand's own experiences were diverse, including contacts with Nehru and Gandhi in India, friendships with the 'Bloomsbury Group', working for the BBC with George Orwell on the Eastern Service, and joining the International Brigades in the Spanish Civil War.[93] Though too young to have been a combatant in the First World War himself, Anand in *Across the Black Waters* works over and reflects upon recent colonial experiences from within the late colonial period itself.

Britain After the War: Claude McKay

The year 1919 was one of political crisis, the so-called 'Red Year', in which European governments were anxious about further revolutions like the ones in Russia in 1917. Populations were depleted not only by the war but also by influenza (the 'Spanish Flu') and faced food shortages, in some cases starvation. In Britain, skirmishes between strikers and police led the authorities to deploy tanks and troops on the streets of Glasgow. Some on the Right linked economic difficulties to the continued presence of colonial troops; demobilisation was a slow process. There were outbreaks of violence in port towns, including Cardiff and London. One of those of African heritage caught up in this violence, Ernest Marke, later wrote about it in his memoirs. In Liverpool, a Black man was lynched.[94]

The police did not help people of colour under attack, and neither did they get support from most on the Left. E. D. Morel remained a hero for many into the mid-twentieth century.[95] He had left the Liberals for the Labour Party and became an MP for Dundee in the 1922 general election, ousting the sitting member of parliament, Winston Churchill. His great achievement was his pioneering human rights campaign against the treatment of Africans in the Congo by their Belgian colonisers. In part because of Morel's campaign, the Congo was transferred from the King of the Belgians' private company to the Belgian state. From 1914, Morel headed the Union of Democratic Control (UDC), which sought to make decisions about going to war democratically accountable in Britain – something that is still not in place in twenty-first-century Britain. Morel's close friend Bertrand Russell was on the UDC's General Council during the war, as was J. A. Hobson; Leonard Woolf joined its Executive Committee after the conflict's end.[96]

Immediately after the war, the UDC spoke up against humiliating the defeated power, something they rightly saw as likely to stoke up resentment. Morel then launched a new UDC campaign with characteristic vigour. His campaign over the Congo did not mean that Morel regarded Black Africans as equals, and the claims involved racialised forms of sexual violence that are hard to read about. Morel took particular issue with the deployment of French colonial troops from Africa in the occupied German Rhineland. He maintained that this was a continuation of the war against the German population because the French authorities knew that the colonial troops would not be able to restrain themselves sexually when near white women.[97] Supposed African male physical attributes were, he said, resulting in murder in addition to rape:

> Primitive African barbarians [. . .] have become a terror and a horror unimaginable to the countryside, raping women and girls [. . .] [F]or well-known

physiological reasons, the raping of a white woman by a negro is nearly always accompanied by serious injury and not infrequently fatal results.[98]

Morel claimed that these crimes – the 'horrors' – were in full swing.

The Jamaican-born Claude McKay responded to Morel's race-based conspiracy narrative. McKay was born in the Blue Mountains of Jamaica, and was encouraged to begin writing poetry, in Creole, by an expatriate Englishman, Walter Jekyll. McKay then went to the United States, becoming part of the Harlem Renaissance, before working his passage to England at the end of the First World War. Indignant at the way those of African descent were being described and represented in the stories he read about in the 'Black Horror on the Rhine', McKay tried to get a letter published in *The Daily Herald*. The daily newspaper's founder and editor, George Lansbury, an MP and future Labour Party leader, refused to print McKay's letter.[99] McKay was, though, able to place it in Sylvia Pankhurst's *Workers' Dreadnought*. He wrote: '[w]hy all this obscene, maniacal outburst about the sex vitality of black men in a proletarian paper?' He drew attention to the sexual behaviour of British men in the colonies and cited his own sexual continence as a man of African descent as evidence. African men were not 'sexually unrestrainable', he said, '[this was] palpably false. I, a full-blooded Negro, can control my sexual proclivities when I care to, and I am endowed with my full share of the primitive passion.'[100] The scrutiny this invited of his own sexual life was perhaps unwise, given that McKay was, according to his friends in London, openly homosexual, and male homosexual acts were illegal in England and Wales until partial decriminalisation in 1967. In time, the dearth of evidence to support Morel's claims was exposed. It was the Black American press – all too used to investigating false stories in the United States – that revealed 'the horrid lack of horrors on the Rhine'.[101]

McKay later claimed that it was through getting this letter published that he met Sylvia Pankhurst and came to write for the *Workers' Dreadnought*.[102] Winston James has established that work for the *Workers' Dreadnought* did not take all of McKay's time in London; he had a patron who supported him financially. McKay spent time engaging in political activities, and he also had the time to write in the reading room of the British Museum. He responded to what he saw elsewhere in the museum, and McKay was to write back to the primitivism of modernist art, maintaining that 'the treasure house of Benin are more complex in conception and more amazing than the strangest works of Picasso'.[103]

According to Peter Fryer, McKay's time on the *Workers' Dreadnought* made him 'Britain's first Black journalist'.[104] His particular focus was labour relations and the London docks. The authorities were very anxious about sailors living in poor conditions while they awaited demobilisation. McKay's stay in Britain came to an end when he became involved in publishing the views of a sailor in the Royal Navy who was in fact a communist agitator.[105] It was to be Sylvia Pankhurst who felt the consequences. Refusing to give up the source of the story, she was imprisoned for five months. McKay left Britain for the United States.

In his sonnet 'England' (1924), McKay was to echo Shakespeare, and specifically the *Sonnets* and John of Gaunt's speech in *Richard II*. The poem describes the island 'like a fixed and fortressed rock', until 'the slaves revolt [. . .] with strong hands and rude,/From thy high eminence to dash thee down'.[106] McKay often chose to write lyrics and sonnets, something that long puzzled Harlem Renaissance critics, who saw a tension between the use of the elite English form and the radical content. McKay can, though, be seen as colonising the form and style of the English poetic canon, including the verse of the national poet himself; they are repurposed to convey an anti-colonial message.[107] It was after his time in Britain, when living mainly in France and North Africa, that McKay wrote fiction that sought to go beyond borders, national identities, and the confines of sexual and gender roles. These novels include *Banjo* (1929) and *Romance in Marseille*, which was written in the early 1930s, left in manuscript, and finally published in 2020.

A Colonialist and Racist Culture

Sylvia Pankhurst's anti-racism and anti-colonialism were rare beliefs at this date. It would be wrong to assume that there was a part of the political spectrum in Britain that was consistently anti-colonial and anti-racist, holding all peoples equal and with the right to determine their own future. Things began to shift in the years immediately before the Second World War, but even then the numbers were small and often involved networks that included writers and thinkers of colour from the colonies.

The Conservatives were the strongest supporters of the empire, though, as we will discuss, they were divided over the issue of preferential tariffs for the colonies in the early decades of the twentieth century. The Liberal Party experienced its 'strange death' after its 1906 election landslide, which was the last time it gained a parliamentary majority. The 'first past the post' electoral system allows just two major parties, and Labour gained increasing numbers of votes from the newly enfranchised working class. While rarely enthusiasts for the empire, Liberal governments had not moved against it. Gladstone had eventually tried, and failed, to enact an Irish Home Rule Bill in the late 1880s and early 1890s, and some reforms were undertaken in India. There was, though, an important group of 'Liberal Imperialist' MPs who advocated national efficiency at home and pro-empire policies abroad. Radical Liberals questioned colonial practices, but it is only really with Wilfred Scawen Blunt that we approach a full form of Liberal anti-imperialism – as seen, for example, in his 1901 pamphlet 'The Shame of the Nineteenth Century: A Letter Addressed to the "Times"'. Summed up as a 'hedonist, poet, and breeder of Arab horses' in his entry in the *Dictionary of National Biography*, Blunt stood a number of times, unsuccessfully, as a Liberal candidate for Parliament. E. M. Forster favourably reviewed the two volumes of Blunt's diaries that were published towards the end of Blunt's life. For a period around the start of the First World War, Blunt was a hero to the *avant-garde* Imagist and Vorticist circles around Ezra Pound; their politics were informed by anarchism and an opposition to the British Empire.[108] (Pound was later, however, to produce propaganda for Italian fascism.)

Anarchism is neglected in studies of modernism and politics.[109] It was never a mass movement in the Irish and British Isles, but it does have a rich intellectual tradition, and there were many writers who can be described as 'left libertarians', combining socialism and anarchism.[110] Against state power and war, anarchists often opposed colonial wars. Not all of them were against empire and racism, however. Winston James notes of Guy Aldred's British anarchist paper, *The Spur*, that in the years after the First World War it was radical on everything except when it came to condemning racist violence.[111]

For its first decade or so, the Communist Party of Great Britain foregrounded an opposition to imperialism. Founded in 1921, the Party adopted the views of the Soviet Union and the analysis of Vladimir Lenin in his *Imperialism: the Highest Stage of Capitalism* (1916). Lenin argued that the world economy of the time was one of competing empires and economic blocs, summarising his argument in his later 'Preface to the French And German Editions' (1920) as follows:

> In the pamphlet I proved the war of 1914–18 was imperialistic (that is, an annexationist, predatory, plunderous war) on the part of both sides; it was a war for the division of the world, for the partition and repartition of colonies, 'spheres of influence' of finance capital, etc. [. . .] Capitalism has grown into a world system of colonial oppression and of the financial strangulation of the overwhelming majority of the people of the world by a handful of 'advanced' countries.[112]

In the decade after Lenin's death in 1924, the Comintern, the organisation controlled by the Soviet Union that aimed to spread communism to the world, pushed an anti-colonial message. However, with the rise of Nazi Germany, Stalin's USSR moved for a period to advocate a broad anti-fascist grouping of nations, the Popular Front. As a result, criticism of the empires of European powers was toned down. Then, after a period of accord with Germany, under the Molotov–Ribbentrop Pact, came Germany's invasion of Russia in June 1940, and the Soviet Union became Britain's ally in the Second World War. Key members of the Communist Party of Great Britain (CPGB) supported colonial independence movements. The books of the arch-loyalist executive committee member, and briefly general secretary of the Party, Rajani Palme Dutt, are an example; they include his *India Today* (1940).

After the Labour Party's electoral defeat in 1924, its party conference passed motions that meant that not only were CPGB members no longer able to stand as Labour parliamentary candidates, as had been the case, but also that no one in the Labour Party could also be in the CPGB.[113] Some in the Labour Party eschewed claims of an age of imperialism not simply on the merits or otherwise of the case, but because they did not want to be seen to hold the same views as their political opponents. Many in the Labour Party anyway strongly supported colonialism. Robert Blatchford had founded the *Clarion* newspaper to facilitate a good, healthy life for the working class, branching out into walking and cycling clubs. He believed such activities could help repair the damage that had been done when workers moved into cities from the countryside. Blatchford became a vocal supporter of colonialism, arguing that the colonies had to be defended and the money they provided used to support better lives for British workers.[114] Unions with members in jobs linked to the colonies often supported the empire. Many in the Party argued that Labour would make itself more electable if it asserted patriotic and pro-empire positions. The first Labour government of 1923–1924, a minority government, undertook what David Torrance has called in his study of the administration 'Imperial business as usual'. Making a toast after the opening of the Empire Exhibition, with King George V present, Colonial Secretary Jimmy Thomas said that in the future no one would question that the Labour government was 'proud and jealous of, and were prepared to maintain, the Empire'.[115]

Some in the Labour movement were critical of this stance, including George Lansbury, a number of local parties, and the wider Independent Labour Party (ILP). (At this point, the ILP was affiliated to the Labour Party.) Colonial violence was an issue because some of its leading members were pacifists. However, when they got into office, leading ILP figures often compromised their principles – indeed, in time, Ramsay MacDonald was to compromise to such an extent that he led a national government, the majority of whom were Conservatives. As we will see later in the chapter, it was only at the end of the 1930s, when the ILP had disaffiliated from the Labour Party – and when it was less of an electoral force – that strongly anti-colonial positions were developed within its ranks, spurred by members of colour.

Paternalism

Many intellectuals and theorists on the Left in the first half of the twentieth century saw Britain as taking on a parental role in relation to its colonies; those of different races were seen as less developed and in need of guidance. Independence might one day come, but that day was in the future. Though those on the Left wanted more enlightened colonial administration, the prevalence of eugenicist views meant that racist positions were common.[116]

It was not the case that progressive positions steadily gained ground. There was a retreat from the strongly anti-imperialist positions articulated by William Morris in the late nineteenth century. Edward Carpenter helped pioneer the case for homosexual rights and espoused socialist, feminist, and anti-carceral positions. He visited South Asia, writing a travel book, *From Adam's Peak to Elephanta*. However, he exoticised the East, and his poetry is bifurcated on colonialism. The empire is dying, yet English values provide the ground for a rebirth. Before Tressell's *The Ragged Trousered Philanthropist* became widely available and known, Carpenter's poetry collection *Towards Democracy* was the most popular literary text on the Left. The poem 'Empire', in Part IV of the collection, which he added in 1902, sees England as a tree and 'the bully of weak nations whom thou wert called to aid'; given its moral decline, the poem continues, 'I fear thou canst but die'. However, England is the 'Mother of the forest' with new growth springing up from its roots. In the same part of *Towards Democracy*, the poem 'India, the Wisdom-Land', despite lauding the insights South Asia offers, sees England as providing 'the precious semen of Democracy'.[117]

Carpenter had been in the Fabian Society in its earliest days, but he soon left as it developed its characteristic position that an elite within the governing class should guide the country to socialism through technocratic government. Believing in social structures that enabled the fullest possible expression of the self, Carpenter would not have agreed with Sidney Webb when he said that 'the perfect and fitting development of each individual is not necessarily the utmost and highest cultivation of his own personality, but the filling, in the best possible way, of his humble function in the great social machine'.[118] Paternalism was central to the Fabian project, whether that be for the working class in Britain or for people in the colonies. In 1913, Sidney and Beatrice Webb published an article in the recently established left-leaning periodical *The New Statesman* titled 'The Guardianship of the Non-Adult Races'. It saw the peoples of the empire as being like children of different ages, with Britain as the parent. The most advanced of those populated by people of colour was India, and it was growing up: 'Whereas it used to be only seven years old, it is now fourteen.'[119]

One-voiced claims are made in modernist studies for Leonard Woolf as a thoroughgoing anti-imperialist. Anna Snaith sees the Woolf's Hogarth Press as establishing a network that facilitated anti-colonial discourse after the First World War. This is a highly partial account. Leonard Woolf's journey from an imperial administrator in Ceylon who believed he could help those who lived there to disillusionment was the subject of his novel *The Village in the Jungle* (1913) and the short story 'Pearls and Swine' from *Stories from the East* (1924). His biographer, Victoria Glendinning, declared that his time in Ceylon made him an anti-imperialist, but Peter Wilson has argued that it is more accurate to call Woolf a disillusioned imperialist until 1920.[120] As Wilson's 2003 reconsideration of Woolf shows, he was a major figure in developing foreign policy for the Fabian Society and the Labour Party, and he was known for his attacks on economic exploitation and his belief in eventual self-government for the colonies. However, he saw European education and values as wholly unrelated to colonialisation and assumed a position as an arbiter of what was appropriate in colonial education, development, and the timing of independence. The primary issue for Woolf was always what he saw as good government.[121] As late as 1945, in an essay titled 'The Political Advance of Backward Peoples', Woolf maintained that 'our object in Africa should be to produce good Africans' and that it would take more 'than one generation to produce by education a sufficient number of educated Africans to make self-government possible'. A start could, though, be made with local government so that 'they may eventually acquire the difficult art of governing themselves'.[122] Woolf's language for describing Africans moved in the 1920s from referring to them as 'non-Adult races', 'primitive peoples', and 'African savages' to instead using 'backward peoples' and 'the native'.[123]

After the First World War, Woolf had supported the League of Nations mandates in the former German and Ottoman Empires, seeing them as offering a structure for guided development. In terms that surprise today, in his 1920 pamphlet *Mandates and Empire*, Woolf maintained that mandates were 'the opposite of imperialism'.[124] It was in the late 1930s that the Trinidad-born Pan-Africanist George Padmore would set out how the mandate system was an adaptation of colonialism rather than something radically different. As Rodney Worrell has argued, '[f]or Padmore the mandatory system was a disguised from of imperialist annexation'.[125] In a 2019 article on Leonard Woolf and imperialism, Luke Reader summarises Woolf's position:

> Woolf may not have been supportive of imperialism, but he thought imperially. He was paternalistic. He considered colonial populations backwards,

and organized people into racial hierarchies, balancing these prejudices with calls for eventual self-government. Woolf was anti-imperialist, but only if empire is viewed solely in economic terms. One effect of his arguments was the tautology that the Labour Party use imperialism to protect against economic imperialism.[126]

As with other writers from the first half of the century, then, Leonard Woolf needs to be seen in a context of a time when thorough going anti-colonial and anti-racist positions were rare.

Virginia Woolf criticism has noted the sustained consideration of colonialism in her writing; it was there at the start of her career with *The Voyage Out*. There has been some work over the decades that has been open both to registering her writing's questioning of colonialism and also its recirculation of colonial attitudes and tropes.[127] In his *Archipelagic Modernism*, John Brannigan sees Woolf's final position in her posthumously published novel *Between the Acts* (1941) as a future-orientated resolution to go beyond the current imperial and national order: 'It is that sense of responsibility, of a vow to imagine Englishness beyond empire, beyond race, which characterises Woolf's ambition in *Between the Acts*, and which is that novel's principal legacy for a post-devolutionary imagination of an independent England.' However, Woolf's novel does not go beyond the promissory.[128]

The leading historian and critic E. P. Thompson wrote in 1963 that anti-colonialism before the Second World War was mainly found amongst 'ultra left groups and communists' and parts of the labour movement. He observes that 'the Fabians were notoriously ambiguous (or plainly compromised) on colonial issues; while there was no Labour leader whose attitude to India was more paternalist than [Ramsay] MacDonald'.[129] Thompson points out that the end of empire in India only became a general feeling and policy on the Left with the successful 1945 Labour election manifesto. That manifesto, though, said little about the empire – but then it was a brief document – redeploying notions of different stages of racial maturation and upholding Britain's role as a guide. Only India is promised independence: 'the Labour Party will seek to promote mutual understanding and cordial co-operation between the Dominions of the British Commonwealth, the advancement of India to responsible self-government, and the planned progress of our Colonial Dependencies.'[130] The manner in which Britain left India in 1947 resulted in the loss of around a million lives, and has ongoing consequences to this day.

Registering Late Colonial Uncertainties

As the mid-century approached, and as the economic strength that underpinned Britain's global position was eroded, confidence in the colonising project started to ebb. Rather than a knowing gaze and a sense of certainty, some of those who made the 'voyage out' began to question what they were doing and why. Writers adapted existing forms and styles of writing to represent their responses.

E. M. Forster's A Passage to India

To capture this interwar change, Forster's image in his essay 'What I Believe' (1938), about his relationship with liberalism, is hard to improve upon. Forster said that he 'has felt liberalism crumbling beneath him'.[131] Beliefs and old certainties were in question, but the image conveys more than that – the sense that the very ground beneath one's feet was becoming uncertain. New understandings and identities would be needed.

A Passage to India is now recognised as a complex text, one that captures a wider slippage in the Occidental confidence needed to rule and dominate. The self, social conventions, and the nation are all in question. The novel asks whether it is possible to know and understand India and the world beyond Britain at all. As Benita Parry noted, considering these issues leads the novel to make particular formal innovations that differ from those found in metropolitan modernism.[132] Though *A Passage to India* asks epistemological questions, it is also a more directly political novel. That claim might surprise some. When writing *A Passage to India*, Forster did yet not believe in Indian independence; his views were only to change subsequently. Edward W. Said was right to note that the novel recirculates tropes that see Indians as emotional and disorganised, and that it eschews a sustained engagement with nationalist politics.[133] However, *A Passage to India* takes aim at one specific group, Anglo-Indians, as the British in India were then called. The novel's narrative reverses one of the central narratives of British India.

The novel explores a number of failed journeys to India. Relationships end there, including the friendship established so promisingly between Fielding and Aziz. What happens to Adela Quested is the cause. Going to India with Mrs Moore as chaperone, Adela wants to assess a possible future life in India as the wife of Ronny Heaslop, the city magistrate, who is Mrs Moore's son. The two women want to see India and Indians, but the trip to the caves that Dr Aziz organises for them ends with Adela accusing him of a sexual assault in one of the caves. At his subsequent trial, Adela, replaying the events in her mind on the witness stand, does not feel able to attest to the claim, and the case is dismissed. An accusation of sexual assault which is not believed and subsequently withdrawn troubles many modern readers. Adela is made to take the weight of responsibility for multiple lives and events in the novel; much rests in *A Passage to India* on the main woman character.

The novel would have had further resonances at that time. The way the British ruled India often invoked stories of the 1857 Uprising, which the British called the 'Mutiny'. The story that was frequently told – often focusing on events at, for example, Cawnpore (now Kanpur) – was that British women had been at risk from Indian men, who could not control themselves. (It is a similar narrative structure, then, to that seen in the 'Black Horror on the Rhine' campaign.) Nancy Paxton has termed this plot the 'rape script', in which the vulnerability of British women to Indian men was said to justify a violent response.[134] Events in Amritsar in 1919 provided early readers of *A Passage to India* with a recent example. After unrest in the Punjab region, Brigadier General Dyer ordered troops in the Jallianwala Bagh to open fire on a peaceful gathering. Forster had early and full news of the massacre – the British tried to suppress reports – in a letter from his friend Malcolm Darling in India. Gerard Wathen, a mutual friend and principal of the local college, played a pivotal role in preventing further British violence. Kim A. Wagner sees Dyer's actions as an example of the '"Mutiny"-motif': 'The British effectively created their own nightmares and this proved to be the Achilles heel of the Raj.'[135] *A Passage to India* exposes an Anglo-Indian group panic, though the Anglo-Indians see their response as entirely rational. As Superintendent of Police McBryde notes: 'Read any of the Mutiny records; which, rather than the Bhagavad Gita, should be your Bible in this country.'[136] The novel was clearly written in part to rile early Anglo-Indian readers. There was a further reversal of expectations because they are treated one-dimensionally in the novel and the Indians are accorded more attention. The novelist Paul Scott later noted that many Anglo-Indian readers 'threw copies overboard from the P. and O. into the Red Sea' in disgust at their treatment.[137]

The novel's continuum of questioning goes beyond Anglo-India. *A Passage to India* also refuses to adopt such conventions of the novel form as the marriage plot and it reaches for ways of expressing what it means not to know, and the conditions in which new meanings emerge. As readers, we are made aware of how things look from different perspectives; we cannot take everything that the narrator says at face value. From the novel's opening chapter, we are made aware that things look different when viewed from alternative standpoints. The narrator is no lodestar, with Paul B. Armstrong observing that the 'narrator is both all-knowing and an eccentric, oddly opinionated commentator who debunks Orientalist prejudices only then himself to deploy them'.[138]

The use of symbolism in *A Passage to India* is part of an exploration of what lies outside European knowledge, but the novel knowingly puts itself in the position of trying to represent the unrepresentable in the novel form. The events in the caves see a crucial gap in the narration. One of Forster's advances in the novel's long gestation was the addition of this absence in the text – paralleling the caves in the Marabar Hills. (In surviving draft material, there is an assault in the darkness of the caves; because it is related from Adela's perspective, however, the reader cannot be certain of the perpetrator.[139]) There is also the novel's innovative use of symbolism. Everything uttered within the cave comes back as the 'same monotonous noise': '"Boum" is the sound as far as the human alphabet can express it, or "bou-oum," or "ou-boum," – utterly dull. Hope, politeness, the blowing of a nose, the squeak of a boot, all produce "boum."'[140] The symbol of the cave does not, then, offer up meaning; rather, it shows the loss and emptying out of signification.

Mrs Moore's Christian understanding fails with her health: of love, she concludes, 'in a cave, in a church – boum, it amounts to the same'.[141] Her earlier kindness, though, takes on a life of its own. There is a belief among the Indians that she had evidence that could have exonerated Aziz. Not knowing that she has recently died on board ship on her way home, those outside the courtroom chant a version of her name, 'Esmiss Esmoor'. Ronny feels that she has been 'travestied' and transformed into 'a Hindu goddess'.[142] The respect Mrs Moore had shown for difference, seen early in the novel in her first encounter with Aziz in the mosque, is also present when she acknowledges an Indian wasp, different in appearance from those in England, that she notices on a coat hook: 'Pretty dear', she says. Professor Godbole remembers this moment – though he was not there and previously knew nothing of it – during his devotions at the end of the novel.[143] There is a stress on other such narratives of return and recurrence, such as when the Nawab of Bahadur fears that the car accident he has been in is caused by a *jinn* related to an earlier crash in which a man had died. Also travelling in his car are Adela and Ronny, and their engagement is briefly renewed in the aftermath of the incident – however, the return of mutual affection does not last.

Meaning proliferates in *A Passage to India*, but it also recedes from view and may not be accessible to the coloniser. The queer aspects of the text – present from the first meeting of Aziz and Fielding when Aziz gives Fielding his collar stud – are often used to suggest meanings and possibilities that cannot be articulated directly. Benita Parry observed that there are 'three superb and marginal Indian male figures' who, for all their objectification, are powerfully silent:

[The] import of silence within the novel resides rather in the lowly Indians, whose aphonia alludes to their habitation of a realm beyond the ken and the control of western knowledge, and who join India's material being and cognitive traditions in resisting incorporation into a western script.[144]

Fielding becomes a less open and more conventional figure after his time back in England and his marriage. His efforts to renew his friendship with Aziz are rebuffed on the novel's last page, suggesting that such connection at an individual level is not possible in late colonial India. However, there is a complex mixture of openness and closure at the end of *A Passage to India*. The penultimate chapter offers what can be seen as another ending, one that involves connection and reconciliation of sorts, when the rowing boat on the lake carrying Aziz and the British characters crashes into the tray with the representation of the village of Gokul, Krishna's birthplace, being used in the Hindu rituals to mark Gokulashtami. Those present, and letters from Ronny and Adela, all end up roiling together in the water.

Robert Byron's The Road to Oxiana

The standout modernist travel book, Paul Fussell maintained in his classic study of interwar travel writing, is Robert Byron's *The Road to Oxiana* (1937): 'perhaps it might not be going too far to say that what *Ulysses* is to the novel between the wars and what *The Waste Land* is to poetry, *The Road to Oxiana* is to the travel book.'[145] Byron's book captures the ebbing of confidence in a British person's authority to know and understand other locations and peoples. *The Road to Oxiana* arose from a car journey Byron undertook with Christopher Sykes – the son of Sir Mark Sykes of the Sykes–Picot Agreement and the future biographer of Evelyn Waugh – in what we now call the Middle East. The goal was to reach the source of the River Oxus (Amu Darya), in order to find support for Byron's claim that it was here that Islamic art originated. Fussell focuses on the formal aspects of *The Road to*

Nation, Empire, and Identity in Late Colonial British Writing 57

Oxiana – for example, its use of short sections over long passages – but it is most remarkable for the way it expresses doubt and uncertainty, including over whether the observer has the right to be there at all.

The Road to Oxiana often subverts narratives of progress and British pre-eminence in the time of the League of Nations mandates. British decline in industry and science is shown through the failure of the vehicles they are testing, which are powered by charcoal and are unreliable, and of the materials the country exports: '"Are you English?" asked the driver in disgust. "Look at that." An inch of British steel had broken clear through.'[146] Islamic art provides the contrast, and is the equal in its formal qualities of that of ancient Greece and Rome. It is also, however, different:

> Such classic, cubic perfection, so lyrical and yet so strong, reveals a new architectural world to the European. This quality, he imagines, is his own particular invention, whatever may be the other beauties of Asiatic building. It is astonishing to find it, not only in Asia, but speaking in an altogether different architectural language.[147]

What he sees is uncannily the same in its quality, and yet also its meanings differ in ways that cannot readily be comprehended.

The power relationship between the colonies and the centre is seen as being flattened, even reversed. Rulers have the same status and simply succeed each other, as in this potted account of recent Indian history: 'Their last ruler died in exile in Rangoon in 1862, to make way for Queen Victoria.'[148] Humour is also used to unsettle the reader, as when the Byron-figure is asked a series of questions: '"What Government do you belong to?" asked the Hazrat Sahib. "The Government of Inglistan [England]." "Inglistan? What is that?" "It is the same as Hindostan [India]?" "Is Inglistan part of Hindostan?" "Yes."'[149] England is subsumed into India, rather than being its coloniser. There is also both a questioning of nationalism – too much complaining – and a rather detached claim of 'sympathy' with the cause of Indian independence, one that is now shared, we are told, by many in England.[150]

The Road to Oxiana depicts a journey undertaken by someone from the elite – Byron was Eton- and Oxford-educated – who moved easily in the 'best' circles. He knew the Mitfords well – Unity Mitford hoped Byron would marry her, before she realised he was only sexually interested in other men. Unlike Unity – and her sister, Diana, who married Oswald Mosley, the British fascist leader – Byron opposed Nazism. Social ease in the highest social circles is not presented straightforwardly in *The Road to Oxiana*. An example is the way the question at the end of this quotation leads us to rethink what has gone before:

> We dined with the High Commissioner, most pleasantly. There were none of those official formalities which are very well at large parties, but embarrass small ones. In fact, but for the Arab servants, we might have been dining in an English country-house. Did Pontius Pilate remind his guests of an Italian squire?[151]

The final question suggests self-reproach; he is perhaps breaking bread with a colonial ruling class that is washing its hands of doing what is right. Cultural richness is often seen as the result of histories of movement and interchange. *The Road to Oxiana* registers Jews being displaced, sympathetically including them within its purview – however, it also shows prejudice against modern-day Arabs.[152]

A crucial scene in *The Road to Oxiana* occurs in Mashhad in Persia (now Iran), which Byron called Meshed. He is keen to visit the interior of the famous mosque, thus disregarding an interdiction on unauthorised visits by foreigners and non-believers. The account in *The Road to Oxiana* is a late colonial correlative of a famous account by Richard Burton of a trip to Mecca in the 1860s. (Among many other works, Burton translated *The Arabian Nights* in 11 volumes.) Burton recounts lying his way into the holiest parts of the site:

> [H]e officially inquired my name, nation, and other particulars. The replies were satisfactory [. . .] I will not deny that, looking at the windowless walls, the officials at the door, and a crowd of excited fanatics below [. . .] my feelings were of the trapped-rat description [. . .] A blunder, a hasty action, a missed word, a prayer or bow, not strictly the right shibboleth, and my bones would have whitened the desert sand. This did not, however, prevent my carefully observing the scene during our long prayer, and making a rough plan with a pencil upon my white *ihram*.[153]

Maintaining his aplomb under pressure, he continues his researches and does not doubt his right to be there.

The Byron-figure in *The Road to Oxiana*, on the other hand, behaves differently in an analogous situation. He resolves to make a second visit to the mosque in Meshed, despite the local guide having cold feet, and dons make-up and a disguise. Once he is inside, an epiphany admiring the calligraphy of 'an inscription whose glory explains forever the joy felt by Islam in writing on the face of architecture' is accompanied by a sense of uncertainty: 'The vision was a matter of seconds. Simultaneously I began to feel insecure.'[154] Rather than relying on his sense of his right to be there as a European, he feels in imminent danger of being found out and departs hurriedly.

Sylvia Townsend Warner – Writing Leaving, Leaving Off Writing

In her writing, Sylvia Townsend Warner reflected deeply on empire, nation, and identity and how these are written about, and did so in the late colonial period itself. She was one of a number of women writers who revitalised the historical novel for the interwar context,[155] and she often mixed fantasy and realism, as seen in her first novel, *Lolly Willowes* (1928), and her late stories in *The Kingdom of Elfin* (1977). Many of Warner's texts can be considered using Michael Löwy's term 'irrealism' because they deploy different combinations of realist and non-realist styles.[156] Though a member of the Communist Party of Great Britain, she did not adopt 'socialist realism'.

There is only space here for brief discussions of three Warner texts, selected for their themes of movement and of not imposing oneself on others. Her second novel, *Mr Fortune's Maggot*, published in 1927, picks up the issues of connection between coloniser and colonised found a few years previously in E. M. Forster's *A Passage to India*. Set in the South Pacific, the British central character, Timothy Fortune, comes to realise that he has no right to intrude on the lives of others, however strong his emotions. Warner never visited the region; hers was a textual engagement, with writing that included Daniel Defoe, Robert Louis Stevenson, Paul Gauguin (in particular his travel book *Noa Noa* (1901)), and missionary writing. Timothy goes to a remote island as a lone missionary. Not only does Timothy fail to convert the islanders, but he also ends up losing his own faith. His 'unconversion' occurs after he falls in love with a boy, Lueli. In time, he comes to realise that he stands in the way of Lueli's development and is but an interloper. At the end of the novel, when Timothy is being taken off the island, he hears about the First World War for the first time, and thus of the very opposite of his newfound respect for the lives of others.[157]

A more active response, this time to fascism and Nazism, is found in Warner's (very) short story 'My Shirt is in Mexico', which was first published in 1941. A waiter in a railway restaurant carriage tells the narrator about giving his shirt to a refugee from Germany bound for the United States. He later heard that the man had, in turn, passed it on to another man who was going to Mexico. The story ends with the following interchange with the narrator: '"You must feel happy about that shirt," I said. "I do," he replied. "It was a blue one, just right for a sunny climate. I've always wanted to go to Mexico."'[158] The reader realises that they are reading an 'irrealist' text in which the shirt's journey connects selfhood, generosity to migrants and personal joy. The waiter finds happiness in the new lives that others have been able to take up. The shirt, something he does not feel the need to possess, gets to have a new experience he had always wanted. Queer-coded travelling and migrating subjects are contrasted with separateness, exclusion, and ownership. 'My Shirt is in Mexico' had a powerful political message in its time and still does when it is read today.

Warner's *The Flint Anchor* of 1954 pushes back against the ideological dominance of the Victorian middle-class family and the values and morals it imposes on its members, communities, nations, and the wider world. In the novel, the family is not nurturing but a site of terrible violence and harm. It is hard and unyielding, hence the image of the anchor on the front of the Barnards' family home, unchanging and flinty, that gives the novel its title. This fixity is, though, built on trade and the mobility, often undertaken by those under the Barnards' sway, either voluntarily or by force. The Barnard money comes from trade with the Baltic across the North Sea, but John's eldest son, Joseph, goes against his father's wishes and becomes a plantation manager in the Caribbean. John's effort to uphold a morality separate from capitalism is punctured by this association with slavery and its legacies, and in time, his long-suffering wife, Julia, develops a taste for the rum Joseph sends; she eventually succumbs to alcoholism.[159]

Deeply constrained emotionally by his evangelical Christianity, John becomes enamoured of Thomas, though he cannot see that he has fallen in love with the younger man. In many ways Thomas is John's opposite, untethered to place or confining social codes. Thomas marries Barnard's daughter and chafes against his home and working life. A rumour that he has had sex with a local fisherman provides Thomas with a way out. He declines to deny the accusation and leaves the country. In time, a letter arrives from Spain saying he is very ill, followed by a death certificate. As Claire Harman first noted, the lack of corroborating testimony means that we are left wondering whether Thomas has really died or if he has found a means of starting anew.[160] The implication is that his future, free life would lie beyond what the bourgeois novel form can represent. Dominant plots fix down and contain identity, for example, the marriage plot and the Bildungsroman, and there is also the novel form's preoccupation with families, homes, and nations. *The Flint Anchor* was to be Warner's last novel; she seems to have come to believe that the genre itself had reached the end.[161]

Nations and Regions Between the Wars

Representing the Empire in Britain in the 1920s

The empire was often at the centre of British politics in the first decades of the new century, with a split in the Conservative Party over trade between Britain and its colonies. The dispute was between the supporters of free trade and those in the Imperial Tariff Reform movement that wanted preferential treatment for the colonies. These divisions in the Conservative Party can be compared with those over Brexit a hundred years later.

For the leading historian of empire and British popular culture, the late John M. MacKenzie, the reach of the British Empire into the consciousness of the wider population reached its peak after the First World War.[162] The empire could be promoted to a population that had now pretty much all had a basic schooling – though secondary education was reserved for the middle classes – through both traditional and new media. 'Empire Day', an innovation from the colonies, was marked in Britain in schools and elsewhere on Queen Victoria's birthday, 24 May. In 1924 and 1925, the British Empire Exhibition in London had 27 million visitors. In the tradition of the Great Exhibition of 1852, it was held at Wembley, where, in addition to the exhibition halls, a new stadium was built.[163] Andrea Levy's historical novel *Small Island* (2004) has the main white British character visit the colonial pavilions at Wembley as a small girl. She is to be open to other peoples and cultures in Britain, though her parents, among others, are prejudiced about race and the colonies. *Small Island* explores a longer-term history that reaches back before the arrival of the Empire Windrush from the Caribbean in 1948. It includes the Empire Exhibition and the responses to Black American servicemen in Britain during the Second World War.

The eventual defeat of those campaigning for a full system of imperial preference was not without concessions, and one of them was the setting up of the Empire Marketing Board. Instead of having preferential tariffs it would promote trade with the colonies. Part of its brief was to encourage people to purchase goods from the colonies and to make them aware of the importance of colonial markets for Britain's future. The advertising posters of the Empire Marketing Board give a fascinating insight into their historical and cultural moment.[164] Landmarks in graphic design, they depicted the empire as sun-drenched and productive, while also recirculating older tropes. The settler colonies, by this stage with Dominion status and much self-government, were seen as modern. Elsewhere in the empire, the posters often placed exoticised and contented native workers in fields, for example harvesting fruit or picking tea leaves. Immaculately dressed white men bring progress under a watchful eye, pipes in hand. The posters emphasised conventional gender and familial roles. The empire was presented as a close-knit community of economic cooperation, with hierarchies of power and race not explicitly dwelt upon, though made clear at times, as happens, for example, in Adrian Allinson's contrasting pair of images, displayed in the winter of 1931–1932, 'East-African Transport Old Style' and 'East-African Transport New Style'.[165]

The Empire Marketing Board helped launch the careers of a new generation of artists and writers who helped develop genres in new visual media, most notably John Grierson and the Documentary Film Movement. Grierson was later to transfer with others to form the General Post Office (GPO) Film Unit. The films they made often depicted the lives of ordinary Britons – most famously of workers sorting the post on a mail train heading north to Scotland in the documentary *Night Mail* (1936), for which W. H. Auden wrote the words and Benjamin Britten the music.

Resurgences: 'English Literature' Breaks Up

The Scottish critic and poet Robert Crawford's *Devolving English Literature* appeared in 1992, with devolution coming to Scotland and Wales at the end of that same decade. Crawford saw a monolithic 'English Literature' giving way to multiple national literatures. Narratives about English Literature were perhaps never quite as unitary as this suggests, and neither are nations the only collective unit.[166] Rather, in the writing of the Irish and British Isles of the first half of the twentieth century, there are multiple overlapping identities – imperial, national, and regional. In addition, the population was now more mobile, moving between locations near and far. As recent work on Welsh modernism has demonstrated, there was an engagement with European trends that was not mediated through London's and artistic literary networks. For example, Dylan Thomas was just one Welsh writer who engaged with European surrealism.[167]

Nationalism was questioned in the first half of the century; among the best-known critiques were those by E. M. Forster and George Orwell. Forster stressed the primacy of personal relationships, saying in 1938, 'If I had to choose between betraying my country and betraying my friend I hope I should have the guts to betray my country'.[168] In his essay 'Notes on Nationalism' (1945), George Orwell set himself the tricky task of distinguishing between nationalism and patriotism. Negative characteristics are attached to the former, while the latter is seen positively.[169] However, there is an earlier and more far-reaching critique of nationalism than either of these. Rabindranath Tagore, in his *Nationalism*, published in

1917 and mostly written during the First World War, argued that nationalism was a discourse developed in European colonising nations and then disseminated to other parts of the world.[170] In his subsequent ongoing dialogue with Mohandas Gandhi and Jawaharlal Nehru, Rabindranath was to question the adoption of the Western nation state as the model for India after British rule. As we noted in the Introduction, those seeking independence embraced nationalist discourse with more or less enthusiasm, but there was no readily available alternative.

Research on the Scottish Revival and Scottish modernism is now a rich and diverse field, encompassing such important issues as the role of language (Scottish Gaelic and Scots as well as English); the establishment of a 'broad church' nationalist party from different class, political, and religious affiliations; and the relationship of Scottish culture to Celtic Revivals. Two interventions will be made here. One is to note how rich and nuanced interwar discussions of nation, regional identity, and economic issues were. The second is to question those critics who claim that the empire did not touch the supposed deep, essential Scottishness of the country's major writers.

One focus of interwar Scottish nationalism and nationalist writing was the response to economic crisis. Industrial areas of Scotland underwent a decline in the 1930s that went deeper, and was more long-lasting, than that experienced just about anywhere else in Britain. The poet and writer Edwin Muir produced some of the most incisive reflections on Scotland, its economy, and nationalism in this decade. (His wife, Willa, and Muir produced the pioneering translations of Franz Kafka into English.) Many of the major Scottish modernist writers did not reside in Scotland – for example, Catherine Carswell lived in London, and Lewis Grassic Gibbon wrote his trilogy the *Scots Quair*, concluded in 1934, while guarding his precarious health in Welwyn Garden City. Muir had spent much of his life in London, and after attending a 1934 PEN conference in Edinburgh, he undertook the journey that he wrote up as *Scottish Journey*. Muir was from an Orkney family, and it is written from an 'insider-outsider' perspective when addressing, for example, the cities of Glasgow and Edinburgh.[171] He comes round in the book to arguing that while he thought Scotland should be a separate nation, the primary issues were economic. Muir shared with the poet Hugh MacDiarmid – though they were to fall out over issues of language – a complex response to the multivalences of the Scottish context and history in their time, of Renaissance and Revival.[172] The resulting ambivalences are caught in Muir's poetry. An example is 'The Solitary Place', first published as 'Poem' in, ironically enough, the June 1937 'English Number' of the American magazine *Poetry*, edited by W. H. Auden and Michael Roberts. Among the poem's many oppositions, at once overwhelming in number and yet also somehow generative, are the forms of 'rending, reuniting/The torn and incorruptible bands/That bind all these united and disunited lands'.[173]

Running against this richness of debate at that time is the simplistic claim, made in the twenty-first century, that Scottish identity is separate from colonialism. One example is Murray Pittock, the leading cultural critic and historian of modern Scotland, writing about John Buchan's *Prester John* (1910). In the novel,

Nation, Empire, and Identity in Late Colonial British Writing 63

the Scottish narrator, David Crawfurd, is embroiled in an adventure that draws on tropes of atavistic regression. An African convert to Christianity, John Laputa, gains a European education and becomes a minister of the Kirk before returning to Africa, changing sides, and leading a violent anti-colonial uprising. Crawfurd, who has been forced by circumstance to move to South Africa to make a living, plays a major role in foiling the uprising. Pittock argues that

> Buchan writes par excellence of the experience of the Scot in the British empire – outward conformity, inner longing, nostalgia, rebellion, fear or simply the existential void of *mauvais foi*, the Sartrean bad faith which indicates that an outward role is compromising inner authenticity.[174]

The invocation of Sartre's existential philosophy provides theoretical scaffolding for the claim that Scottish identity and a role in the empire can be wholly differentiated, with the former the pure authentic selfhood.

Industry, Regions, the Working Class, and Empire

Mark Crinson's *Shock City: Image and Architecture in Industrial Manchester* (2022) argues that in accounts of modernism, industrialisation is often either omitted or elided with the coming of consumer culture. It is the latter that Walter Benjamin spoke about so influentially, for example in his 'Paris: City of the Nineteenth Century' (1938). Neither Paris nor London had much heavy industry, and for Crinson industrial cities produced their own forms of modernism.[175] We should respond to the culture of industrial centres, as well as the centres of power, and think about the distinct and particular forms of culture that emerged there.

The publishing industry in Britain was based mainly in London, and those from outside the capital and from the working class struggled to get published – that is, if they found the time to write in the first place. The process of reclamation of the work that was produced is still ongoing and often takes place outside university English departments.[176] The partial nature of the representation of people in nations, regions, and communities in this period – where it swells and ebbs – always needs to be kept in mind.

Regional artists had to work out the forms and styles to adopt. Sometimes the best that could be done was to repeatedly work over the prevailing conditions in their place and time. In the visual arts, T. J. Clark has said of L. S. Lowry's paintings that:

> There is a 'Lowry question'. [. . .] How could it be that England ended up having *this* painting – this deliberately limited and repetitive body of work – as the best visual record it possesses of the great fact of England's recent history: its experience as pioneer of the Industrial Revolution, and the intricate (appalling, resilient, humane, inhuman) social order that emerged from the shock?

For Clark, Lowry is 'exceptional' – in multiple senses – in representing the 'landscape and social fabric of industrialism', but strikingly his art also 'deliberately' enacts its entrapment through repetition.[177]

The Wall Street Crash of 1929 and the Depression that followed made industrial areas of national concern, with visitors from elsewhere coming to undertake an 'anthropology from within', often doing so from the perspective of a different class. Books on Englishness in the interwar period often involved journeys using such modern forms of transport as the motor bus and the car. H. M. Morton's 1927 travel book *In Search of England* did not spend long looking for the nation's essence in the North; only 2 of his 12 chapters are set there. The best known of these internal travel books from the 1930s is J. B. Priestley's *English Journey* (1934). (It was because of its success that the publisher Gollancz commissioned Muir's *Scottish Journey*.) The Yorkshire-born Priestley was already well known as the author of the warm-hearted *The Good Companions* (1929). Alick West's reading of Priestley's fiction from 1958 is persuasive. Beyond the appreciation of community and his writing's strong sense of injustice, the texts offer no route through which change might come about. Social problems are seen as the consequence of nature or made inevitable by history. West's close analyses show how the powerful sense of scene and incident is undermined by generalisations and a collapse into sentimentality.[178] Priestley's centre left politics and his openness also had its limits. Writing of the 'Irish quarter' of Liverpool in *English Journey*, he bemoans 'what Ireland has done to England' and calls for 'a grand clearance' of the Irish, which in his view would be 'a fine exit of ignorance and dirt and drunkenness and disease'.[179]

As a riposte to privileged if socially engaged travellers, Jack Hilton journeyed across England, staying with other working-class people and writing up his journey in *English Ways: A Walk From the Pennines to Epsom Downs in 1939* (1940). George Orwell was a friend of his, but Hilton felt that Orwell's *The Road to Wigan Pier* had failed to engage with the Northern working class as equals. It seems that Orwell had not imagined that there would be any Northern readers of *The Road to Wigan Pier*, writing that 'when you go to the industrial North you are conscious, quite apart from the unfamiliar scenery, of entering a strange country'.[180] For those that lived there this was the landscape of home.

Jack Hilton found it hard to sustain a career. After a long period of neglect, the Oldham-born writer's first book, *Caliban Shrieks* (1935), was republished in 2024. As its title suggests, it is a howl of rage in the face of authority. Hilton published five books before he returned to work as a plasterer.[181] Another writer who was briefly picked up as a representative voice of his class, only to be dropped when the publishing industry felt the vogue for proletarian voices had passed, was Walter Brierley. The Nottinghamshire writer's novel about the demeaning process for applying for help when unemployed, *Means-Test Man* (1935), was published by Methuen. However, he struggled to get published after his next novel, the impressive and powerful *Sandwichman* (1937). Like Hilton, Brierley got a job and gave up writing books. James Hanley did manage to sustain a career. Born into the working-class Liverpool of Irish descent but long resident in South Wales, he had been seen by John Fordham as deploying expressionist techniques in his writing.

He was prolific and worked in different genres; when his plays were taken up by the BBC that provided a further source of income.[182]

Ellen Wilkinson grew up in the working class in Manchester and gained a scholarship to the city's university. She became an MP and participated in the Jarrow March. In the post–Second World War Labour government of Clement Attlee, she became Minister of Education, with a seat in the Cabinet. Her novel *Clash* (1929) addressed experiences of both women and men during the miners' strike that continued after the end of the General Strike of 1926. Also among texts that utilised realist modes was Louis Golding's *Magnolia Street* (1932). It addresses Manchester's Jewish community, exploring proximity and prejudice in the context of war and the rise of fascism. One side of the eponymous street is Christian, the other Jewish. October 1936 was to see the Battle of Cable Street in London, with anti-fascists stopping a march by Sir Oswald Mosley's British Union of Fascists through an area of the East End with a large Jewish population.

Other authors wrote back to much-praised metropolitan novels by also adopting the 'day novel' form. For example, David Sommerfield focused on London's working class and the docks in *May Day* (1940), and the Yorkshire-born Storm Jameson's *A Day Off* (1933) mounts an extraordinary response to Woolf's *Mrs Dalloway* and the essay 'Mr Bennett and Mrs Brown'. It unflinchingly explores how poverty and experience has formed the main (unnamed) character's subjectivity. That her resultant behaviour does not align with middle-class morality troubles many readers.

A different tone is adopted in W. C. Sellar and R. J. Yeatman's *1066 and All That* (1930), illustrated by John Reynolds, which humorously ridicules nation, empire, and traditional British historical narratives. Raphael Samuel thought it a 'much underrated anti-imperialist tract'.[183] More conventionally framed histories also aimed at a wide readership, including A. L. Morton's classic *A People's History of England* (1938, revised edition 1948). It focuses on how economic change, power, and class made English history, giving colonialism much attention. Also from the Left came the anthology *Spokesmen for Liberty* (1941), compiled by Edgell Rickword and Jack Lindsay, which used excerpts from earlier writers to construct a radical, dissenting tradition. It draws on writing by William Morris, Edward Carpenter, Olive Schreiner – so not quite all 'spokesmen', then – and Wilfrid Scawen Blunt.

Colonial subjects who questioned the empire often found allies among the working class. Visiting the cotton town of Darwen in Lancashire in 1931, Mohandas Gandhi received a warm reception from large crowds – unexpectedly so at first sight, given his support for the boycott of British textiles called by the Indian National Congress.[184] Paul Robeson, the African American singer, actor, anti-imperialist, and communist, developed close connections with South Wales mining communities between the wars; he had an uncle who lived in Tiger Bay in Cardiff. Learie Constantine became a hero in the North-West as a cricketer in the Lancashire League. A lawyer and politician, he was later to become Trinidad and Tobago's first high commissioner in London and the first Black member of the House of Lords. While staying with Constantine, his friend C. L. R. James underwent a political awakening, coming to the conclusion that the working class in 'Red Nelson' was shaped by the same processes that he had seen operating in colonial Trinidad. He wrote in 1936, 'Tyranny and oppression in the Colonies, and lies and hypocrisy at home, in order that the British worker may be acquiescent and peaceably assist in forging his own chains'.[185]

The Rural and the Environment

Englishness in this period is often seen as rooted in the countryside. Work on rural modernisms has explored writing about modernisation in the countryside and how its communities were changing.[186] Winifred Holtby's *South Riding* focuses on local institutions and councils – a particular interest of the Fabians Sidney and Beatrice Webb – to address changing gender and class dynamics. Raymond Williams's classic study *The Country and the City* (1973) explored a key relationship within Britain, between the city and the rural, but as Corinne Fowler has set out, the colonial dimension long went unaddressed. Those who had made huge sums of money in the colonies bought country estates and advocated, often as members of parliament, for the enclosure acts. This gave them a path to ownership of what had previously been common land, which rural workers had farmed so they could sustain themselves. Many in the countryside were forced to either seek poor relief from the parish or to move to industrialising cities in search of work. Having participated in a land grab and exploitation abroad, colonisers who had made their money in the Caribbean or India undertook a form of internal colonialism at home. The countryside was transformed by 1900, then, and the myth of an unchanging rural England has always done much ideological work.[187]

For those living in cities, access to nature was not possible if the countryside was behind walls and fences with farmers and gamekeepers' guns warning you off. In 1932, the Manchester-born Benny Rothman organised the Mass Trespass of Kinder Scout in Derbyshire. This and other acts of civil disobedience eventually led to the establishment of National Parks in Britain, the first of which was to be the Peak District, encompassing Kinder Scout, in 1951. The right to roam exists in Scotland under the Scottish Land Reform Act of 2003, and pressure groups campaign for its extension to Wales and England.

Jed Esty has noted 'a new kind of shaped temporality and bounded spatiality' in English modernism around the year 1940.[188] T. S. Eliot's *Four Quartets* (1936–1942) is one of his main examples. Eliot's England is rooted in the countryside, and in *Four Quartets* there is an underlying unity between religion, nation, the land, and art. In 1928, T. S. Eliot had declared himself a 'classicist in literature, anglo-catholic in religion, royalist in politics'.[189] The final quartet, *Little Gidding* (1942), published in wartime, shows time and nation resolving into a state beyond change and mutability. It takes its title from the church and community in Little Gidding which was buffeted and renewed over the centuries. *Four Quartets* had given voice to Eliot's own sense of return from his family's American generations in the third quartet, *The Dry Salvages* (1941), thus sharing a theme with Kipling's 'An Habitation Enforced'. *Four Quartets* culminates in the claim in *Little Gidding* that 'while the light fails/On a winter's afternoon, in a secluded chapel/History is now and England'. A final homecoming is brought about:

We shall not cease from exploration
And the end of all our exploring
Will be to arrive where we started
And know the place for the first time.[190]

Meaning is located not in the earthly but in the divine, and specifically in the language of Pentecost, and in a return to the Garden of Eden. Issues from poverty to colonialism are left to one side. To view the modern world in this way requires Eliot's religious and political allegiances, but even without them, *Four Quartets* is powerfully seductive. C. L. R. James said when discussing *Little Gidding* that Eliot 'is of special value to me in that in him I find more often than elsewhere, and beautifully and precisely stated, things to which I am completely opposed'.[191]

Eliot's Anglo-Catholicism allowed him to place himself in a Catholic tradition – for Anglo-Catholics the Reformation is no rupture – whilst being within the Established Church. As Roman Catholics, Evelyn Waugh and Graham Greene viewed Englishness and the empire from within and without. It gave them a basis for their social comment but meant that they viewed individual actions and responses from within the frame of the Roman Catholic Church, with sin and evil to the fore. However – and there are many examples to choose from here – Greene's texts have a refreshing range of different settings and are rich in context. Examples include the fraying social fabric in England in *Brighton Rock* (1938) and, after the Second World War, French colonialism in Vietnam as it gave way to American control in *The Quiet American* (1955). As Rebecca Dyer observes of Greene's 1940s writing on class and colonialism, 'by depicting masters destroying themselves when they recognize the human costs of the hierarchal arrangement of society both at home and abroad, Greene anticipates in the 1940s a less rigid world emerging in the post-war period'.[192]

The writing of Greene's friend Evelyn Waugh includes the *Sword of Honour* trilogy (1952–1961), some of the best British fiction to emerge from the Second World War. Much of his writing stresses personal responsibility and is averse to the levelling of the classes and to modernity. *Brideshead Revisited* (1945) laments the decline of landed estates and old Catholic families and utilises discourses of degeneration in the depiction of the queer character Sebastian. Lacking what is seen as true masculine purpose, Sebastian takes to drink and dies. Waugh's comic, satiric mode often raises the questions: What are we being asked to find amusing? In his fiction on Africa, *Black Mischief* (1932), Waugh only appears to satirise all sides. His late travel book, *A Tourist in Africa* (1960), is less extreme in its racial language than his earlier *Remote People* (1930), which draws on his time in Africa as a correspondent for *The Times*. *A Tourist in Africa* both declares that '[r]acialism is dotty' and maintains that Black Africans are incapable of governing themselves.[193]

A number of writers in this period – indeed it is a staple of fantasy writing – invoke a disruptive essence in nature that returns to unsettle modern complacencies, a twentieth-century form of the stories of Pan and the Dionysian that had been so popular at the end of the previous century. Examples include the work of the Dorset writers T. F. Powys and his brother, John Cowper Powys, author of *Wolf Solent* (1929). T. F. Powys's *Mr Weston's Good Wine* (1927) is striking – the wine merchant of the title is also God, but manifested in an often discomforting way. In Sylvia Townsend Warner's *Lolly Willowes* (1926), Lolly reconnects with nature on her journey to becoming a witch and as she questions received gender roles. Denton Welch's *In Youth is Pleasure* (1945) draws on Decadent models and demonstrates an acute attentiveness to place and location that queers norms of gender and sexuality.

Writers such as John Cowper Powys reacted to the damage being done to nature, which is also a concern of E. M. Forster's two 1930s pageants. Part of the pageant movement which had started in the Edwardian period,[194] the short 'The Abinger Pageant' (1934), intended for local performance, was followed by *England's Pleasant Land* (1938). Both had music written or arranged for them by Ralph Vaughan Williams. The text of *England's Pleasant Land* was published by the Woolfs' Hogarth Press in 1940, and may well have influenced Virginia Woolf's last novel, *Between the Acts*, published posthumously in 1941, which depicts the performance of a pageant. In 'The Abinger Pageant' it is the trees that are front and centre and not the local people.[195] The narrator is the Woodman, the voice of a worker who harvests and tends self-regenerating woodland. The pageant is aligned with what William Greenslade has called the 'diffused guardianship and fellowship' that characterised the ecological imagination in the decades around the turn of the century.[196] The Woodman says of the historical survey in the area that the pageant will depict people who 'will pass like the leaves in autumn but the trees remain'. Reference is made to 'one great tree that shall not be cut down. It is the Kingdom of England'. Whilst the tree presides over the final thousand years of the pageant, the internal logic of the image suggests that nation and monarchy will not last forever, just as a tree has a natural lifespan.

The Epilogue sees the Woodman address the audience:

Houses, houses, houses! You came from them and you must go back to them. Houses and bungalows, hotels, restaurants and flats, arterial roads, by-passes, petrol pumps and pylons – are these going to be England? Are these man's final triumph? Or is there another England, green and eternal, which will outlast them? I cannot tell you, I am only the Woodman, but this land is yours, and you can make it what you will. If you want to ruin our Surrey fields and woodlands it is easy to do, very easy, and if you want to save them they can be saved. Look into your hearts and look into the past, and remember that all this beauty is a gift which you can never replace, which no money can buy, which no cleverness can refashion. You can make a town, you can make a desert, you can even make a garden; but you can never, never make the country, because it was made by Time.[197]

This is offered as a 'lesson'. The need to make choices from the perspective of the *longue durée* is stressed, as is the acknowledgement that humans are part of nature, rather than somehow set apart from it. A deep essence of England and its 'beauty' is invoked in the face of what is seen as an encroaching modern nation in which humans have increasing sway over the natural world and its continuance.

Women's Writing, Politics, and the Modern

There has been much work that has followed Alison Light's observation in 1991 that '[i]t is extraordinary how much the literary history of "the inter-war years", for example, has been rendered almost exclusively in male terms'.[198] Light's own book *Forever England: Femininity and Conservatism Between the Wars* focuses on just three women writers – Ivy Compton Burnet, Agatha Christie, and Daphne du Maurier – noting a shift from the public sphere to the middle-class home. She relates this change to the need for damaged body to find the space to recuperate after the traumas of the First World War. Though women are seen as adopting many of the codes of imperial masculinity, the nation as a whole was 'feminise[d]', creating a private and retiring people that featured pipe-smoking 'little men', a nation of gardeners and competent housewives.[199]

Not all were comfortable adopting such a domestic role, something seen in women's poetry of the period.[200] Naomi Mitchison's poem 'New Verse' from the early 1930s appears at first sight to offer a stirring feminist rallying cry: 'You have lost your power, young men.' However, these young men are seen as failing by not having 'baby sons'. The response is probably to W. H. Auden and the queer male writers of his circle, and the poem's assertion of a new place for women also recirculates tropes that linked male homosexuality to misogyny. The future the poem appropriates is that of the doublets 'dams and pylons', 'anode and cathode', and 'dyes and test-tubes'. The rally crying for women is, finally, a call for them to become a new modernising elite in a society that has no space for diverse identities.[201]

In the run-up to the war, alternatively, a number of women writers analysed the relationship between politics, gendered identities, sexuality, and the middle-class family. In her novel *In the Second Year* (1936), Storm Jameson carefully uses first person narration to explore the relationship between sexuality, male bonding, and fascism in an imagined British fascist state in the near future, reworking the recent events leading up to the Night of the Long Knives in Hitler's Germany.[202] Katherine Burdekin's *Swastika Night* (1937, under the name Murray Constantine), imagined a more distant time, the seventh century of Nazi control of Europe, and an emergent crisis due to the long-term dominance of extreme forms of masculinity.

Nancy Cunard used her writing, money, and influence in support of the Republic in Spain, for example, as an editor of *Authors Take Sides on the Spanish Civil War* (1937). Writers were asked to state their allegiance and write about their choice. Though there was overwhelming support for the Republican side, some did support Franco and fascism, including Evelyn Waugh. A larger group than those who supported Franco were neutral, and some, including George Orwell, refused to respond at all. Cunard's most enduring focus was on those of African heritage, and she was active in the Caribbean and the United States, also working with communities in Liverpool and Cardiff in the 1940s as they faced racism. As well as many essays on race and empire, she edited and published *Negro Anthology* (1934).[203] Cunard called for legislation against race discrimination, a position, Maroula Joannou notes, that was 'greeted with incomprehension and hostility whenever she tried to broach it in white circles as she frequently did'.[204] As we will now see, Cunard's collaboration with George Padmore during the Second World War helps show that clusters of anti-colonial and anti-racist thought very often involved writers of colour.

George Padmore in Britain and the British Left

The Trinidad-born activist and writer George Padmore came to Britain in the 1930s after he had left the service of the Comintern and no longer supported the Soviet Union's positions. He moved from a 'class before race' approach back to the Pan-Africanism he had espoused as a young man. He continued to maintain that racist discourses were deployed to justify appropriating land and resources for the colonial power; this was 'part and parcel of the capitalist system'.[205] As we have already noted, Padmore was also sharply critical of the League of Nations mandates, which he saw as a form of colonial rule. In the 1930s Padmore saw European empires that purported to be democracies opposed to fascism as hypocritical because they were themselves perpetrating a 'colonial fascism'. Padmore did not see colonialism and fascism as distinct; indeed, '[t]hat is why we maintain that Colonies are the breeding ground for the type of fascist mentality which is being let loose in Europe today'.[206] With fascism and Nazism, conventional valencies of power and violence were being reversed: 'Now that imperialism has come home to roost, the victims are white. Europe has taken the place of Africa as "the Dark Continent."'[207]

Fascism and Nazism were not wholly generated within Europe, nor should theories and histories of colonialism be put on one side when they are addressed. For example, medical experiments conducted in Germany's African colonies were continued in Europe by the very same doctors after Hitler's rise to power.[208] After the Second World War, a number of writers and theorists, including Hannah Arendt in *The Origins of Totalitarianism* (1951), noted the often-shared history of colonialism and fascism. For Aimé Cesaire, in his *Discourse on Colonialism* (1950, revised 1955), Europeans failed to comprehend Nazism, fascism, and their legacies by confining their thinking to Europe's borders, 'before they were its victims, they were its accomplices; that they tolerated that Nazism before it was inflicted on them; that they absolved it, shut their eyes to it, legitimised it, because, until then, it had only been applied to non-European peoples'. Cesaire saw fascism as the 'terrific boomerang effect' of colonialism.[209] (The original French for the word translated here as 'boomerang' is 'choc en retour', which is more strictly rendered in English as 'recoil, return shock or backlash'.[210])

Among other Caribbean anti-colonial intellectuals in London was C. L. R. James, a friend of Padmore's. James arrived in Britain from Trinidad with the manuscript of a novel. *Minty Alley* (1936) became the first by a man of African heritage to be published in England. James's play *Toussaint Louverture* was performed twice in London in March 1936, with Paul Robeson in the title role; it was to be the only time the actor was to appear in work by a Black writer. The text of the play was rediscovered in the archive in 2005, and it is no mere pendant to James's later classic historical study of the Haitian Revolution, *The Black Jacobins: Toussaint L'Ouverture and the San Domingo Revolution* (1938). In the play, Toussaint is a tragic figure because he embodies a split between the European enlightenment and revolutionary values he has taken on, and his commitment to the liberation of those of African heritage from within their own traditions. He comes to realise at the end of his life that the fellow revolutionaries who took the latter position had been right.[211] James thus notes the complicity of European narratives of progress and rationality in colonialism that Theodor W. Adorno and Max Horkheimer were shortly to theorise in respect of Nazism in *Dialectic of Enlightenment* (1944). Intellectuals like James and Padmore were in many ways well positioned to provide a critical account of their late colonial moment, but James acknowledged how difficult it was for him to negotiate his expectations, reading, and thinking and what he actually found on arrival in Britain: 'For a non-white colonial to adjust his sights to England and not to lose focus is the devil's own job and the devil pays great attention to it.'[212]

Toussaint Louverture was not the only play by a writer from the Caribbean to be staged in 1930s London. Una Marson's co-written play *At What a Price* had earlier been performed in two amateur productions.[213] Marson spent two periods in Britain, in the 1930s and early 1940s; between them she had acted as secretary to Emperor Haile Selassie in Ethiopia and then recuperated back home in Jamaica. For the BBC she worked on the *Caribbean Voices* radio programme, which helped bring forward a distinguished generation of male Caribbean writers. Best known today as a poet, she felt the need to make different formal and stylistic choices than the European and American writers lauded by post–Second World War modernist studies, something she shares with Claude McKay.[214]

In the late 1930s, Padmore and James were active in the Independent Labour Party. The ILP had been part of the Labour Party before tensions led to it disaffiliating in 1932. Though it had declined under the first past the post-electoral system, it still had a group of MPs and was a site of open debate for socialists and Marxists not aligned with the Soviet Union. As Priyamvada Gopal has persuasively argued, from the late 1930s Padmore in particular helped 'radicalise' the ILP on issues of race and empire. She notes how figures who had been cautious when it came to calling for an end to British colonial rule became more assertive, including Reginald Reynolds and Fenner Brockway. The latter was the editor of the ILP weekly, then called the *New Leader*.[215] A striking example of how they were perhaps persuaded to take a strong line by Padmore is the 'Empire Special' issue of May Day 1938 which included a number of penetrating critiques of the Britain's Empire.[216]

Padmore's main focus after he left the service of the Comintern was on Africa, those of African heritage, and independence movements. An example is his organisation of the 1945 Pan-African Congress in Manchester which brought together many union and representative groups, political leaders who were to lead their nations on independence, and leaders of African Americans, including Amy Garvey and W. E. B. Du Bois. The resolutions that were passed often reflected the views of the group Padmore coordinated, the Pan-African Federation. Padmore helped articulate, through his writing and correspondence with an extraordinarily wide set of contacts, a commitment to ending colonialism, by force when needed, and establishing truly independent new nations.

Paternal guidance from the British Left was no longer needed, though support from that quarter could be useful. This is the context for Nancy Cunard's dialogue with Padmore in their *The White Man's Duty* (1945).[217] Cunard was among the most receptive of writers in England to Padmore's message, but even she seems to find the perspective he articulates new and challenging. (Though this might in part be the way the dialogue is staged for its readers.) Both C. L. R. James and Padmore had a role in George Orwell's late 1930s response to colonialism, which saw him at his most critical of empire. As Christian Høgsbjerg has argued, Orwell was then a member of the ILP and was in contact with C. L. R. James, having positively reviewed a book of his, and it seems that he met George Padmore through James.[218] Orwell powerfully attacked the erasure of colonial peoples and their experience in his 1939 review of Clarence K. Streit's *Union Now*. Streit advocated a federation among the major democracies so as to resist fascism that left the *status quo* in the colonies in place because it was the less pressing problem. In Orwell's view that meant he was 'bolstering up a far vaster injustice': 'For of course it *is* vaster. What we always forget is that the overwhelming bulk of the British proletariat does not live in Britain, but in Asia and Africa.'[219] The word 'British' here is used in the sense of those who live under the British state, rather than just those who live in the archipelago. As we will soon see, however, Orwell's wartime writing of just a few years later crafted influential images of England that saw it as separate and distinct from colonialism and its history.

Nation, Empire, and the Second World War

During the war writers were called on to articulate what defined the nation they were defending. They wanted to make the style and tone different from Nazi propaganda, but something had to be presented that held the different nations, regions, and classes together, and this was not straightforward. Fragmentary images were used to imply a whole that could not be articulated – just as the concept of a fragment implies a former wholeness, even if it is not known what that whole looks like. Though the use of the fragment is a modernist technique, here its use was more a matter of strategy. It provided a way of avoiding such awkward issues as colonial history and an unequal society.

The work of Michael Powell and Emeric Pressburger, including their *The Life and Death of Colonel Blimp* (1943) and *A Canterbury Tale* (1944), provided thoughtful reflections on national identity, masculinity, and empire during wartime.[220] They feel different from more straightforwardly propagandistic projects, such as Laurence Olivier's film version of *Henry V* (1944). The GPO Film Unit was taken on by Crown Film Unit and charged with making films supportive of the war effort. Humphrey Jennings had joined the GPO Film Unit in 1934, and his most famous wartime film for the Crown Film Unit was *Listen to Britain* (1942).

It has no words – though it does include overheard speech – and proceeds through a series of scenes that seek to capture the spirit and range of the nation at war. The scenes have a cumulative effect, intended to produce an increasingly full sense of the nation, with meaning conveyed by the interplay of the visual and a soundtrack of sounds as diverse as music, different factories, and those made by tanks on the move. The music includes both Flanagan and Allen singing 'Underneath the Arches' in a works canteen and Myra Hess playing a Mozart piano concerto at one of the National Gallery concerts for an audience that includes the Queen. The short film aims to show all classes united in a common purpose and seeks to enfold regions and forms of difference – though we see no people of colour. Other films Jennings made in wartime include *Fires Were Started* (1943), about the London fire service and its response to bombing, and *Letter to Timothy* (1945). The latter had words by E. M. Forster and imagines the different kind of life to be lived by a baby born towards the end of the conflict. There was a determination to break with a past shaped by wars and the Depression years.

At the time of his death, Jennings was pursuing a similar strategy to *Listen to Britain*, but this time using writing from the past. He compiled a manuscript comprising quotations that addressed the change brought about by economic, social, and intellectual change and the coming of industrial processes. Each excerpt can be seen as being like the scene of a film, or it can be compared with what Robert Byron does with particular impressions of travel and place in *The Road to Oxiana*. A shortened version was first published in 1985 – though it is only about one-third of Jennings's manuscript – as *Pandæmonium, 1660–1886: The Coming of the Machine as Seen by Contemporary Observers* (composed 1937–1950). Frank Cottrell-Boyce acknowledged this book as a major influence on the opening ceremony of the 2012 London Olympic Games, on which he worked with Danny Boyle.[221] Widely praised though that ceremony was, the use of fragments and scenes meant that colonialism could go unaddressed.

George Orwell deployed a similar strategy to Jennings in his wartime writing. Opinions about Orwell divide sharply. His champions tend to stress progressive intentions, while critics alight on his reception and popularity on the Right. Raymond Williams was characteristically insightful about Orwell, noting that with the real name of Eric Blair, he was an outsider, largely because of his family background in the colonies and his own period in Burma. However, he was not prepared to give up on also being an insider, the old Etonian. The result for Williams was a constructed persona as a writer, George Orwell, that attempted to bridge that gap. His was a 'double vision, rooted in the simultaneous positions of dominator and dominated, [that] is at once powerful and disturbed'.[222]

Orwell was a libertarian, where freedom from an encroaching state was seen as under increasing threat in the 1930s. The National Council for Civil Liberties (now known as Liberty) was formed in 1934 to campaign for individual freedoms in the face of state encroachment; E. M. Forster became its first president. Like the fiction of Leonard Woolf, Orwell's early writing drew on his times as a colonial administrator and was critical of the colonial administration. Douglas Kerr's deeply researched *Orwell and Empire* (2022) sees Orwell as formed by

Anglo-India: 'Orwell struggled all his life, and not with complete success, to exorcise the Orientalism (in Said's sense) which came with his Anglo-Indian patrimony.'[223] For all their questioning of British, *Burmese Days* (1934) and the essay 'Shooting an Elephant' (1936) repeat tropes about the colonised; they are not seen as the equal of Europeans.

Orwell's 'England Your England' in *The Lion and the Unicorn: Socialism and the English Genius* (1941) adopts the viewpoint of an outsider. It views the nation from the perspective of the returning traveller, of someone making a 'voyage in'. In one of two well-known passages from that text that will be examined here, Orwell moves to define Englishness not with a fully coherent definition but by recourse to representative images:

> When you come back to England from any foreign country you have immediately the sensation of breathing a different air. [. . .] And the diversity of it, the chaos! The clatter of clogs in the Lancashire mill towns, the to-and-fro of the lorries on the Great North Road, the queues outside the Labour Exchanges, the rattle of pin-tables in the Soho pubs, the old maids biking to Holy Communion through the mists of the autumn mornings – all these are not only fragments, but *characteristic* fragments, of the English scene. How can one make a pattern out of this muddle?[224]

There is no pattern, and so the question goes unanswered, but one is implied through the '*characteristic* fragments'. These 'fragments' have now all dated – there are still lorries on the Great North Road, though now it is called the A1 (a busy road was perhaps never anyway uniquely English); Soho is now prosperous and characterless; and the cotton mills have largely been demolished or repurposed. The reference to 'old maids' is ageist and misogynistic.

In the 1990s, the Conservative prime minister John Major sought, after the divisive government of his predecessor, Margaret Thatcher, to advocate a 'country at ease with itself'. He recast this Orwell passage, removing the sensitive reference to 'Labour Exchanges', the job centres of their time, while introducing some new '*characteristic* fragments': 'Fifty years on from now, Britain will still be the country of long shadows on county [cricket] grounds, warm beer, invincible green suburbs, dog lovers, and – as George Orwell said – old maids bicycling to Holy Communion through the morning mist.'[225] As a story that brought a nation together, it was already dated and threadbare, but it was all that was ready to hand.

The second of Orwell's influential ways of talking about England is as a dysfunctional but resilient family:

> England is not the jewelled isle of Shakespeare's much-quoted passage, nor is it the inferno depicted by Dr Goebbels. More than either it resembles a family, a rather stuffy Victorian family, with not many black sheep in it but with all its cupboards bursting with skeletons. It has rich relations who have to be kow-towed to and poor relations who are horribly sat upon, and there is a deep conspiracy of silence about the source of the family income. It is a

family in which the young are generally thwarted and most of the power is in the hands of irresponsible uncles and bedridden aunts. Still, it is a family. It has its private language and its common memories, and at the approach of an enemy it closes its ranks. A family with the wrong members in control – that, perhaps, is as near as one can come to describing England in a phrase.[226]

That there are, as the popular phrase has it, 'skeletons in the cupboard' and the 'deep conspiracy of silence about the source of the family income' suggests an awareness that Britain's wealth has relied on slavery and colonial exploitation. Otherwise, however, those in the colonies are omitted. The analogy of an upper-middle-class family serves to exclude, among others, those of other races, the queer in terms of gender or sexuality, those of other classes, and the single and child free. With this image of Orwell's we are a long way from the explorations of crossing borders and boundaries that have characterised many of the texts explored in this chapter. National identity now seems haunted by an empire it will not name directly. This construction of England was to have consequences for those who came to Britain from elsewhere in the empire from towards the end of the 1940s on. They had been brought up to believe that Britain was the Mother Country – that they were part of the same 'family'– but found themselves, to use Orwell's language, rendered outsiders by a self-defined national family that 'closes its ranks', as it had done against the Axis powers during the war.

Claiming there is a home culture separate from the empire in the first half of the twentieth century is pervasive but not sustainable. It has been termed by Stuart Ward the 'minimal impact thesis'. It is not credible, he counters, to claim that 'the idea of a world-wide British identity – the myth of a Greater Britain – that resonated at all levels of metropolitan culture' ended so quickly.[227] Indeed, many did not think that the empire would cease with Indian independence. There was still confidence in its future in Africa and an expectation in the Foreign Office that its Middle East interests could be maintained.[228] Jed Esty's influential study *A Shrinking Island: Modernism and National Culture in England* (2004) sees Britain as being reconfigured into a national culture as the empire ends. This is an argument that relies on the texts selected for analysis and the sleight of hand of claiming that the end of empire happened rather earlier than was the case. Britain's relationship with empire after the Second World War saw, as Graham MacPhee has noted, no simple 'withdrawal into the national', rather there is a 'much messier, more complicated and more contradictory picture'. English 'parochialism and insularity', as Bill Schwarz observes, has functioned as 'screens that have obscured an entire stratum of colonial realities'.[229] Chapter 2 will explore these issues further.

Coda – Late Colonialism and Founding Myths of Modernist Studies

In May 1960, Clement Attlee gave the Chichele history lectures at the University of Oxford; they were published the following year by Oxford University Press under the title *Empire into Commonwealth*. The Labour prime minister from 1945 to 1951 addressed 'changes in the conception and structure of the British Empire

76   *British Writing from Empire to Brexit*

during the last half century'. He helped promulgate a powerful and pervasive myth about late colonialism, one that modernist studies was to build itself upon. Attlee clearly expected his audience to be in ready agreement. As a practised politician, albeit one by this point retired to the House of Lords rather than in the Commons, he knew how to construct narratives that built on people's existing opinions and which did not make them feel uncomfortable.

It is an exculpatory narrative that begins with his memories of being a boy in London in 1897 and seeing the elderly Queen Victoria, with many colonial soldiers, celebrate her last jubilee. Support for the empire is placed in the hands of a few persuaders – Kipling is mentioned, as is the champion of Imperial Tariff Reform, Joseph Chamberlain – and, stretching credulity, everything was to change utterly but a few years later because of the Second South African War. Attlee slides from discussing how the conflict revealed problems with the British military power into making the claim that everyone then decided that Britain's empire would have to end as soon as practicable. Attlee thus disseminates a post-Second World War position summarised as follows by Raphael Samuel: imperialism is 'no more than a brief passage' that 'is narrowly defined – as a passion which burned brightly in the last two decades of the nineteenth century, but was then snuffed out, "discredited" (as a recently published primer puts it) by the disappointments of the Boer War'.[230] In Attlee's view, when the flame dimmed the British quickly decided to bring the empire to an ordered and decent end.

The rest of Attlee's book describes decolonisation as the major task of twentieth-century British statecraft. Bill Schwarz has seen the book as the 'purest expression' of the view that 'there had occurred an easy evolution from an old colonialism to a new and benevolent Commonwealth, overseen by the far-sighted men of reason placed at the imperial centre of things' – as Schwarz continues, as a case, '[i]t fails on every count'.[231] Attlee ignores such events as the Bengal Famine while he was deputy prime minister during the Second World War, and the violence that attended the Partition of India after Britain's sudden decision, made by his own administration, to leave India. The violent British response to insurgencies after the Second World War by communists in Malaya and by the Mau Mau in Kenya is given scant attention. The latter are briefly mentioned as 'troubles' that arose from the gap between 'educated Africans' and those 'emerging from primitive conditions' that are somehow wholly unrelated to British rule.[232]

Attlee argues that pride can be taken in an empire that had no fall:

There have been many great Empires in the history of the world that have risen, flourished for a time, and then fallen. Some on account of attack by a rival or by insurgent barbarians; some have decayed through internal weakness; while others have been resolved into a number of separate and contentious national States. There is only one Empire where, without external pressure or weariness at the burden of ruling, the ruling people has voluntarily surrendered its hegemony over subject peoples and has given them their freedom, where also the majority of the people so liberated have continued in political association with their former rulers. This unique example is the British Empire. The process of the transformation of an Empire into a Commonwealth, an association of free and equal States, has taken place during the last sixty years, a period which covers my adult life. I have seen it happen, and have taken some share in bringing it about.[233]

The colonies' new 'freedom' is invoked, but what and whom they were being 'liberated' from is left vague. There has been no 'weariness at the burden of ruling' – the choice of vocabulary echoes Kipling's 'white man's burden' – but since 1900 all dedicated and enlightened public servants, Attlee among them, had put their shoulders to the wheel to bring about a new order. It is a national achievement that places Britain's empire above all others in history. Britons should not feel the loss of the empire but rather take pride in it. Such a narrative only served to defer the working through of the colonial past.

The writing and culture of nations and regions in late colonial Britain respond to the emergence of new identities – across, for example, race, class, gender, and sexuality – and led to writing in new and adapted forms and styles. As we have seen, a number of writers tried to examine and push beyond late colonial modernity – with increasing success by the end of the 1930s. Black and Asian writers around the turn of the twenty-first century can be seen as stepping past the fatally flawed discourse of modernist studies to establish their own canon of writing and thematic concerns. For example, both *Tono-Bungay* and Hanif Kureishi's *The Buddha of Suburbia* (1990) explore moving from the suburbs to living with the well-off in central London. Kureishi mentions Wells's Bromley upbringing in the novel, and it was where he too lived as a child.[234]

Zadie Smith established her career in sustained dialogue with E. M. Forster. She stressed attentiveness to an 'ethical realm' and forms of narrative that explored 'the consequences of human actions as they unfold in time, and the multiple interpretive possibilities of those actions'. Andrzej Gasiorek has seen Smith as establishing 'continuities with a mode of writing' with other twentieth-century writing that has sought to address 'ethical concerns':

> This is as true of *White Teeth* (2000) as it is of *On Beauty* (2005), Smith's most obviously Forsterian work. These novels represent the mundane, mixed-up, and often haphazard reality of people's lives in the late twentieth and early twenty-first centuries, coupled with scepticism about the redemptive narratives and the patterned aesthetic forms that promise to transcend that reality.[235]

The relationship of Kureishi and Smith to the writing of the late colonial period, and the criticism it has spurred, provide examples of the remapping of the archipelago's late colonial culture that is now underway. The hope is that this chapter, in its effort to operate after and beyond modernist studies, has been a further contribution to that wider project.

Notes

1. Rudyard Kipling, 'The Return', in *Service Songs* in *The Cambridge Edition of the Poems of Rudyard Kipling, Volume I, Collected Poems I*, ed. Thomas Pinney, Cambridge: Cambridge University Press, 2013, pp. 611–3. Here and elsewhere, 'England' in this period is often used to stand in for the whole of Britain. One demonstration of this is George Orwell's 'England Your England', from 1941, which gives the population of England as 46 million – that was, in fact, the size of the population of the United Kingdom in the 1931 census. Later on, Orwell acknowledges that he extrapolates from London and the Home Counties when he talks about England and Britain. George Orwell, 'England Your England', in *The Lion and the Unicorn: Socialism and the English Genius* in *Orwell's England*, ed. Peter Davison, London: Penguin, 2020, pp. 251–74: 252 and 274 n. 2, 259. On Kipling and the Second South African War, see Sarah LeFanu, *Something of Themselves: Kipling, Kingsley, Conan Doyle and the Anglo-Boer War*, London: Hurst, 2020.
2. Rudyard Kipling, 'The Recall', in *Actions and Reactions*, London: Macmillan, 1926, p. 51.
3. Bill Schwarz, Introduction to Bill Schwarz, ed., *The Expansion of England: Race, Ethnicity and Cultural History*, London: Routledge, 1996, p. 4. The Seeley text is not unique. Other influential texts on similar themes include the Radical Liberal politician Charles Dilke's *Greater Britain* (1879) and the historian J. A. Froude's *Oceana, or England and Her Colonies* (1886).
4. Catherine Hall and Sonya Rose, 'Introduction: Being at Home with the Empire', in *At Home with the Empire: Metropolitan Culture and the Imperial World*, eds. Catherine Hall and Sonya O. Rose, New York: Cambridge University Press, 2006, pp. 1–31: 21, 2.
5. Raymond Williams, 'When Was Modernism?', in *Culture and Politics: Class, Writing, Socialism*, ed. Phil O'Brien, London: Verso, 2022, pp. 203–20: 207, 217.
6. Douglas Mao and Rebecca L. Walkowitz, 'The New Modernist Studies', *PMLA*, 123:3 (2008), 737–48: 737. As Paul K. Saint-Amour argues, coinages such as 'transnational, global, and planetary' modernisms suggest '*expansionism*' (Paul K. Saint-Amour, 'Weak Theory, Weak Modernism', *Modernism/modernity*, 25:3 (2018), 437–59: 441.) Returning to these debates in 2021, Douglas Mao says that this expansionary phase is now over, calling for a return, in a context of in beleaguered humanities departments, to the text. Mao's modernist studies melancholia is a subset of imperial melancholia and the result of a refusal to fully address and work through the past. (Douglas Mao, 'Introduction: The New Modernist Studies', in *The New Modernist Studies*, ed. Douglas Mao, Cambridge: Cambridge University Press, 2021, pp. 1–22.)
7. See, for example, Elleke Boehmer, *Empire, the National, and the Postcolonial, 1890–1920: Resistance in Interaction*, Oxford: Oxford University Press, 2002; and Priyamvada Gopal, *Insurgent Empire: Anticolonial Resistance and British Dissent*, London: Verso, 2019.
8. Vincent Sherry, 'Modernism under Review: Edmund Wilson's *Axel's Castle: A Study in the Imaginative Literature of 1870–1930*', *Modernist Cultures*, 7:2 (2012), 145–59: 145 drawing on Lewis M. Dabney, *Edmund Wilson: A Life in Literature*, New York: Farrar, Straus, and Giroux, 2005, p. 159.
9. Jason Harding and Ronald Schuchard, eds., *The Complete Prose of T. S. Eliot: The Critical Edition, Volume 4, English Lion, 1930–1933*, Baltimore: Johns Hopkins University Press, 2015, pp. 758–809: 761.
10. George Bernard Shaw, ed., *Fabianism and the Empire: A Manifesto of the Fabian Society*, London: Grant Richards, 1900.
11. Duncan Bell, 'Founding the World State: H. G. Wells on Empire and the English-Speaking Peoples', *International Studies Quarterly*, 62 (2018), 867–79: 875.
12. W. E. B. Du Bois et al., 'To the Nations of the World', in *W. E. B. Du Bois: International Thought*, eds. Adom Getachew and Jennifer Pitts, Cambridge: Cambridge University Press, 2022, pp. 18–21: 19, 20.

13 Boehmer, *Empire, the National, and the Postcolonial, 1890–1920*, pp. 17–8.
14 Eliot does not include writers of colour, and he has very little to say about women's writing in his lecture notes.
15 Ralph Darlington, *Labour Revolt in Britain, 1910–1914*, London: Pluto Press, 2023. There was also an international dimension as shown by the formation of the Industrial Workers of the World union. As well as seeking improved pay and working conditions for workers of all races across the globe, it advocated living alongside nature rather than exploiting it. See Peter Cole, David Struthers and Kenyon Zimmer, eds., *Wobblies of the World: A Global History of the IWW*, London: Pluto Press, 2017.
16 Bernard Semmel, *Imperialism and Social Reform: English Social-Imperial Thought 1895–1914*, Cambridge, MA: Harvard University Press, 1960, pp. 46–51; G. R. Searle, 'The Politics of National Efficiency and of War, 1900–1918', in *A Companion to Early Twentieth-Century Britain*, ed. Chris Wrigley, Oxford: Blackwell, 2003, pp. 56–71.
17 Rudyard Kipling, 'The Lesson', in *The Five Nations* in *The Cambridge Edition of the Poems of Rudyard Kipling, Volume I*, ed. Thomas Pinney, Cambridge: Cambridge University Press, 2013, pp. 550–1.
18 See Elleke Boehmer, Introduction to Robert Baden-Powell, *Scouting for Boys: A Handbook for Instruction in Good Citizenship*, Oxford: Oxford University Press, 2004, pp. xi–xxxix. Allen Warren, 'Citizens of Empire: Baden-Powell, Scouts and Guides and an Imperial Ideal, 1900–40', in *Imperialism and Popular Culture*, ed. John M. MacKenzie, Manchester: Manchester University Press, 1986, pp. 232–56.
19 Joseph L. Zornado, *Inventing the Child: Culture, Ideology, and the Story of Childhood*, New York: Routledge, 2001, pp. 118–24. See also J. S. Bratton, 'Of England, Home and Duty: The Image of England in Victorian and Edwardian Juvenile Literature', in *Imperialism and Popular Culture*, ed. John M. MacKenzie, Manchester: Manchester University Press, 1986, pp. 74–93.
20 C. R. L. Fletcher and Rudyard Kipling, *A History of England*, Oxford: Oxford University Press, 1911, p. 239. They say of India: 'Our rule has been infinitely to the good of all the three hundred millions of the different races who inhabit that richly peopled land', p. 241.
21 H. E. Marshall, *Our Island Story*, London: Civitas, 2005. On David Cameron and H. E. Marshall, see Andrew Hough, 'Revealed: David Cameron's Favourite Childhood Book is *Our Island Story*', *The Daily Telegraph*, 29 October 2010. www.telegraph.co.uk/culture/books/booknews/8094333/Revealed-David-Camerons-favourite-childhood-book-is-Our-Island-Story.html and Tom Holland, '*Our Island Story*: Not as Conservative as David Cameron Imagines', *The Guardian*, 7 February 2014. www.theguardian.com/books/booksblog/2014/feb/07/our-island-story-conservative-david-cameron.
22 See David Glover, *Literature, Immigration, and Diaspora in Fin-de-Siècle England: A Cultural History of the 1905 Aliens Act*, Cambridge: Cambridge University Press, 2012.
23 Labour shortages in Southern Africa after the Second South African War saw the introduction of Chinese workers. There were concerns that their conditions were tantamount to slavery. Glover, *Literature, Immigration, and Diaspora in Fin-de-Siècle England*, p. 140.
24 Shiel, who was of mixed race and born in Monserrat in the Caribbean, later became a pioneer of science fiction and was convicted of the sexual assault of a minor. See Albert R. Vogeler, 'Shiel, Matthew Phipps (1865–1947)', in *Oxford Dictionary of National Biography*, Oxford: Oxford University Press, 2004; and Kirsten MacLeod, 'M. P. Shiel and the Love of Pubescent Girls: The Other "Love That Dare Not Speak Its Name"', *English Literature in Transition, 1880–1920*, 51:4 (2008), 355–80.
25 Glover, *Literature, Immigration, and Diaspora in Fin-de-Siècle England*, pp. 131–7.
26 Glover, *Literature, Immigration, and Diaspora in Fin-de-Siècle England*, p. 144.
27 Glover, *Literature, Immigration, and Diaspora in Fin-de-Siècle England*, p. 14.
28 Edward Marsh presented the first Georgian anthology 'in the belief that English poetry is now once again putting on a new strength and beauty'. E. M. [Edward Marsh], Prefatory Note to *Georgian Poetry, 1911–12*, London: The Poetry Bookshop, 1912, p. v.

29 Rupert Brooke, 'The Old Vicarage, Grantchester', in *Georgian Poetry, 1911–1912*, London: The Poetry Bookshop, 1912, pp. 33–7: 37, 33.
30 H. G. Wells, *Tono-Bungay*, eds. Edward Mendelson and Patrick Parrinder, London: Penguin, 2005, p. 3. Subsequent references in parentheses in the text to this edition as *TB*.
31 Leon Edel and Gordon N. Ray, eds., *Henry James and H. G. Wells: A Record of Their Friendship, Their Debate on the Art of Fiction, and Their Quarrel*, London: Rupert Hart-Davis, 1958.
32 H. G. Wells, *Experiment in Autobiography: Discoveries and Conclusions of a Very Ordinary Brain (since 1866)*, London: Victor Gollancz, 1934, Vol. 2, pp. 494–5.
33 David Lodge, '*Tono-Bungay* and the Condition of England', in *Language of Fiction: Essays in Criticism and Verbal Analysis of the English Novel*, London: Routledge, 2001, pp. 227–58: 231.
34 Henri Lefebvre, *The Production of Space*, trans. Donald Nicholson-Smith, Oxford: Blackwell, 1991, p. 25.
35 See Jonathan Wild, 'Sex and the Single Edwardian Girl: Sex and Censorship in the Edwardian Novel', in *Edwardian Culture: Beyond the Garden Party*, eds. Naomi Carle, Samuel Shaw and Sarah Shaw, New York: Routledge, 2018, pp. 223–35.
36 George Townsend Warner, *Landmarks in English Industrial History*, London: Blackie & Son, 1899, p. 360.
37 Gauri Viswanathan, 'Value: H. G. Wells' Tono-Bungay and the "Romance of Modern Commerce"', *Journal of the American Academy of Religion*, 87:3 (2019), 618–24, citing Theodor W. Adorno, *The Stars Down to Earth and Other Essays on the Irrational in Culture*, trans. Stephen Crook, London: Routledge, 1994, pp. 172–80: 174.
38 Modern gender roles were not simply made in Europe and America and then exported elsewhere. Jules Gill-Peterson discusses how colonial anxieties helped mould gender norms in the colonising country. Jules Gill-Peterson, *A Short History of Trans Misogyny*, New York: Verso, 2024.
39 Rudyard Kipling, 'The Destroyers', in *The Cambridge Edition of the Poems of Rudyard Kipling, Volume I, The Collected Poems I*, ed. Thomas Pinney, Cambridge: Cambridge University Press, 2013, pp. 480–2: 481.
40 The long coda is shortened in the symphony's subsequent revisions, and the Vaughan Williams estate has only allowed the original version to be recorded once, by Richard Hickox and the London Symphony Orchestra (Chandos, 2001). On Vaughan Williams linking the symphony's coda to *Tono-Bungay*, see Eric Saylor, *Vaughan Williams*, Oxford: Oxford University Press, 2021, p. 76. See also Alain Frogley, 'H. G. Wells and Vaughan Williams's *A London Symphony*: Politics and Culture in Fin-de-Siècle England,' in *Sundry Sorts of Music Books: Essays on the British Library Collections*, eds. Chris Banks, Arthur Searle and Malcolm Turner, London: British Library, 1993, pp. 299–308. For music and empire in Britain in this period see, Jeffrey Richards, *Imperialism and Music, 1873–1953*, Manchester: Manchester University Press, 2001.
41 C. F. G. Masterman, *The Condition of England*, London: Methuen, 1909, p. 237.
42 Masterman, *The Condition of England*, p. 62.
43 Masterman, *The Condition of England*, p. 103.
44 Benita Parry, 'Tono-Bungay: The Failed Electrification of the Empire of Light', in *Postcolonial Studies: A Materialist Critique*, London: Routledge, 2004; Benita Parry, 'A Departure from Modernism: Stylistic Strategies in Modern Peripheral Literatures as Symptom, Mediation and Critique of Modernity', in *The Bloomsbury Companion to Modernist Literature*, eds. Ulrika Maude and Mark Nixon, London: Bloomsbury, 2018, pp. 349–73; Timothy Brennan, 'Against Modernism', in *Marxism, Postcolonial Theory, and the Future of Critique: Critical Engagements with Benita Parry*, eds. Sharae Deckard and Rashmi Varma, New York: Routledge, 2019, pp. 21–36.
45 T. J. Clark, *Picasso and Truth*, Princeton: Princeton University Press, 2013, p. 4.
46 E. M. Forster, 'The Machine Stops', in *Collected Short Stories*, London: Penguin, 1954, pp. 109–46: 146.

47 Paul B. Armstrong, 'The Narrator in the Closet: The Ambiguous Narrative Voice in *Howards End*', *Modern Fiction Studies*, 47:2 (2001), 306–28.
48 E. M. Forster, *Howards End*, ed. Oliver Stallybrass, London: Penguin, 1989, p. 188.
49 See Robert K. Martin, '"It Must Have Been the Umbrella": Forster's Queer Begetting', in *Queer Forster*, eds. Robert K. Martin and George Piggford, Chicago: University of Chicago Press, 1997, pp. 255–73.
50 Forster, *Howards End*, p. 58.
51 Nicholas Royle, *E. M. Forster*, Plymouth: Northcote House, 1999, p. 49; Andrew Thacker, 'Of Dust and Rubber: Rereading *Howards End*', *Études britanniques contemporaines*, 58 (2020). https://doi.org/10.4000/ebc.8856; Kelly Sultzbach, *Ecocriticism in the Modernist Imagination: Forster, Woolf, and Auden*, New York: Cambridge University Press, 2016, pp. 25–81; Ted Howell, 'An Imperialist Inherits the Earth: *Howards End* in the Anthropocene', *Modern Language Quarterly*, 77:4 (2016), 547–72.
52 Forster, *Howards End*, p. 196.
53 David Bradshaw, '*Howards End*', in *The Cambridge Companion to E. M. Forster*, ed. David Bradshaw, Cambridge: Cambridge University Press, 2007, pp. 151–72: 163–6.
54 Forster, *Howards End*, p. 197.
55 Forster, *Howards End*, pp. 177–8.
56 Fredric Jameson, *Modernism and Imperialism*, Derry: Field Day, 1988, pp. 11, 19. The pamphlet was reprinted in Seamus Deane et al., *Nationalism, Colonialism and Literature*, Minneapolis: University of Minnesota Press, 1990, pp. 43–66.
57 Combines E. M. Forster, *Howards End*, ed. Oliver Stallybrass, London: Edward Arnold, 1972, p. 42 and E. M. Forster, *The Manuscripts of Howards End*, ed. Oliver Stallybrass, London: Edward Arnold, 1973, p. 39.
58 James T. Boulton, ed., *The Letters of D. H. Lawrence, Volume I, 1901–13*, Cambridge: Cambridge University Press, 1979, pp. 127, 119.
59 F. R. Leavis, *D. H. Lawrence: Novelist*, London: Chatto and Windus, 1955, p. 173.
60 D. H. Lawrence, *The Rainbow*, ed. Mark Kinkead-Weekes, Cambridge: Cambridge University Press, 1989, p. 377.
61 Lawrence, *The Rainbow*, p. 289.
62 Lawrence, *The Rainbow*, p. 459.
63 See also Howard J. Booth, '*The Rainbow*, British Marxist Criticism of the 1930s and Colonialism', in *New D. H. Lawrence*, ed. Howard J. Booth, Manchester: Manchester University Press, 2009, pp. 34–58; Howard J. Booth, 'D. H. Lawrence's *The Rainbow* and the Dream of a Better World', *Journal of D. H. Lawrence Studies*, 4:1 (2015), 19–44.
64 See Jeremy MacClancy, 'Anthropology: "The Latest Form of Evening Entertainment"', in *A Concise Companion to Modernism*, ed. David Bradshaw, Oxford: Blackwell, 2003, pp. 75–94.
65 See Paddy Docherty, *Blood and Bronze: The British Empire and the Sack of Benin*, London: Hurst, 2021; and Dan Hicks, *The Brutish Museums: The Benin Bronzes, Colonial Violence and Cultural Restitution*, London: Pluto, 2020.
66 For Digital Benin on the Manchester Museum holdings, see https://digitalbenin.org/institutions/21?id=21&page=1. For the museum's policy on return and repatriation, see www.museum.manchester.ac.uk/making-the-museum/futureofcollections/.
67 Boehmer, *Empire, the National, and the Postcolonial, 1890–1920*, p. 170.
68 Frances Fowle, 'The Celtic Revival in Britain and Ireland: Reconstructing the Past', in *Celts: Art and Identity*, eds. Julia Farley and Fraser Hunter, London: British Museum, 2015, pp. 234–59.
69 Ralph Vaughan Williams and A. L. Lloyd, eds., *English Folk Song*, London: Penguin, 2009 [1959]; Ralph Vaughan Williams, *National Music* (1934) in *National Music and Other Essays*, ed. Michael Kennedy, Oxford: Oxford University Press, 1986, pp. 1–82.
70 Christopher Caudwell, *Romance and Realism: A Study in English Bourgeois Literature*, ed. Samuel Hynes, Princeton: Princeton University Press, 1970, p. 99.

71 Rudyard Kipling, 'The English Flag', in *Barrack-Room Ballads* in *The Cambridge Edition of the Poems of Rudyard Kipling, Volume I, Collected Poems I*, ed. Thomas Pinney, Cambridge: Cambridge University Press, 2013, pp. 291–4: 291.
72 Terry Eagleton, *Exiles and Émigrés: Studies in Modern Literature*, London: Chatto & Windus, 1970.
73 Anna Snaith, *Modernist Voyages: Colonial Women Writers in London, 1890–1945*, Cambridge: Cambridge University Press, 2014.
74 Fredric Jameson, 'Cognitive Mapping', in *Marxism and the Interpretation of Culture*, eds. Cary Nelson and Lawrence Grossberg, Basingstoke: Macmillan, 1988, pp. 347–57: 350.
75 Boehmer, *Empire, the National, and the Postcolonial, 1890–1920*, pp. 169–214.
76 William Radice, Introduction to Rabindranath Tagore, *Gitanjali*, trans. William Radice, New Delhi: Penguin India, 2011, pp. xv–lxxxvi.
77 See Jade Munslow Ong, *Olive Schreiner and African Modernism: Allegory, Empire and Postcolonial Writing*, New York: Routledge, 2018; and Jade Munslow Ong and Andrew Van der Vlies, eds. *Olive Schreiner: Writing Networks and Global Contexts*, Edinburgh: Edinburgh University Press, 2023.
78 D. H. Lawrence, 'With the Guns', in *Twilight in Italy and Other Essays*, ed. Paul Eggert, Cambridge: Cambridge University Press, 1994, pp. 81–4.
79 G. R. Searle, *The Quest for National Efficiency: A Study in British Politics and Political Thought, 1899–1914*, Oxford: Basil Blackwell, 1971.
80 Rudyard Kipling, 'Sons of the Suburbs', in *The Cambridge Edition of the Poems of Rudyard Kipling, Volume III, Uncollected Poems*, ed. Thomas Pinney, Cambridge: Cambridge University Press, 2013, pp. 2105–7: 2106.
81 Rudyard Kipling, *A Diversity of Creatures*, London: Macmillan, 1917, pp. 442, 440. See David Bradshaw, 'Kipling and War', in *The Cambridge Companion to Rudyard Kipling*, ed. Howard J. Booth, Cambridge: Cambridge University Press, 2011, pp. 80–94: 84–8. Jan Montefiore surveys critics who have seen Mary's response as sexual, while noting the story's complex ambivalence. Jan Montefiore, *Rudyard Kipling*, Tavistock: Northcote House, 2007, pp. 151–5.
82 Rupert Brooke, *The Poetical Works*, ed. Geoffrey Keynes, London: Faber and Faber, 2014, pp. 5, 9.
83 *The War Poems of Wilfred Owen*, ed. Jon Stallworthy, London: Chatto and Windus, 1994, pp. 83, 35–6: 36.
84 *Isaac Rosenberg: Complete Writings*, ed. Vivien Noakes, Oxford: Oxford University Press, 2008, p. 104.
85 Cited in Samantha Rayner, 'David Jones, *In Parenthesis*', in *Handbook of British Literature and Culture of the First World War*, eds. Ralf Schneider and Jane Potter, Berlin: de Gruyter, 2021, pp. 323–35: 323.
86 Edward Thomas, 'As the Team's Head Brass', in *The Collected Poems of Edward Thomas*, ed. R. George Thomas, Oxford: Oxford University Press, 1981, pp. 108–9: 109.
87 David Olusoga, *The World's War: Forgotten Soldiers of Empire*, London: Head of Zeus, 2014.
88 See, for example, Michael J. K. Walsh, and Andrekos Varnava, eds., *The Great War and the British Empire: Culture and Society*, Oxford: Routledge, 2017.
89 John Connor, 'Home and Away: The Enlistment of Australian, Canadian, New Zealand, and South African Men in Dominion Expeditionary Forces in the United Kingdom during the Great War', *Itinerario*, 38 (2014), 45–58: 55.
90 James Barr, *A Line in the Sand: Britain, France and the Struggle that Shaped the Middle East*, London: Simon & Schuster, 2011.
91 See Kate Kennedy, '"A Tribute to My Brother": Women's Literature and Its Post-War Ghosts', *Journal of War and Culture Studies*, 8:1 (2015), 7–23; Graham Dawson, *Soldier Heroes: British Adventure, Empire and the Imagining of Masculinities*, London: Routledge, 1994, p. 23.

92 See Andrew Frayn, *Writing Disenchantment: British First World War Prose, 1914–30*, Manchester: Manchester University Press, 2014; and Andrew Frayn and Fiona Houston, 'The War Books Boom in Britain, 1928–1930', *First World War Studies*, 13:1 (2022), 25–45.
93 Santanu Das, *India, Empire, and First World War Culture: Writings, Images, and Songs*, Oxford: Oxford University Press, 2018, pp. 343–66: 343. See also Samraghni Bonnerjee, 'Indian Writings of the First World War', in *Handbook of British Literature and Culture of the First World War*, eds. Ralf Schneider and Jane Potter, Berlin: de Gruyter, 2021, pp. 167–79.
94 David Olusoga, *Black and British: A Forgotten History*, London: Macmillan, 2016, pp. 427–66; Jacqueline Jenkinson, *Black 1919: Riots, Racism and Resistance in Imperial Britain*, Liverpool: Liverpool University Press, 2009; and Ernest Marke, *Old Man Trouble*, London: Weidenfeld and Nicolson, 1975.
95 See, for example, A. J. P. Taylor, 'The Great War: The Triumph of E. D. Morel', in *The Trouble Makers: Dissent Over Foreign Policy, 1792–1939*, London: Faber and Faber, 1957, pp. 132–66.
96 Marvin Swartz, *The Union of Democratic Control in British Politics during the First World War*, Oxford: Oxford University Press, 1971, pp. 47, 94 n. 44; Sally Harris, *Out of Control: British Foreign Policy and the Union of Democratic Control, 1914–1918*, Hull: University of Hull Press, 1996.
97 See E. D. Morel, *The Horror on the Rhine*, 8th edition, London: Union of Democratic Control, August 1920. See Iris Wigger, *'The Black Horror on the Rhine': Intersections of Race, Nation, Gender and Class in 1920s Germany*, Basingstoke: Palgrave Macmillan, 2017.
98 E. D. Morel, 'Black Scourge in Europe', *The Daily Herald*, 10 April 1920.
99 Claude McKay, *A Long Way from Home*, London: Pluto, 1985 [1937], p. 75.
100 Claude McKay, 'A Black Man Replies', *The Workers' Dreadnought*, 24 April 1920. See also Wayne F. Cooper, *Claude McKay: Rebel Sojourner in the Harlem Renaissance*, Baton Rouge: Louisiana State University Press, 1987, pp. 131, 393, 396.
101 Keith L. Nelson, 'The "Black Horror on the Rhine": Race as a Factor in Post World War I Diplomacy', *Journal of Modern History*, 42:4 (1970), 606–27: 622.
102 In fact, Max Eastman in New York had made Pankhurst aware of McKay and that he was in London; a number of his poems and an article had already appeared in the *Workers' Dreadnought*. Winston James, *Claude McKay: The Making of a Black Bolshevik*, New York: Columbia University Press, 2022, pp. 279–80.
103 James, *Claude McKay*, pp. 281–3; Claude McKay, *The Negroes in America* (1923) cited in James, *Claude McKay*, p. 315.
104 Peter Fryer, *Staying Power: The History of Black People in Britain*, London: Pluto, 1984, p. 318.
105 James, *Claude McKay*, pp. 288–90.
106 Claude McKay, *Complete Poems*, ed. William J. Maxwell, Chicago: University of Illinois Press, 2004, p. 233.
107 See Howard J. Booth, 'Claude McKay in Britain: Race, Sexuality and Poetry', in *Modernism and Race*, ed. Len Platt, Cambridge: Cambridge University Press, 2011, pp. 137–55: 144–51.
108 Elizabeth Longford, 'Wilfrid Scawen Blunt (1840–1922)', in *Dictionary of National Biography*. https://doi.org/10.1093/ref:odnb/31938; Gopal, *Insurgent Empire*, 127–66; Helen Carr, 'Imagism and Empire', in *Modernism and Empire*, eds. Howard J. Booth and Nigel Rigby, Manchester: Manchester University Press, 2000, pp. 64–93; and E. M. Forster, 'Wilfrid Blunt', in *Abinger Harvest and England's Pleasant Land*, ed. Elizabeth Heine, London: André Deutsch, 1996, pp. 263–74.
109 For example, the word 'anarchist' is used only a small number of times in passing in Christos Hadjiyiannis and Rachel Potter, eds., *The Cambridge Companion to Twentieth Century Literature and Politics*, Cambridge: Cambridge University Press, 2023.

110 See David Goodway, *Anarchist Seeds Beneath the Snow: Left Libertarian Thought and British Writers from William Morris to Colin Ward*, Oakland, CA: PM Press, 2012.
111 James, *Claude McKay*, p. 283.
112 V. I. Lenin, 'Preface to the French and German Editions' of *Imperialism: The Highest Stage of Capitalism*, London: Penguin, 2010, pp. 4–10: 4, 5. Lenin wrote this preface when he no longer had to worry about Tsarist censorship; that had led him be cautious about drawing wider conclusions in the pamphlet itself. A. L. Morton provides a summary of Lenin's 'exact definition' of imperialism, and thus a sense of how the word was understood in mid-century British communism, in his *A People's History of England*, London: Lawrence and Wishart, 1989 [1938, 1948], p. 423.
113 James Klugmann, *History of the Communist Party of Great Britain, Volume 1, Formation and Early Years, 1919–1924*, London: Lawrence and Wishart, 1969, pp. 300–9, 321.
114 Semmel, *Imperialism and Social Reform*, pp. 222–33.
115 Quoted in David Torrance, *The Wild Men: The Remarkable Story of Britain's First Labour Government*, London: Bloomsbury, 2024, pp. 151, 148.
116 Historical texts on questioning the empire, which offer a different account from the one that circulates in modernist studies, include Stephen Howe, *Anticolonialism in British Politics: The Left and the End of Empire*, Oxford: Oxford University Press, 1993; Gregory Clays, *Imperial Sceptics: British Critics of Empire, 1850–1920*, Cambridge: Cambridge University Press, 2010; Nicholas Owen, *The British Left and India: Metropolitan Anti-Imperialism 1885–1947*, Oxford: Oxford University Press, 2007; and Mira Matikkala, *Empire and Imperial Ambition: Liberty, Englishness and Anti-Imperialism in Late Victorian Britain*, London: I. B. Tauris, 2011.
117 Edward Carpenter, *Towards Democracy*, London: George Allen and Unwin, 1915, pp. 462–7: 466, 440–2: 442.
118 Sidney Webb, 'Historic', in *Fabian Essays in Socialism*, ed. G. Bernard Shaw, London: Fabian Society, 1889, pp. 30–61: 58.
119 Sidney Webb and Beatrice Webb, 'What is Socialism: XVII The Guardianship of the Non-Adult Races', *The New Statesman*, 2 August 1913, 525–6: 526. See J. M. Winter, 'The Webbs and the Non-White World: A Case of Socialist Racialism', *Journal of Contemporary History*, 9:1 (1974), 181–92.
120 Anna Snaith, 'Leonard and Virginia Woolf: Writing Against Empire', *The Journal of Commonwealth Literature*, 50:1 (2015), 19–32. Victoria Glendenning, *Leonard Woolf: A Biography*, New York: Simon and Schuster, 2006. Peter Wilson, 'Leonard Woolf: Still Not Out of the Jungle', *The Round Table: The Commonwealth Journal of International Affairs*, 47 (2008), 154–6.
121 Peter Wilson, *The International Theory of Leonard Woolf: A Study in Twentieth-Century Idealism*, New York: Palgrave Macmillan, 2003, pp. 83–141.
122 Leonard Woolf, 'The Political Advance of Backward Peoples', in *Fabian Colonial Essays*, ed. Rita Hinden, London: George Allen and Unwin, 1945, pp. 83–98: 92, 97, 98.
123 Wilson, *The International Theory of Leonard Woolf*, p. 135.
124 Leonard Woolf, *Mandates and Empire*, London: British Periodicals, 1920, p. 7.
125 Rodney Worrell, *George Padmore's Black Internationalism*, Kingston, Jamaica: The University of West Indies Press, 2020, p. 160.
126 Luke Reader, '"An Alternative to Imperialism": Leonard Woolf, The Labour Party and Imperial Internationalism, 1915–1922', *The International History Review*, 41:1 (2019), 157–77: 170.
127 See, for example, Patrick McGee, 'The Politics of Modernist Form; or, Who Rules *The Waves*?,' *Modern Fiction Studies*, 38:3 (1992), 631–50 and Matt Franks, 'Serving on the Eugenic Homefront: Virginia Woolf, Race, and Disability', *Feminist Formations*, 29:1 (2017), 1–24.
128 John Brannigan, 'Virginia Woolf and the Geographical Subject', in *Archipelagic Modernism: Literature in the Irish and British Isles, 1890–1970*, Edinburgh: Edinburgh University Press, 2014, pp. 107–36: 136.

129 E. P. Thompson, 'Where Are We Now?', in *E. P. Thompson and the Making of the New Left*, ed. Cal Winslow, London: Lawrence and Wishart, 2014, pp. 215–46: 228–29.
130 1945 Labour Manifesto, *Let Us Face the Future*, The Labour Party, 1945. www.labour-party.org.uk/manifestos/1945/1945-labour-manifesto.shtml.
131 E. M. Forster, 'What I Believe', in *Two Cheers for Democracy*, ed. Oliver Stallybrass, London: Edward Arnold, 1972, pp. 65–73: 72.
132 Benita Parry, 'Materiality and Mystification in *A Passage to India*', in *Postcolonial Studies: A Materialist Critique*, London: Routledge, 2004, pp. 162–75.
133 Edward W. Said, *Culture and Imperialism*, London: Chatto and Windus, 1993, pp. 241–8.
134 Nancy L. Paxton, *Writing Under the Raj: Gender, Race, and Rape in the British Colonial Imagination, 1830–1947*, New Brunswick, NJ: Rutgers University Press, 1999, pp. 5–6. See also Benita Parry, *Delusions and Discoveries: India in the British Imagination, 1880–1930*, London: Verso, 1998 [1972], pp. 225–44.
135 Kim A. Wagner, *Amritsar 1919: The Empire of Fear and the Making of a Massacre*, New Haven: Yale University Press, 2019, pp. 39–41, 173–6; Kim A. Wagner, '"Treading Upon Fires": The "Mutiny"-Motif and Colonial Anxieties in British India', *Past and Present*, 218 (2013), 159–97: 196.
136 E. M. Forster, *A Passage to India*, ed. Oliver Stallybrass, London: Edward Arnold, 1978, p. 176.
137 Paul Scott, 'How Well Have They Worn?', *The Times*, 6 January 1966, 15.
138 Paul B. Armstrong, Introduction to E. M. Forster, *A Passage to India*, ed. Paul B. Armstrong, New York: Norton, 2021, p. xii.
139 E. M. Forster, *The Manuscripts of A Passage to India*, ed. Oliver Stallybrass, London: Edward Arnold, 1978, p. 320.
140 Forster, *A Passage to India*, p. 159.
141 Forster, *A Passage to India*, p. 213.
142 Forster, *A Passage to India*, p. 228.
143 Forster, *A Passage to India*, pp. 55, 283–4, 287–8.
144 Parry, 'Materiality and Mystification in *A Passage to India*', pp. 172, 173.
145 Paul Fussell, *Abroad: British Literary Traveling between the Wars*, Oxford: Oxford University Press, 1980, p. 95.
146 Robert Byron, *The Road to Oxiana*, London: Penguin, 1992, p. 80.
147 Byron, *The Road to Oxiana*, pp. 58–9. See also pp. 196–200.
148 Byron, *The Road to Oxiana*, p. 92.
149 Byron, *The Road to Oxiana*, p. 117.
150 Byron, *The Road to Oxiana*, p. 289. See also Byron's *An Essay on India*, London: George Routledge, 1931.
151 Byron, *The Road to Oxiana*, p. 25.
152 See also Howard J. Booth, 'Beyond Europe's Borders: Late Colonial Uncertainty in Robert Byron's *The Road to Oxiana*', in *European Travel Writing in the 1930s*, eds. Charles Burdett and Derek Duncan, Oxford: Berghahn Books, 2002, pp. 159–72: 169–70. As a counter to the popular belief that Jewish refugees met with sympathy from the British authorities around the time of the Second World War, finding it straightforward to settle and live in Britain, see Louise London, *Whitehall and the Jews, 1933–1948: British Immigration Policy, Jewish Refugees and the Holocaust*, Cambridge: Cambridge University Press, 2000.
153 Richard F. Burton, *Narrative of a Pilgrimage to Meccah and Medinah*, 3rd edition, London: William Mullan, 1879, pp. 436–7.
154 Byron, *The Road to Oxiana*, p. 244.
155 Janet Montefiore, *Men and Women Writers of the 1930s: The Dangerous Flood of History*, London: Routledge, 1996. For Warner's engagement with George Lukács's *The Historical Novel* and her exchange with Lukács, see Ksenia Shmydkaya, 'Georg Lukács, Sylvia Townsend Warner and *The Historical Novel*', *The Journal of the Sylvia Townsend Warner Society*, 23:1 (2023), 97–111.

156 Michael Löwy, 'The Current of Critical Irrealism: "A Moonlit Enchanted Night"', in *Adventures in Realism*, ed. Matthew Beaumont, Oxford: Blackwell, 2007, pp. 193–206.
157 See further Howard J. Booth, 'Colonialism and Time in Sylvia Townsend Warner's *Mr Fortune's Maggot* and "The Salutation"', *Literature Compass*, 11:12 (2014), 745–53.
158 Sylvia Townsend Warner, 'My Shirt is in Mexico', in *A Garland of Straw*, London: Chatto and Windus, 1943, pp. 81–4: 84. It was originally published in *The New Yorker* (January 1941) as 'My Shirt in Mexico'. The story is republished in Sylvia Townsend Warner, *English Climate: Wartime Stories*, London: Persephone, 2020, pp. 9–13.
159 Jennifer P. Nesbitt, 'Rum Histories: Decolonizing the Narratives of Jean Rhys' *Wide Sargasso Sea* and Sylvia Townsend Warner's *The Flint Anchor*', *Tulsa Studies in Women's Literature*, 26:2 (2007), 309–30.
160 Claire Harman, Introduction to Sylvia Townsend Warner, *The Flint Anchor*, London: Virago, 1997, p. xi.
161 See Howard J. Booth, 'Sylvia Townsend Warner's *The Flint Anchor* and Modernism', *The Journal of the Sylvia Townsend Warner Society*, 18:2 (2019), 60–71.
162 John M. MacKenzie, Introduction to John M. MacKenzie, ed., *Imperialism and Popular Culture*, Manchester: Manchester University Press, 1986, pp. 1–16.
163 John M. MacKenzie, 'The Popular Culture of Empire in Britain', in *The Oxford History of the British Empire, Volume IV: The Twentieth Century*, eds. Judith M. Brown and Wm. Roger Louis, Oxford: Oxford University Press, 1999, pp. 212–31.
164 Stephen Constantine, '"Bringing the Empire Alive": The Empire Marketing Board and Imperial Propaganda, 1926–33', in *Imperialism and Popular Culture*, ed. John M. MacKenzie, Manchester: Manchester University Press, 1986, pp. 192–231.
165 Stephen Constantine, ed., *Buy and Build: The Advertising Posters of the Empire Marketing Board*, London: Public Record Office, 1986, plates 48 and 49.
166 This stress on the national level remains in place in John Brannigan's often insightful *Archipelagic Modernism: Literature in the Irish and British Isles, 1890–1970* (2014).
167 Laura Wainwright, 'Cadaqués and Carmarthenshire: The Modernist "Heterotopias" of Salvador Dalí and Dylan Thomas', in *New Territories in Modernism: Anglophone Welsh Writing, 1930–1949*, Cardiff: University of Wales Press, 2018, pp. 105–26.
168 Forster, 'What I Believe', p. 66.
169 George Orwell, *Notes on Nationalism* in *Orwell and Politics*, ed. Peter Davison, London: Penguin, 2001, pp. 355–411.
170 Rabindranath Tagore, *Nationalism*, London: Macmillan, 1917.
171 Margery Palmer McCulloch, *Edwin and Willa Muir*, Oxford: Oxford University Press, 2023, pp. 146–58.
172 Scott Lyall, '"That Ancient Self": Scottish Modernism's Counter-Renaissance', *European Journal of English Studies*, 18:1 (2014), 73–85.
173 Edwin Muir, 'The Solitary Place', in *Collected Poems*, London: Faber and Faber, 1963, pp. 80–8: 83.
174 Murray Pittock, 'Scotland, Empire and Apocalypse: From Stevenson to Buchan', in *The Edinburgh Companion to Twentieth-Century Scottish Literature*, eds. Ian Brown and Alan Riach, Edinburgh: Edinburgh University Press, 2009, pp. 25–36: 29. Pittock's argument is quoted with approval by Angela Smith in her 'Scottish Literature and the British Empire', in *Scotland and the British Empire*, eds. John M. MacKenzie and T. M. Devine, Oxford: Oxford University Press, 2011, pp. 255–79: 278.
175 Mark Crinson, *Shock City: Image and Architecture in Industrial Manchester*, Yale: Yale University Press, 2022, pp. 3–11.
176 Andy Croft, *Red Letter Days: British Fiction in the 1930s*, London: Lawrence and Wishart, 1990; and, for the decade before, John Lucas, *The Radical Twenties: Aspects of Writing, Politics and Culture*, Nottingham: Five Leaves, 1997.
177 T. J. Clark, 'Lowry's Other England', in *Lowry and the Painting of Modern Life*, eds. T. J. Clark and Anne M. Wagner, London: Tate, 2013, pp. 21–73: 21.

178 Alick West, 'J. B. Priestley', in *Mountain in the Sunlight: Studies in Conflict and Unity*, London: Lawrence and Wishart, 1958, pp. 155–83. See also John Baxendale, *Priestley's England: J. B. Priestley and English Culture*, Manchester: Manchester University Press, 2014.
179 J. B. Priestley, *English Journey*, London: Heinemann; Gollancz, 1934, p. 248.
180 George Orwell, *The Road to Wigan Pier* in *Orwell's England*, ed. Peter Davison, London: Penguin, 2020, pp. 57–216: 130.
181 See Jack Chadwick, 'Two Calibans', in *Caliban Shrieks*, ed. Jack Hilton, London: Vintage, 2024, pp. xv–xxiv.
182 John Fordham, *James Hanley: Modernism and the Working Class*, Cardiff: University of Wales Press, 2002.
183 Raphael Samuel, 'Empire Stories: The Imperial and the Domestic', in *Island Stories: Unravelling Britain – Theatres of Memory, Volume II*, London: Verso, 1998, pp. 74–97: 82.
184 See Hester Barron, 'Weaving Tales of Empire: Gandhi's Visit to Lancashire, 1931', in *The British Labour Movement and Imperialism*, eds. Billy Frank, Craig Horner and David Stewart, Newcastle-upon-Tyne: Cambridge Scholars Publishing, 2010, pp. 65–87.
185 C. L. R. James, 'Review of George Padmore's *How Britain Rules Africa*', *New Leader*, 29 May 1936.
186 See Dominic Head, *Modernity and the English Rural Novel*, Cambridge: Cambridge University Press, 2017; Neal Alexander and James Moran, eds., *Regional Modernisms*, Edinburgh: Edinburgh University Press, 2013; and Andrew Frayn, 'Rural Modernity, Rural Modernism and Deindustrialisation in Norman Nicholson's Poetry', *English Studies*, 104:3 (2023), 478–99.
187 Corinne Fowler, *Our Island Stories: Country Walks through Colonial Britain*, London: Allen Lane, 2024, 215–7.
188 Jed Esty, *A Shrinking Island: Modernism and National Culture in England*, Princeton: Princeton University Press, 2004, p. 50.
189 T. S. Eliot, Preface to *For Lancelot Andrewes: Essays on Style and Order*, New York: Doubleday, Doran, 1928, p. vii.
190 T. S. Eliot, *Little Gidding, Four Quartets* in *The Poems of T. S. Eliot, Volume 1, Collected and Uncollected Poems*, eds. Christopher Ricks and John McCue, London: Faber and Faber, 2015, pp. 208, 209.
191 C. L. R. James, *Beyond a Boundary*, London: Vintage, 2019 [1963], p. 79.
192 Rebecca Dyer, 'Masters and Servants, Class, and the Colonies in Graham Greene's 1940s Fiction', in *The 1940s: A Decade of Modern British Fiction*, eds. Philip Tew and Glyn White, London: Bloomsbury, 2022, pp. 156–79: 177.
193 Evelyn Waugh, *A Tourist in Africa*, London: Chapman and Hall, 1966, p. 166.
194 Alexander Hutton, Angela Bartie, Linda Fleming, Mark Freeman and Paul Readman, eds., *Restaging the Past: Historical Pageants, Culture and Society in Modern Britain*, London: UCL Press, 2020.
195 When Forster's *A Passage to India* sold well in the United States, he used some of the money to buy an area of open woodland, Piney Copse, near his house at West Hackhurst, Abinger. He wrote about the wood and owning property in his essay 'My Wood' of 1926 (E. M. Forster, *Abinger Harvest and England's Pleasant Land*, ed. Elizabeth Heine, London: André Deutsch, 1996, pp. 21–4.) He left the wood to the National Trust.
196 William Greenslade, 'Guardianship and Fellowship: Radicalism and the Ecological Imagination 1880–1940', in *Ecology and the Literature of the British Left: The Red and the Green*, eds. John Rignall, John H. Gustav Klaus and Valentine Cunningham, Farnham: Ashgate, 2011, pp. 151–63: 152.
197 E. M. Forster, 'The Abinger Pageant', in *Abinger Harvest and England's Pleasant Land*, ed. Elizabeth Heine, London: André Deutsch, 1996, pp. 335–49: 337, 338, 349.

198 Alison Light, *Forever England: Femininity, Literature and Conservatism between the Wars* London: Routledge, 1991, p. 6.
199 Light, *Forever England*, p. 211.
200 See Janet Montefiore's pioneering 1994 essay 'Undeservedly Forgotten: Women Poets of the 1930s' reprinted in Janet Montefiore, *Arguments of Heart and Mind: Selected Essays, 1977–2000*, Manchester: Manchester University Press, 2002, pp. 66–79; Jane Dowson, ed., *Women's Poetry of the 1930s: A Critical Anthology*, London: Routledge, 1996; and Jane Dowson, *Women, Modernism and British Poetry, 1910–1939: Resisting Femininity*, Farnham: Ashgate, 2002.
201 Naomi Mitchison, 'New Verse', cited in Jill Benton, *Naomi Mitchison: A Life*, London: Pandora, 1992, p. 90.
202 See Stan Smith, Introduction to Storm Jameson, *In the Second Year*, Nottingham: Trent Editions, 2004, pp. vii–xxx.
203 See also Nancy Cunard, *Essays on Race and Empire*, ed. Maureen Moynagh, Peterborough, Ontario: Broadview, 2002.
204 Maroula Joannou, 'Nancy Cunard's English Journey', *Feminist Review*, 78 (2004), 141–63: 160. See also Barbara Bush, '"Britain's Conscience on Africa": White Women, Race and Imperial Politics in Inter-war Britain', in *Gender and Imperialism*, ed. Clare Midgley, Manchester: Manchester University Press, 1998, pp. 200–23.
205 George Padmore, *How Britain Rules Africa*, London: Wishart, 1936, p. 335.
206 Padmore, *How Britain Rules Africa*, p. 4.
207 Gopal, *Insurgent Empire*, p. 169 citing George Padmore, 'Not Nazism! Not Imperialism! But Socialism!', *New Leader*, 27 December 1941.
208 David Olusoga and Casper W. Erichsen, *The Kaiser's Holocaust: Germany's Forgotten Genocide and the Colonial Roots of Nazism*, London: Faber and Faber, 2010.
209 Aimé Césaire, *Discourse on Colonialism*, trans. Joan Pinkham, New York: Monthly Review Press, 2000, p. 36.
210 Albert Toscano, *Late Fascism: Race, Capitalism and the Politics of Crisis*, New York: Verso, 2023, p. 216, n. 16.
211 Christian Høgsbjerg, Introduction to C. R. R. James, *Toussaint Louverture: The Story of the Only Successful Slave Revolt in History: A Play in Three Acts*, ed. Christian Høgsbjerg, Durham, NC: Duke University Press, 2013, pp. 1–39.
212 James, *Beyond the Boundary*, p. 146.
213 Colin Chambers, *Black and Asian Theatre in Britain: A History*, Oxford: Routledge, 2011, p. 99.
214 Alison Donnell, 'Una Marson: Anti-Colonialism, Feminism and a Forgotten Struggle', in *West Indian Intellectuals in Britain*, ed. Bill Schwarz, Manchester: Manchester University Press, 2003, pp. 114–31.
215 Brockway had been a member of the League Against Imperialism and Colonial Oppression from its foundation in 1927. Though the organisation failed, it was a stepping stone to international anti-colonial collaboration. See Michele Louro, Carolien Stolte, Heather Streets-Salter, and Sana Tannoury-Karam, eds., *The League Against Imperialism: Lives and Afterlives*, Leiden: Leiden University Press, 2020.
216 Gopal, *Insurgent Empire*, pp. 375–6.
217 Again Kipling is reworked, in this case the poem 'The White Man's Burden' (1899).
218 Christian Høgsbjerg, 'C. L. R. James, George Orwell and "Literary Trotskyism"', *Orwell Studies*, 1:2 (2017), 43–60.
219 George Orwell, Review of Clarence K. Streit, *Union Now* (*The Adelphi*, July 1939) in *Orwell and Politics*, 66–70: 69.
220 See Andrew Moor, *Powell & Pressburger: A Cinema of Magic Spaces*, London: I. B. Tauris, 2005.
221 Humphrey Jennings, *Pandæmonium, 1660–1886: The Coming of the Machine as Seen by Contemporary Observers*, eds. Marie-Louise Jennings and Charles Madge,

London: Icon, 2012. The Foreword by Frank Cottrell-Boyce is on pp. vii–xii. See also Ros Cranston, 'Humphrey Jennings: How the Documentarian Inspired Danny Boyle's London 2012 Olympic Ceremony' on the British Film Institute website: www.bfi.org.uk/features/humphrey-jennings-danny-boyle-olympics-london-2012#:~:text=This%20scene%2C%20along%20with%20the,greatest%20documentary%20filmmakers%2C%20Humphrey%20Jennings.

222 Raymond Williams, *Orwell*, London: Fontana/Collins, 1971, pp. 16–28: 19.
223 Douglas Kerr, *Orwell and Empire*, Oxford: Oxford University Press, 2022, p. 4.
224 Orwell, 'England Your England', p. 252.
225 John Major, *Speech to the Conservative Group for Europe*, 22 April 1993. https://johnmajorarchive.org.uk/1993/04/22/mr-majors-speech-to-conservative-group-for-europe-22-april-1993/.
226 Orwell, 'England Your England', p. 264. To show the influence of this passage, John Brannigan uses it to provide the frame for his *Orwell to the Present: Literature in England, 1945–2000*, Basingstoke: Macmillan, 2003.
227 Stuart Ward, Introduction to *British Culture and the End of Empire*, ed. Stuart Ward, Manchester: Manchester University Press, 2001, pp. 1–20: 4, 13.
228 Matthew Whittle, *Post-War British Literature and the 'End of Empire'*, Basingstoke: Palgrave Macmillan, 2016, pp. 11–2.
229 Graham MacPhee, *Postwar British Literature and Postcolonial Studies*, Edinburgh: Edinburgh University Press, 2011, p. 65; and Bill Schwarz, 'Introduction: End of Empire and the English Novel', in *End of Empire and the English Novel since 1945*, eds. Rachel Gilmour and Bill Schwarz, Manchester: Manchester University Press, 2011, pp. 1–37: 5.
230 Samuel, 'Empire Stories: The Imperial and the Domestic', p. 86. For the 'primer' see Norman Lowe, *Mastering Modern British History*, Basingstoke: Macmillan, 1984, p. 252.
231 Bill Schwarz, 'The End of Empire', in *A Companion to Contemporary Britain, 1939–2000*, eds. Paul Addison and Harriet Jones, London: Blackwell, 2005, pp. 482–98: 482 and 497 n. 1.
232 See Yasmin Khan, *The Raj at War: A People's History of India's Second World War*, London: Vintage, 2016; Caroline Elkins, *Legacy of Violence: A History of the British Empire*, London: Vintage: 2023, pp. 460–579; Clement Attlee, *Empire into Commonwealth*, London: Oxford University Press, 1961, p. 49.
233 Attlee, *Empire into Commonwealth*, p. 1.
234 Regina Martin, 'London and Professional Society in H. G. Wells's *Tono-Bungay* and Hanif Kureishi's *The Buddha of Suburbia*', *Studies in the Humanities*, 42:1–2 (2015), 82–107.
235 Zadie Smith, 'Love, Actually', *The Guardian*, 1 November 2003, based on her 2003 Orange Word Lecture 'E. M. Forster's Ethical Style: Love, Failure and the Good in Fiction'. www.theguardian.com/books/2003/nov/01/classics.zadiesmith; and Andrzej Gasiorek, '"A Renewed Sense of Difficulty": E. M. Forster, Iris Murdoch and Zadie Smith on "Ethics and Form"', in *The Legacies of Modernism: Historicising Postwar and Contemporary Fiction*, ed. David James, Cambridge: Cambridge University Press, 2011, pp. 170–86: 175–6.

2 Post-War Unsettlement, 1948–1980

The years following the Second World War saw the emergence of what the historian David Edgerton has called the British nation. The dissolution of empire, a process undertaken haphazardly and often reluctantly, but then with gathering speed in the three decades after 1945, brought into being a national rather than imperial formation for the first time, one characterised increasingly by borders controlling the movement of goods, capital, and people. Britain was now 'a distinct political and ideological unit with a certain internal homogeneity', Edgerton argues in *The Rise and Fall of the British Nation* (2018), his important revisionist account of post-war British history.[1] Britain's tenure as world hegemon finally came to an end during the war, its finances dependent on American loans, its overseas assets mostly destroyed or expropriated, its prize colonies too difficult or too expensive to retain.[2] After 1945, debates about the rival merits of free trade and imperial protectionism that had raged since the nineteenth century gave way to a national-productivist consensus on jobs, housing, and economic sovereignty. The historian Peter Hennessy calls this the 'British New Deal', 'a fusion of philosophies of social justice and national efficiency'.[3] In addition to the nationalisation of coal mining, public utilities, railways, healthcare, and the Bank of England, Britain's was now a national economy hedged by tariffs, quotas, and import surcharges. Britain was hardly a socialist culture or society, but it was dedicated to a specifically and, to a degree, inclusively *national* development process. Needless to say, this project and its accompanying ideological vision of cultural homogeneity were built on a number of insufferable and unsustainable tensions and exclusions that, we argue, are amplified in the literature of the period.

To be sure, full employment, powerful trade unions, massive council house building programmes, the foundation of the National Health Service, and the expansion of secondary and, later, higher education meant that the three decades after the war were years of unprecedentedly rapid, albeit extremely uneven, social progress. They were characterised by the so-called 'post-war settlement' or social democratic compromise, as in other leading capitalist economies, with unprecedented rates of economic growth allied to rising wages and living standards. But by the early 1960s, the air was already filled with laments for Britain's supposed 'decline', such as Anthony Sampson's *Anatomy of Britain* (1962), Michael Shanks's *The Stagnant Society: A Warning* (1961), Anthony Hartley's *A State of*

DOI: 10.4324/9781003230816-3

England (1963), and Arthur Koestler's *Suicide of a Nation* (1963). We do not agree that Britain was in decline: to adapt the historian A. J. P. Taylor's verdict on the first half of the century, which we quoted in our introduction, after 1945, Britain's empire collapsed and the condition of its people rapidly improved. What looked to some like decline was, from a different viewpoint, actually progress: the dissolution of empire, the swingeing taxation imposed on the very rich, the ability of trade unions to secure wage increases, plus the loosening of conservative moral strictures of all kinds and, most of all, the advent of a society in which greater numbers of working-class people enjoyed the amenities necessary to lead more comfortable and happier lives. Where Britain clearly was weakening, economically in comparison with powerful new exporting economies, such as West Germany and Japan, or socially, as a consequence of, for example, the racist hostility that greeted many immigrants, this was because Britain's economy and society had not broken with its imperial past forcefully or rapidly enough. We see post-war and postcolonial Britain not as a story of *decline* but of uneven and halting and, alas, eventually postponed and partly retarded *progress*.

One prominent critique of Britain in the late 1950s and early 1960s was that it was not modern enough. Sampson's gripe in his *Anatomy of Britain* was that the British establishment was too hidebound and complacent; after empire, it lacked a clear sense of purpose, an 'ethos' to replace the 'invincible imperial machine'.[4] C. P. Snow, the novelist and later adviser to the Ministry of Technology in the Labour prime minister Harold Wilson's first government, likewise blamed decline on a 'Luddite' intelligentsia in his famous 1959 Rede Lecture at Cambridge, 'The Two Cultures and the Scientific Revolution'.[5] Our argument, by contrast, is that Britain in this period was nowhere near *democratic* enough. Nor had it really begun to break away from consoling fantasies about being a go-ahead island race.[6] The nation, in our view, had not stalled or declined and was not simply in need of more up-to-date and less-stuffy managers in the fields of politics and business; what it required was a fundamental transformation in the direction of more democratic participation, more equality, and therefore, more diversity in order to make good the uneven social progress made since the war. For the Shakespeare scholar and pioneer of cultural studies Alan Sinfield, the politics and culture of post-war Britain were defined by the brief efflorescence, the incomplete fulfilment, and then, alas, after the late 1970s, the steady abandonment of the political promises of 1945: promises of equality, democracy, higher living standards, secure work and more free time, plus an end to the hierarchies and injustices of imperialism.[7] Those aspirations were broadened by social movements in the 1960s, extending and enriching these visions of equality to include sexuality, gender, and race and to explore forms of liberation beyond the worlds of work and the family. How literary texts articulated those aspirations and thereby contested the dominant meanings that secured British society in the period is the subject of this chapter.

Chapter 2, therefore, addresses the precarious refinement of a Britishness focused on the national rather than the imperial, at the same time as it echoes Edgerton's stress on the internal fissures and tensions in the British nation during this period, what we call post-war Britain's covert *un*settlement. The social democratic compromise introduced under the reforming Labour government elected in 1945 and then refined by Tory administrations in the 1950s was profoundly unstable and hierarchical. For example, the productivist vision of the British state, including full employment and the Fordist living wage, relied on the restriction of working-class women to the largely non-unionised service sector and to the unremunerated domestic labour of social reproduction, principally housework and care work. Moreover, the national industries in textiles, cars, shipping, and steel suffered from sustained under-investment that left them ill-prepared for increasing international competition. Exorbitant military spending, plus the insistence of the City of London and of US governments on maintaining sterling's role as a global reserve and trading currency meant frequent bouts of deflation, wage controls, and government spending cuts during the fifties and especially the sixties. Social and economic inequalities were by no means eradicated, therefore. The age-old schism between North and South and between the overprivileged South-East of England and the United Kingdom's various peripheries was exacerbated; the City sat pretty while British industry started to rot.[8] The post-war consensus or post-war settlement was neither consensual nor settled.

We are not convinced, incidentally, by Edgerton's claim that the formation of a British nation after 1945 constituted a wholesale break with the previous articulation of Britain as an empire. British imperialism was always an extension and a product of the unitary British state, and the British state was, from its inception, an imperial project. Moreover, imperialism did not simply expire after 1945. The supposedly post-imperial British state waged counter-insurgencies in Greece, Palestine, Kenya, Malaya, Korea, Yemen, Cyprus, and Northern Ireland. Military spending remained sky-high after 1945 (and spending on welfare very low) because of Britain's remaining imperial commitments. Sterling was the world's second reserve currency. For a time, at least, Britain maintained a continued presence 'East of Suez' with bases in Iraq, Egypt, Aden, Hong Kong, and Singapore, in addition to large numbers of troops stationed in Austria and Germany. In short, Britain sought to remain *Great* Britain, a 'geopolitical projection', in the words of Perry Anderson's stringent review of Edgerton's study.[9] The state simply adapted its colonial role to the status of the new American hegemon's junior adjutant. Moreover, the utterly toxic racism with which empire infused British culture and society was hardly brought to an end in the decades of large-scale immigration after the war. So the British nation was a reasonably novel but, at best, unevenly progressive social, economic, political, and cultural formation, one characterised by its continuing commitment to imperial structures now presided over mainly by the United States and by enduring economic and regional as well as gender and increasingly racial inequalities within Britain itself. Writers attuned to these tensions, including those from immigrant backgrounds, in addition to queer, working-class, and women writers (we are, of course, aware that these are overlapping categories), articulated the exclusions that marked the British nation in the decades after the Second World War.

We therefore see the 1970s, which is where this chapter ends, as a moment of social, economic, political, and cultural crisis in which these various tensions came to the surface. The social democratic compromise between capital and labour became untenable in Britain in the 1970s, as it did elsewhere. Faced by economic stagnation, high inflation, and a general crisis of profitability, governments trimmed their commitment to social democratic goals in favour of greater freedom for capital, which is what happened under the Labour government of James Callaghan in the late 1970s, and then much more extensively under those of Margaret Thatcher and her successors. The 1980s and 1990s saw radical reductions in expenditure on education, social security, and health, much greater freedom for the City of London to make speculative profits, the cannibalisation of state assets by private companies, and the reduction of labour costs by weakening the powers of trade unions. Yet the 1960s and 1970s had also seen the development of radical plans to break out of the now-moribund post-war settlement in the other direction, towards more freedom for workers rather than more freedom for capital. All kinds of exciting proposals for extending democracy and equality and for addressing the persistent exclusions of the post-war order emerged in the shape of socialist, feminist, and anti-racist projects and movements for gay liberation. This period also saw the efflorescence of nationalism in Wales, and especially Scotland, in addition to the turbulent consequences of the British state's tolerance since 1922 of an undemocratic ethno-statelet in the six counties of Northern Ireland. Campaigns for workers' control of industry, such as the Upper Clyde Shipbuilders work-in in Glasgow in 1971 (plus the radical humanist vision of one of its leaders, Jimmy Reid) and the 1976 Lucas Plan of Lucas Aerospace shop stewards to convert their company from arms manufacture to socially useful and pioneering green technologies, proposals to overturn the power of finance, or popular anti-racist organisations like the Black and Asian youth movements and the Anti-Nazi League, presaged more equality and democracy and diversity and not less, a radical extension of the post-war settlement rather than its abandonment.[10]

For us, the key moment in post-war British history is 1968, provided that that year is understood as an inflection point at which the social, economic, and cultural progress of the previous two decades began to stall; though it might have been radicalised and extended, that progress was, in fact, subsequently rolled back. A central figure in this second chapter is therefore the Tory Member of Parliament and ex-minister Enoch Powell, whose notorious 'Rivers of Blood' speech in Birmingham in April 1968 immediately popularised his campaign, in the historian David Olusoga's words, to re-energise 'a new national and racial self-consciousness' in the wake of empire.[11] Before we begin to trace how literary texts articulated the characteristic tensions and choices facing the British nation in these years, we want briefly to describe how the year of 1968 and the figure of Powell symbolise a moment in which the stakes in post-war and postcolonial British history were vividly clarified: restoration or radicalisation.

Intriguingly, Olusoga's magnificent historical study *Black and British* focuses not on Powell's 1968 speech but on his 1961 speech to the Royal Society of St George. Speaking about a year after Prime Minister Harold Macmillan had urged the South African parliament in Cape Town, in his 'Winds of Change' speech, to acknowledge the inevitability of the end of empire, Powell argued that Britain or, rather, as he said, England had been somehow 'uninvolved' in the colonial project. The empire had been acquired almost accidentally, he claimed, as the result of a serendipitous but brief 'conjunction of cheap and invincible sea power with industrial potential' and had now just as casually been given away. The nation's institutions, particularly the Crown-in-Parliament, as well as its character, by which Powell meant its racial identity or its whiteness, were miraculously unchanged by four centuries of empire-building: 'looser connections which had linked her with distant continents and strange races fell away.' But modern Britain, Olusoga shows, was precisely the product of these connections, politically, economically, culturally, and demographically, connections which were therefore not 'loose' at all but extremely extensive and integral. What he calls Powell's 'deeply emotional appeal to romantic ethnic nationalism' was, Olusoga shows, 'a vision that required much of the history of the past four hundred years to be set aside'.[12] Powell's ideas about England's 'continuity' and 'homogeneity' are, in fact, belied by the very long history of migration of various peoples, including people of colour, to Britain over the centuries and by the usually violent interconnections between Britain and its colonies, including the transplantation of millions of people of African descent to the Caribbean and the Americas by British slave traders, as well as Britain's centuries of economic dependence on the profits of empire.

Powell's objectives, of course, were primarily political. By seeking to erase the many links between Britain and its former colonies and by agitating for the expulsion (or, as he called it, the 're-emigration') of people of colour, as well as by denouncing the new 1968 law against racial discrimination, Powell was seeking to remodel the nation state along profoundly reactionary lines. Post-imperial England would thereby become 'an ethnic and racial state',[13] in Olusoga's words, albeit in a defensive and insular rather than extroverted imperial mode. Powellism should therefore be understood, in Camilla Schofield's view, as 'a distinctively English, post-war and *postcolonial* version of nationalism'. Powell's was a vision of what England and Britain might become after empire. He allied 'an obsessive preoccupation with community decline and victimhood'[14] to conservative anxieties about moral decay and working-class militancy.[15] Powell himself became a backbench exile and later an MP for the Ulster Unionists. But what the cultural theorist Paul Gilroy, in *There Ain't No Black in the Union Jack* (1987), his classic study of the cultural politics of race and nation, calls Powell's populist 'new racism' – 'new' because it was now national rather than imperial – rapidly gained ground after 1968.[16]

The thesis of what was the first and is still one of the best books on Powell, by the radical journalist Paul Foot, is that by effectively legitimising the arguments of the Far Right about the need to end emigration and enforce 'repatriation', Powell had injected a form of racist nativism into the political mainstream. Moreover, while his Tory and Labour critics found Powellism vulgar and considered Powell himself persona non grata, they were not willing substantively to oppose his programme. This ideology had a profound effect in reshaping British politics, the scapegoating of immigrants providing a kind of alibi or symbolic compensation for the much-greater levels of social and economic inequality presided over by Thatcher and her successors.[17] The most effective way to oppose the malignant ideology of ethnic nationalism, Foot reasoned, was with a popular politics that addressed the sense of alienation, insecurity, and disenfranchisement off which ethnic nationalism fed. Instead, as Peter Fryer argued in his pioneering history of Black people in Britain, subsequent immigration legislation surrendered to the belief that the cause of white racism was not white racists but the presence of too many Black people. 'Fearful of being outflanked by fascists and each other, fearful of losing votes and seats, Tory and Labour politicians progressively accommodated themselves to racism.'[18] Nobody in power advocated for repatriation, at least until the coalition government after 2010 began deporting Black Britons, but the national community has certainly been defined along implicitly racial lines, membership for people of colour being made provisional, qualified, and conditional. Successive immigration acts after 1968 relegated Black Britons to second-class status, redefined them as immigrants, and implicitly characterised them as a problem. Powellism, if we might call it that, never went away. It was, as Schofield contends, a way of responding to the end of empire not with some major transformation of Britain's structures and ideologies but with a rearguard defence and expedient adaptation of them in the changed circumstances caused by a myriad of new developments, including European integration, immigration, the civil rights movement in Northern Ireland, and the volubility of a militant and multicultural working class.[19]

Maya Goodfellow notes the peculiar juxtaposition of the 1968 Race Relations Act and the Commonwealth Immigrants Act of the same year, both passed by Harold Wilson's Labour government:

> The former stated that people of colour should be treated equally; the latter, based on the premise that people of colour were a problem to be dealt with, implied 'too many' of 'them' shouldn't be allowed here in the first place.[20]

As Ian Sanjay Patel also demonstrates in his exhaustive *We're Here Because You Were There: Immigration and the End of Empire*, the journey from the 1948 British Nationality Act (which recognised citizens of British colonies and of many newly independent Commonwealth countries as British subjects) through to the 1962 and 1968 Commonwealth Immigrants Acts (that restricted British citizenship to those citizens of the Commonwealth who could demonstrate an ancestral connection to Britain, that is, overwhelmingly white people) was a journey towards the implicit racial encoding of British citizenship. The 1968 Commonwealth Immigrants Act distinguished between British citizens with ancestral connections to Britain, who might therefore freely enter the country (such as white Kenyans and Rhodesians), and British citizens whose entry to Britain was heavily restricted (such as East African Asians), what the 1971 Act called 'patrial' and 'non-patrial' British citizens. 'Gone was an inclusivity based on imperial largesse, and replacing it was an implicit racial exclusivity that dictated who belonged in Britain and who did not.'[21] Britain and Britishness would be implicitly coded as white even in the aftermath of empire.

In 1979, a government took power committed to impugning and disciplining radical movements and trade unions, restricting local democracy, reimposing the state's 'right to govern', liberating capital (especially finance capital) from the constraints placed on it during the immediate post-war period, and asserting an imagined community based on nostalgia for racial homogeneity and imperial greatness. This project is usually known in Britain as Thatcherism or, more generally, by the innocuously technical term 'neoliberalism'. A better term for it, in our view, is Ralph Miliband's 'class war conservatism', which has the virtue of ditching neoliberal propagandists' hypocritical twaddle about individual liberty and the greater efficiencies of markets in favour of emphasising what has been essentially a class project to enrich and empower rentiers, monopolists, and speculators.[22] Quinn Slobodian, who is one of the few observers to link the end of empire to class war conservatism, sees the latter straightforwardly as a project 'to inoculate capitalism against democracy', within nation states and at the global level.[23] The end of empire in Britain saw the emergence of a new form of racialised nationalism, one purpose of which was to disguise the Thatcherites' 'class war' programme of inequality and deindustrialisation beneath a vaguely (though conditionally) inclusive rhetoric of greatness and renewal. Under an exceedingly well-worn nationalist banner, Conservative class warriors pushed back the various forces striving to reform Britain's structures and institutions to make them reflect the diverse perspectives and priorities of its citizens. Yet what happened was not inevitable or irreversible; it could have happened differently. It is the chief task of this chapter to show how writers and their texts portrayed Britishness in the three decades or so after the war, its tensions and exclusions, and the emergent possibilities taking shape in opposition.

One of the texts we read in the following pages, Kamala Markandaya's *The Nowhere Man* (1972), is more or less directly about Powell's 1968 speech, which we see as a turning point in post-war British history. This was an opportunity for Britain to radically make itself over with the erasure of a unitary British polity, of sclerotic class hierarchies, of embedded ideas about sexuality and gender, and of the pernicious ideology of whiteness, a moment at which the nation might gladly have ceased to be Britain at all. The last two of Sam Selvon's celebrated novel trilogy, *The Lonely Londoners* (1956), *Moses Ascending* (1975), and *Moses Migrating* (1983), unfold, as it were, in Powell's shadow; this celebrated series charts in intriguingly ambiguous and sometimes ambivalent ways the elaboration between the 1950s and 1980s of a racialised postcolonial form of British identity. We read John Osborne's plays *Look Back in Anger* (1956) and *The Entertainer* (1957) as failures to find the right terms and dramatic forms to register the end of empire in anything other than an unhelpful mode of melancholy and elegy. From a different, more avowedly socialist perspective, J. B. Priestley's play *Summer Day's Dream* (1948) also falls back on dominant forms of national identity even as it tries to picture an appealingly post-imperial and even post-capitalist England. Raymond Williams's *Border Country* (1960) and, from a more overtly feminist angle, Kate Roberts's *The Awakening* (1956) are two Welsh novels that identify the enduring social, political, and cultural tensions of post-war and post-imperial Britain's apparent peripheries in order to explore tentative possibilities of liberation. John McGrath's radical play *The Cheviot, the Stag and the Black Black Oil* (1973) and Caryl Churchill's equally formally and politically bold *Cloud 9* (1979) show how the theatre in the 1970s was optimistically, but also at times anxiously, weighing up projects of liberation alongside deep colonial histories and the emergence of new forces on the radical right.

Postcolonial Possibilities in the Post-War Novel

Our story begins with the 'Windrush generation'. Once a signifier for the emergence of a post-imperial and much more inclusive or multicultural form of Britishness, the arrival of the SS *Empire Windrush* at Tilbury docks in 1948, carrying several hundred British subjects from Jamaica, Guyana, Bermuda, and Trinidad (as well as dozens of Poles previously stranded in Mexico), now carries a rather different meaning, as Paul Arnott's detailed history of that ship contends: 'At first it was a positive, shorthand description for a generation of migrants of black origin arriving in the United Kingdom in the decades after the war.' Now, 'Windrush' signifies the 'Windrush scandal', 'gross maladministration by the UK government in denying two generations of black British people their birthright', in many cases 'sending them back' (the long-cherished goal of the British far right) 'to places to which they had no allegiance, even though under every legal definition – except that they had not got round to applying for passports – they were British subjects'.[24] We think the hounding and deportation of Black Britons by the 2010–2015 Tory-Lib Dem coalition, as though their rights of citizenship were somehow contentious and revocable, change the way post-war writing should be read. The work of the Trinidad-born Sam Selvon, for example, especially his seminal novel *The Lonely Londoners* (1956) and its lesser-known sequels, *Moses Ascending* (1973) and *Moses Migrating* (1983), can no longer be seen as narratives of settlement and confident cultural assertion. *The Lonely Londoners*' episodic and lyrical narratives of Caribbean immigrants' experiences, for example, convey both the impressive ways which in which these (mostly) men stake a claim to the city, its pleasures and opportunities for connection and expression, *and* their confrontation with what now seems, in retrospect, to be a formidably powerful and durable set of exclusions.

The Lonely Londoners, according to Nick Bentley's persuasive reading, describes but also embodies a series of unresolved but productive tensions.

> Selvon's fiction produces, on the one hand, a culturally specific 'resistance' literature that relates to his position as a marginalized Caribbean writer, while on the other, claims a right to be judged against, and ultimately incorporated into, the universalizing discourses of literary value imposed by the dominant institutions of literature in the West.[25]

The text both abrogates English literary tradition and seeks to appropriate it. Jed Esty makes a similar claim when he argues that *The Lonely Londoners* repudiates the structuring opposition between empire's heart (London) and its apparent margins (the colonies), though in a way that registers the continuing fascination or magnetism of the former imperial centre:

> The colonial writers of the 1950s [such as Selvon] represent a distinct phase in the remaking of English culture insofar as their work participates in the

transformation of centre-periphery relations at the end of Empire. . . . These immigrant writers look on inherited conventions of English culture through the lens of alien knowability, generating a tension between a recuperative romance of Englishness and a disillusioned critique of Englishness.[26]

In other words, the Trinidadian writer finds himself well positioned to view England 'at the end of empire' perceptively and quite unmercifully even as he is drawn towards it.

At the interconnected levels of the novel's language, form, and themes, *The Lonely Londoners*, like its characters, both forcefully rejects dominant constructions of 'England' while also seeking to occupy a bridgehead within them. There are two ways of reading the novel's attitudes to the old imperial centre that is England and, more specifically, London, rejection and assimilation. We think, reading the novel again in the wake of the 'Windrush scandal', that rejection is *The Lonely Londoners*' dominant theme. This is a less gloomy reading than it might appear, however, since the novel describes its characters' rejection *of* and not only their rejection *by* the waning imperial centre. Here is the novel's opening paragraph, where these kinds of tension are established:

> One grim winter evening, when it had a kind of unrealness about London, with a fog sleeping restlessly over the city and the lights showing in the blur as if is not London at all but some strange place on another planet, Moses Aloetta hop on a number 46 bus at the corner of Chepstow Road and Westbourne Grove to go to Waterloo to meet a fellar who was coming from Trinidad on the boat-train.[27]

This is the novel's signature technique, a lucid free indirect discourse in which an apparently third-person and omniscient narrator assumes the idiomatic speech of his characters. The narrator is at once appraising his characters but also speaking through them, peering at them inquisitively like the journalists who accost newcomers at Victoria Station but also challenging that prying gaze from the voices and perspectives of the newcomers themselves. The first thing to note, then, is the radically estranging or defamiliarising perspective of the new arrival who sees London as a 'strange place on another planet' and therefore succeeds, if we might adapt an influential formulation of the Russian formalist critic Viktor Shklovsky, in imparting the sensation of the city as it is freshly perceived not as it is already known.[28] To investigate 'the wider world within which "England" and "Englishness" find their meaning . . . we have to work from the outside in'[29], as Krishnan Kumar advises in *The Making of English National Identity*. The novel presents 'grim' London as an exciting but also inhospitable place, replete with possibilities for pleasure and prosperity, but also scarred by exclusion and exploitation. There is also a foretaste in this opening of the narrator's and his characters' confident occupation and inhabitation of the city; knowledge of the city's bus routes is surely one definition of a Londoner. Moses and company enjoy naming and navigating, and thus occupying, the city's streets. The narrator will repeatedly rename 'Brit'n' itself, and later, big city exhaustively defamiliarises the entire metropolis in a series of humorous but also ingenious errors: 'Pentonvilla', 'Musket Hill', and 'Claphand Common' (*LL*, 91). As always in *The Lonely Londoners*, in this opening passage, there are distance and intimacy, alienation and belonging, appraisal and esteem. The emphasis that a reader will give to these two clashing dimensions of the novel depends, obviously, on where and when she encounters it. Our claim is that recent readings and re-readings are likely to stress the novel's critical attention, indeed, as we shall see, Selvon's whole oeuvre's critical attention, to the durability of the dominant exclusionary constructions of England.

Bentley's point about how Selvon's novel both abrogates and appropriates the value of a Western or specifically English literary tradition can be illustrated by the fact that the action of the novel is, at first, chokingly enveloped in a 'fog sleeping restlessly over the city'. At one level, of course, this is simply a depiction of the toxic pea-soupers that formed the backdrop of London fiction from Charles Dickens to Henry James, Arthur Conan Doyle to Selvon, before the introduction of the Clean Air Act in 1956.[30] Fog, or more exactly, the deadly post-war smog that resulted from a combination of cold weather, factory emissions, domestic fires, and exhaust fumes, is also a metaphor in *The Lonely Londoners* for the kinds of separation and invisibility that afflict the inhabitants of the big city, particularly 'lonely' new arrivals in their scattered bedsits. London is 'divide up in little worlds' (*LL*, 60). That kind of alienation is registered in the novel's form, with its disconnected anecdotes that never quite coalesce into a coherent or purposeful narrative. Importantly, Moses's references to the fog are another means by which the novel assertively joins the ranks of canonical representations of London, such as the 'brown fog of a winter dawn' in the 'Unreal City' of T. S. Eliot's 'The Waste Land'[31] or the 'fog everywhere' at the start of Dickens's *Bleak House* and in *Our Mutual Friend*.[32] The 'unrealness' of London in the opening paragraph cited earlier is surely a status-affirming allusion to Eliot's seminal modernist poem. These deft accumulations of cultural capital are a vigorous appropriation of the English literary tradition's value, even as the novel seeks to modify established ways of seeing London and narrates new arrivals' attempts to make it into their home.

The narrator's idiomatic style is another example of this important tension between abrogation and appropriation. The narrator is initially omniscient as well as extra-diegetic, that is, he often speaks authoritatively and dispassionately from outside the events of the novel. Yet the narrator is also, as the end of the novel implies, when our protagonist, Moses, learns how it is possible to go from 'sweating in the factory' to becoming 'a new literary giant' (*LL*, 139), Moses himself. Indeed, the narrator can hardly be fully extra-diegetic since he uses the demotic speech of the characters, though intriguingly he does so not in, say, Jamaican Patois or Trinidadian Creole, but in a kind of lightly, as it were, Caribbeanised standard English featuring distinctive vocabulary and grammatical constructions: 'a modified dialect which could be understood by European readers, yet retains the flavour and essence of Trinidadian speech', in Selvon's own words.[33] The language of the novel both assimilates itself into the received language of English fiction and keeps its critical distance. Moreover, *The Lonely Londoners* is a realist novel committed to verisimilitude and to explaining the experiences and outlooks of new arrivals to an implied white middle-class readership whom it strives to intrigue but not alienate. Yet it is also a modernist novel, one that lacks an overarching plot and a secure and reliable narrative standpoint, that moves in and out of its characters' voices and their fragmented lives and that features ten pages of virtuosic Joycean interior monologue (referred to as a 'ballad' (*LL*, 98)) in the middle of the text. The realist dimension takes the novel closer to an almost-anthropological or journalistic, Colin MacInnes–like effort to introduce Caribbean immigrants sympathetically to a largely middle-class and white audience. The modernist elements of the text, meanwhile, lay stress on alienation and disconnection, on the characters' distinctive voices, and on the absence of resolution and integration.

It is clear that after 1948, the experiences of immigrants from the Caribbean who, in an important sense, are not immigrants at all since, as Moses asserts, they are 'British subjects' (*LL*, 21), with as much right to reside in London as anyone else, demanded a new kind of English fiction. *The Lonely Londoners*, therefore, forges a hybrid narrative style and voice, a multifarious and inconclusive structure in place of a unidirectional plot, in addition to those dual impulses of attraction and abrogation. But does the novel, as John McLeod argued nearly 20 years ago in his study of the literature of postcolonial London, ultimately reach towards the hybrid London that is exemplified in his view by the inclusive party that Harris hosts in St Pancras in the second half of the novel? Does *The Lonely Londoners*, in McLeod's words, envision a city that is 'tolerant, racially inclusive, pleasurable, mobile, negotiating between . . . past and present, inside and outside, the Caribbean and London'?[34] In 2011, as New Labour's increasingly authoritarian nativism prepared the way for Theresa May's 'hostile environment' – and even the perfunctory multiculturalism of the 2000s was officially denounced by Prime Minister David Cameron's Munich speech of that year – Graham MacPhee offered a rather different reading of Selvon's novel. MacPhee did not claim that McLeod's 'optimistic' reading was wrong exactly, but he did suggest that it 'needs to be qualified, and the pervasive nexus of isolation, objectification and racism that pervades the novel also needs to be emphasised'.[35] Now, even more than before, these seem to us to be the dominant notes sounded by Selvon's oeuvre. Reading *The Lonely Londoners* again in the 2020s means highlighting the disconcerting shortage of women's perspectives in the novel. Not only that, but these mostly male characters' encounters with women are also characterised by exploitation, objectification, resentment, and even violence. As Paul Mendez has recently noted, other works by Selvon's contemporaries, such as Andrew Salkey's *Escape to an Autumn Pavement* (1960), Edgar Mittelholzer's *A Morning at the Office* (1950), and Harold Sonny Ladoo's *Yesterdays* (1974), dealt much more overtly with queer sexuality.[36] Any new reading of *The Lonely Londoners*, we insist, is also obliged to reckon with its wider and disturbingly topical vision of violence and segregation: Moses is a prophet, of course, though readers must now wonder with MacPhee whether it was continued exclusion rather than a process of growing inclusion that he was foretelling, after all.[37]

Moses Ascending (1975) is a knottier and much more problematic novel that we think should finally preclude the celebratory way in which *The Lonely Londoners* is often read. The sequel sheds further light on some of the problems that the earlier work identifies and that MacPhee emphasises. *Moses Ascending* registers a profoundly important transitional moment in which Black British writers start to negotiate both old and new preoccupations in the context of the considerable economic, social, and cultural dislocations of the 1970s. Moses, however, the putative author of these reflections, as in *The Lonely Londoners*, reveals himself to be no longer a very effective guide to the problems and possibilities of this period. He has become the owner of a tumble-down terraced house in Shepherd's Bush. Moses is now a man of property, promisingly enough, not just a paying guest. He might even be viewed as an example or a herald of a type that, in the subsequent 40 years or so, would become dominant in British life, the rentier or landlord who lives not by working but by charging rent on an asset. This later novel retains the dialectic of abrogation and appropriation we saw in its predecessor's response to English culture. Its title might even be a mischievous nod to Ralph Vaughan Williams's 'The Lark Ascending', though the specifically urban setting of Selvon's run-down and chaotic seventies London could scarcely be less like the composer's earlier folk-infused Romantic vision of the English countryside. Shakespeare's oeuvre is a more obvious high-cultural intertext that is being both claimed and parodied, less at the level of plot or character (though the tale of racialised master and servant calls to mind *The Tempest*) than in the playfully archaic idiom that Moses frequently adopts. 'Fie' and 'God's blood', he exclaims in his ironical and accusatory account of night-time in the city, 'when the civilized world is in bed or about to hit the hay' and 'the stalwart blacks' 'come tumbling out of the ghettoes' to work.[38] Most obviously, the relations of power in Defoe's *Robinson Crusoe*, which, of course, is a kind of Ur-text of British imperialism, are temporarily subverted in the novel's central relationship between Moses and his factotum, or 'man Friday, a white immigrant name Bob from somewhere in the Midlands' (*MA*, 6). A proudly propertied Moses quaffs Scotch from his drinks tray while Bob tidies the house, cooks Moses peas and rice, and sees to the needs of the querulous tenants. Yet this inversion of colonial power relations is disappointingly short-lived.

The novel continues Selvon's preoccupation in *The Lonely Londoners* with the unequal and insecure (and often squalid) housing conditions of post-war urban Britain. This is a domestic drama in which, as in Kamala Markandaya's *The Nowhere Man*, which we will look at presently, the large and dilapidated house provides a metaphor for Britain itself, and especially for the difficulties and possibilities of settlement and for relations between owners and tenants, discontented long-term residents and insecure newcomers. The possibilities include Moses's own new status as 'master of the house' (*MA*, 5), both owner and occupier in this figurative inversion of colonial power relations. The difficulties are the new impediments thrown up by the 1962 and 1968 Immigrants Acts that, for the first time, as we have seen, implicitly coded British citizenship as white. The increasingly exclusionary intentions of British immigration policy are starkly spelt out when his Pakistani tenant, Faizull, inveigles a reluctant Moses into turning the property into a safe house for illegally trafficked South Asian families.

The cultural form to which *Moses Ascending* most insistently, and perhaps surprisingly, alludes, as Hari Kunzru suggests in his introduction to the new Penguin edition, is undoubtedly the TV sitcom. Moses often sounds, as Kunzru observes, 'like a black version of Rigsby, the craven, scheming landlord in the ITV sitcom *Rising Damp*'.[39] *Moses Ascending* is an even more comical text than *The Lonely Londoners*, the house serving not just as a metaphor for the problems and possibilities of settlement but also as a site for jokes, pranks, and farcical inversions and confusions of both class and race. *Moses Ascending* pokes fun at the white majority (Bob's doltishness; the hypocrisy of his prim fiancée, Jeannie; their addiction to the telly; their insularity and antiquated class consciousness), but also much more dubiously, in the manner of notoriously racist seventies sitcoms, like *Love Thy Neighbour* and Spike Milligan's *Curry and Chips*, at the culinary tastes and religious observances of Moses's Pakistani tenants, one of whom he regrettably nicknames 'P*ki'.

Incessantly worrying about the capacity of new arrivals to 'integrate', Moses is himself the personification of a very hard-won but also troubling process of assimilation. '"It will be over soon," Moses reassures Bob as they panic over Faizull's immigration scam, "and we shall revert to our former way of life"' (*MA*, 95), sounding here like the racist neighbours and employers who had blighted the lives of the new arrivals in *The Lonely Londoners*, or even like the minatory figure of Powell, who looms over the novel and whose name is invoked on several occasions. At one point, Moses is arrested and briefly jailed at a Black Power march; what he sees as the implausibly revolutionary aims of the 'party' and its credulous indulgence of a swindling American visitor are ferociously satirised. Moses remains implacably hostile to the kind of collective solidarity propounded by his tenant Brenda and his old friend Galahad. Alas, the portrayal of Brenda, the young woman who runs the party's newspaper from Moses's basement, is relentlessly sexist. These attitudes are Moses's, of course, not necessarily the novel's, though since this novel purports to be Moses's own memoirs, his is the dominant perspective on the problems and possibilities of Black Londoners in the 1970s. Moses tells Galahad that 'literary masterpieces have been written in garrets by candlelight, by men who shut themselves away from the distractions of the world' (*MA*, 57). His narrative is a profoundly misanthropic project. 'The whole structure of my work', Moses admits, 'would have to be drastically altered if I was to incorporate these other aspects' (*MA*, 60), such as the perspectives of women, South Asian immigrants, or new generations of Black Britons.

Moses's viewpoint is, therefore, insistently monologic, not to mention flagrantly outmoded: police violence is a mere inconvenience to him, collective political organisation a waste of time, Asian immigrants a joke, women mere bodies, and 'this new generation of Black Britons' (*MA*, 19) a sociological phenomenon, but also a perplexing mystery. Moses, disarmingly, has no interest in 'black power, nor white power, nor any fucking power but [his] own' (*MA*, 18). He does remain exceptionally perceptive in some ways; there is the virtuosic section, which recalls the lengthy interior monologue in the earlier work, that offers a paean to 'the black people in Brit'n' on whose unrecognised and underpaid toil the country is now dependent. Moses assumes a kind of jocular familiarity with his 'Dear Reader' or 'Dear R' and affectingly confides 'a kind of sad feeling that all black people was doomed to suffer, that we would never make any headway in Brit'n' (*MA*, 46). *Moses Ascending* does its 'Dear Rs' the service of identifying many of the salient issues in Black British life in this period, to do with continuing exclusion and inequality and with poor housing, police violence, and the necessity for new forms of political organisation. Yet it has precious few answers to these questions. The novel ends with Moses consigned to the basement and Bob, now styling himself less familiarly as Robert, in the drawing room, 'holding the reins and cracking the whip' (*MA*, 178). The white man, you might say, again holds 'the whip hand' over the Black man, as Enoch Powell had wished, a surprising and disturbing conclusion. Bob is learning French in preparation for Britain's entry into the Common Market, and as ever, 'it is the white man who ends up Upstairs and the black man who ends up Downstairs' (*MA*, 185), a conclusion that Moses obviously resents, though he has only the vaguest plans to overturn this state of affairs. *Moses Ascending* shows how much had changed since Galahad and others had arrived at Victoria Station in *The Lonely Londoners* and how much had disappointingly stayed the same. From our own perspective, reading Selvon's work afresh in the 'hostile environment' of twenty-first-century Britain, we want to highlight both its preoccupation with maddeningly persistent forms of racial exclusion and its candid inability to see a way out of them.

Moses Migrating (1983) is the final instalment of Selvon's trilogy. Here, the promised land for Moses, who, like his namesake, was an orphan found 'in an old wicker basket' (*MM*, 84), surprisingly turns out to be not Trinidad, to which our irascible protagonist briefly returns with his usual cast of hangers-on, but, perversely, Brit'n or, specifically, 'merry England' itself.[40] Moses writes a jocose letter to the man he familiarly calls 'Enoch' before he sets sail, in order to request passage money and some additional capital to help him when he reaches Trinidad: 'I am writing you to express my support for your campaign to keep Brit'n White' (*MM*, 30). The rich comedy of the novel comes from these kinds of ironical inversion and reversal. In Trinidad, Moses sets out to show 'the British bulldog still had teeth, that Britannia still ruled the waves' (*MM*, 56), and even to 'plant the Union Jack on the land like Raleigh or one of them fellars and get some new subjects for the Queen' (*MM*, 82). He wins a prize for playing Britannia in the carnival, framed in silver like a giant 50p coin to show that Britain and its beleaguered currency still have value. Moses undertakes the role, he says, in order to burnish the tarnished image of his motherland. But carnival is actually the space in which established identities and hierarchies should be overturned, including stubborn colonial ones; Moses's taxi driver tells him that he will be appearing there in a band called Rhodesian Terrorists! (*MM*, 162). Moses's use of Jeannie as a scantily attired handmaiden and of a reluctant Bob to pull the float gives the performance an air of uncanny reversal, of racial, if not gender, hierarchies; indeed, it appears that Moses's routine has been interpreted by the judges as a lampoon, and he is awarded a silver cup for

Most Original Individual Costume. Britishness, this final novel reveals, is a deeply felt and compelling, but also unstable and probably outdated, colonial identity to which Moses remains drawn, albeit perhaps ironically or unconvincingly, or at least in an ostentatiously enthusiastic way that draws attention to its absurdity and obsolescence. The novel ends with Moses's rejection of Trinidad and his return to London; 'even more restrictions on black immigration' have been introduced while Moses was away, Brenda tells him (*MM*, 170), so the immigration officers leave Moses in a liminal space between the two as they go to check his passport and decide if he can re-enter, 'leaving [him] holding the cup in the air like [he] was still playing charades' (*MM*, 194). For a perennial exile like Moses, despite his ostentatious loyalty to the old country, Britishness remains unreachable and implausible, a charade or masquerade, especially under the prying gaze of the state on the nation's increasingly fortified borders.

The republication in 2019 of Kamala Markandaya's 1972 novel *The Nowhere Man* gives us an opportunity to examine an important and prescient work set in the crucial year of 1968.[41] Srinivas, a lugubrious widower and decades-long resident of a South London suburb, invites Mrs Pickering, an elderly white woman, to live with him after he is effectively disowned by his social-climbing son. This is an intensely allegorical work about the possible futures of postcolonial Britain, one that presents the late sixties, and specifically 1968, the year of Powell's notorious speech, as a supremely fateful moment of crisis and decision. Britain might choose either to prolong its antiquated identities of class, nation, and especially race in chauvinistic and even, the novel uncompromisingly suggests, fascistic form or start to remodel an extremely troubled nation state along more inclusive lines. Srinivas's pariah status in an increasingly inhospitable neighbourhood is written on his body in the form of leprosy. His auspiciously peaceable habitation is eventually invaded and set on fire by a local lout, Fred, who has been fired up by racist invective and is decked out in military regalia and redcoat to 'lead his countrymen in the fight to overthrow the evil, hidden forces that were threatening them in their homeland'.[42] We wish to establish the central place of this critically neglected novel in post-war British fiction.

One of the most important things to note about *The Nowhere Man* is the ornateness of its omniscient narrator's syntax, the force and assurance with which this eloquent voice maps the unpromising milieu of late-1960s suburbia. The enormous discernment with which both the despotic environment of colonial India and the oppressive atmosphere of an ostensibly postcolonial London are rendered strikes us as being itself a very confident assertion of presence within England and within the form of the English novel. For example, the following extremely elegant sentence describes how the colonial authorities persecuted Srinivas's family so that 'people and events' assumed for him, as they do, hopefully, for the novel's readers, a 'sharp clarity':

They swam up closer, acquired incised outlines as if cut by a diamond, as if they were to be lifted out and placed, in full dimension and illuminated, in niches along corridors beyond the natural elisions of time.

(*NM*, 177)

This sumptuous sentence is both an example and a description of the novel's own signature technique. The ornate syntax, the cumulative rhythm, and the originality and faintly modernistic surrealness of the metaphor remind us of Virginia Woolf, or perhaps Elizabeth Bowen, though this text has a directness and anger quite unlike theirs. Elegant sentences like this one form an implicit contrast with the sheer crudeness of British colonialism and its legacies. Markandaya employs a precise and even lapidary style to illuminate for us people and events that might otherwise be elided. Such sentences need to be read and re-read closely, appreciated with a quality of attention that the novel rightly considers to be lacking from most narratives of empire and its aftermath in post-war Britain.

We also want to stress the novel's unusually insistent moral tone. Srinivas himself, a pacifistic vegetarian, feels considerable compassion for his tormentors. Dr Radcliffe, who diagnoses him with leprosy at the start of the novel and pronounces his death at the end, is more judgemental about the moral failings of the affluent society, such as 'the washing machine and TV wants that eased the drab lives of his patients' (*NM*, 9), though here, as elsewhere, it is intriguingly hard to tell if these judgements are being asserted by the narrator or by the character. The portrayal of Dr Radcliffe's grasping wife is certainly extremely disapproving, moralistic even. Furthermore, Mrs Pickering denounces the widespread neglect of the poor and the old (*NM*, 192). The novel's all-seeing and all-judging narrator also condemns the growing coarseness, violence, and chauvinism of England in the late 1960s. On reflection, though, 'moralistic' might not be quite the right word here, nor even 'morality'. Rather, what the narrator evinces and what the novel itself counsels, the absence of which from everyday life in Britain in this period it forcefully reprehends, is not exactly a prescriptive moral code. An emergent ethos for a genuinely and substantively postcolonial Britain can be found not in inherited structures or characteristics of race and class but in something more provisional and inclusive: specifically, an ethic of neighbourliness.

Srinivas's rambling Victorian house, which his wife, Vasantha, originally envisages as a home for their grown-up sons and their families, itself becomes a kind of metaphor, as so often in post-war English fiction, for the nation's own structures. The house is a means of exploring wider questions about property and habitation: Who gets to live where, with whom, with what kinds of security, and under what systems of ownership? The housing problem in Britain's slums and bombed-out cities was only partly alleviated by the massive council house building programmes of the 1950s and by the clearances, new towns, and high-rise developments of the 1960s. Of course, in Powell's speech, the issue of competition over housing was both a catalyst and a pretext for racist agitation, as it is in the novel. The increasingly straitened Srinivas and Mrs Pickering take in lodgers, whom they later evict in order to keep his leprosy from becoming known. The ensuing dispute intensifies Fred's bitterness, as Srinivas's tenants are characterised in local gossip as victims of a sharp-elbowed 'intruder' (*NM*, 214). Soon, 'man-sized messages of hate' (*NM*, 209) and crude drawings of a hanged man begin to appear on the hoardings opposite Srinivas's house, where a high-rise block is being erected. Testifying all the while to the centrality of housing as both social problem and versatile metaphor in English fiction of the period, Srinivas's house goes from being an augury of tenuous settlement in post-war suburbia ('[a] place of [their] own', as Vasantha calls it, 'where [they] can live according to [their] lights although in alien surroundings' (*NM*, 24)) to an image of tentative coexistence between Srinivas and Mrs Pickering, and then finally to a burnt-out wreck that signifies the destructive consequences of fascistic demagoguery when Fred clambers into the cellar and sets it alight.

We wonder if the house, besieged by suspicious neighbours and racist hooligans, is an inversion of the scenario sketched in Powell's 'Rivers of Blood' speech. There, the apocryphal Wolverhampton landlady who refuses to rent rooms to 'immigrants' and the 'immigrant-descended population', whose street is 'taken over' and becomes 'a place of noise and confusion', with 'excreta pushed through the letterbox', is the apparent victim. In Markandaya's novel, the source of barbarism is Powell's speech itself and the racists it emboldens, while the house represents not, as the landlady's residence did for Powell, the rights and territory of true-born English folk but an embattled shelter from the violence and hate that Powell himself had unleashed. *The Nowhere Man*, and especially the ominous and claustrophobic atmosphere of its final chapters, therefore, constitutes a warning. It does not pull any punches in its frank depiction of the consequences of Powell's speech. When Fred tries to burn down Srinivas's house at the end of the novel, he kills them both in the process. Srinivas's 'grimy, decent face' laid out on the stretcher assumes a quality of martyrdom, just as earlier this valiant scapegoat thinks of himself as 'a stranger' and 'an unwanted man'; at one point, Srinivas even expects to see 'stigmata' on his hands (*NM*, 285). Dr Radcliffe, the upright figure who has diagnosed and cared for his elderly patient, pronounces an indictment: '"He is dead", he said ruthlessly, "and we have all had a hand in it"' (*NM*, 372). The novel emphasises the murderous consequences of Britain's failure to surmount or even acknowledge empire's physical and ideological legacies.

By shuttling back and forth between Srinivas's present and past, England and India, the action of the novel sketches the often-unacknowledged centrality of empire to the history of modern Britain. It contrasts the complacent amnesia of Powellism with, for example, the death of Srinivas's peaceable younger son, the 'conchie' (*NM*, 38), Seshu, while driving an ambulance during the Blitz: Britain's colonial subjects shared the sacrifices of its 'finest hour'. We learn also about Srinivas's journey to London in 1919 and about the expropriation of his family's teakwood plantation, as well as his career as a spice importer. There are lengthy chapters covering the political tumult in India after the First World War, including the massacre at Jallianwala Bagh and the internment of Indians accused of nationalist sympathies by the colonial authorities. Even the detailed characterisation of the deluded Fred in the later chapters succeeds in explaining, if not, of course, in excusing, the origin of his violent hatred of Srinivas in the distress of unemployment and in Fred's anxieties about status and the unavailability of established models of working-class masculinity. Having failed to settle in the 'white dominion' of Australia, Fred has lost his place in the queue for council housing and projects these resentments onto Srinivas. For those 'on lengthening housing lists', 'their numb misery fermented, waiting for obscene voices to nominate scapegoats on whom they could offload the frustrations of their living' (*NM*, 201). The eruption, or rather, intensification, of racist demagoguery and violence after 1968 is thus placed in the longer histories of British imperialism and the failures and limitations of the post-war settlement.

We go so far as to read *The Nowhere Man* as a cautionary novel about post-war British fascism, which was being kept alive by the anti-Semitic and ultra-nationalist groups around people like Oswald Moseley and John Tyndall and by such organisations as the League of Empire Loyalists in the 1950s and 1960s.[43] It effloresced after 1968 with the rise of the National Front and then the appropriation of NF themes and, to a degree, even anti-immigration NF policies by Tory administrations after 1979. The Tory Party's Monday Club was founded in 1961; the 'Monday' referred to Macmillan's Cape Town speech. It opposed the retreat from empire and then focused increasingly on immigration. Thatcher talked repeatedly in the election year of 1979 of communities being 'swamped' by immigrants.[44] Obviously, Conservatism is not the same thing as fascism, though Conservative politicians from Powell and Thatcher to May and Johnson have had few compunctions about appropriating far right rhetoric and talking points in order to consolidate their electoral base. Srinivas ponders the ways in which fascist groupings in Britain in the 1960s adopted the tactics and rituals as well as the dehumanising ideologies of German and Italian fascism.[45]

> He recalled them now, almost phrase by phrase, presenting hate as a permissible emotion for decent German people. Not only permissible but laudable, and more than that, an obligatory emotion, which they summoned up subtly and starkly from a reading of a checklist, or charge sheet, of the differences between men, their customs and observances, their sexual, religious, and pecuniary habits, sparing nothing as they peeped and probed, neither bed nor bathroom nor tabernacle, citing in the end, without shame, the shape and size of their noses, lips, balls, skulls, and the pigment of their skins.
> (*NM*, 209)

Again, the ornateness of the syntax is itself an implicit rebuke to the divisive simplifications of imperialism and fascism.

Srinivas is a leprous pariah in Powell's Britain, just as Indians in the Raj, according to his father, Narayan, were 'like lepers', 'a copy of human beings' (*NM*, 155). We are informed that the colonial policeman who assaults Vasantha during an inspection of the family's house had been poisoned by 'imperial implants', his natural human sympathies deranged by 'potent drugs that bore him to spheres from which he looked down, cold distant eye above the common run: an attitude which annihilated any basis of parity between the two human sides, substituting the split levels of vassal and overlord' (*NM*, 164). This essentially feudal language of class hierarchy might provide the clue to understanding the allegorical significance of Srinivas's leprosy. Snubbed by hostile neighbours and harassed by racist yobs, the unfailingly urbane Srinivas is described as a victim of 'atavistic urges and old refrains that put bell and clapper on a man and sent him wandering' (*NM*, 241). The fabled ostracism of lepers in the Middle Ages is, for our assertive and judgemental narrator, the measure of a fundamentally primitive society, which neatly turns the arrogant colonial rhetoric about development and modernisation on its head. British racism and fascism, like British imperialism, are portrayed throughout as 'crude and repulsive' (*NM*, 310) eruptions of veritably barbaric desires, objects for the narrator of disgust and aversion.

If it detects the disturbing growth of a distinctively British fascism in the aftermath of empire, *The Nowhere Man* also anticipates many of the themes and concerns of later generations of postcolonial British writers. These are writers whose multiple origins and identities will make them and their work, like Srinivas, 'aware of incongruity as the islanders were not' (*NM*, 105–6). The novel's title obviously foreshadows another demagogic speech by a Tory politician, Prime Minister Theresa May's inflammatory denunciation of 'citizens of nowhere' in her 2016 party conference address. Srinivas is even worn down by what the novel refers to as a 'hostile climate' (*NM*, 212), which is a chilling portent of May's 'hostile environment', the harassment and deportation of Black Britons after 2010 that represents for Maya Goodfellow the grim culmination of 'decades of exclusionary politics' since the Commonwealth Immigrant Acts of 1962 and especially 1968.[46] 'Nowhere Man' is also a track from The Beatles' influential 1965 album *Rubber Soul*, which reminds us how, in the late sixties, the group produced not only a kind of celebratory psychedelia or Victorian nostalgia or upbeat Americana but (as the novel does) much more earnest evocations of those who remain on or have been pushed to the margins of British life in the supposed decade of liberation. This angry and disenchanted novel has even less faith than its better-known successors, such as Salman Rushdie's *The Satanic Verses* (1988) or Zadie Smith's *White Teeth* (2000), that England will learn from its imperial history. Abdul, Srinivas's Zanzibari friend and former business partner, tells him that immigrants are 'coming here – right here to England – to take up their share in the prosperity which was built on their backs. Only the islanders won't see it that way' (*NM*, 50). Abdul's French wife, Odile, 'thought the British were so full of their own virtues that no dialogue with them was possible' (*NM*, 97). Pessimistically but, alas, presciently, *The Nowhere Man* anticipates the zombified perpetuation of nationalist and racist ideologies after the end of empire, while hinting at the best way to finish these revenants off.

The novel refers obliquely to Powell's speech, though he is actually never mentioned. For example, the nosy Mrs Glass has 'no great hate' but spreads malevolent tittle-tattle about Srinivas nonetheless, 'bearing in mind the issued warnings of leaders of opinion and moulders of men' (*NM*, 250). Srinivas's tenants do not fault 'his fastidious personal cleanliness', 'although they would later on, after tuition' (*NM*, 72), in the way that, the novel implies, people are taught to suppress their hospitable inclinations by malevolent instructors like Powell and to associate immigrants with excrement and dirt. It was precisely in its use of scatological imagery, in addition to its motifs of invasion and defilement, that Powell's speech most effectively conjured up the phantasmagorical nightmares and fantasies of empire, as Stuart Hall and the other authors of an important study of conservative backlash contended: 'The symbolism of the race-immigrant theme was resonant in its subliminal force, its capacity to set in motion the demons which haunt the collective subconscious of a "superior" race; it triggered off images of sex, rape, primitivism, violence and excrement.'[47] Towards the end of the novel:

> The following day words spewed out.
> A speech.
> An explosion.
>
> (*NM*, 339)

Powell's anti-immigrant demagoguery harnessed the anxieties and revulsions characteristic of imperialist racism. *The Nowhere Man* makes that demagoguery itself the object of an appalled disgust so profound that the novel cannot bring itself to pronounce the detestable Powell's name.

Neighbourliness and love hold the line against Powell's adherents. Mrs Pickering is told in the novel's final lines not to blame herself for Srinivas's death:

> 'Blame myself,' said Mrs Pickering. 'Why should I? I cared for him.'
> And, indeed, that seemed to her to be the core of it.
>
> (*NM*, 373)

The question is not rhetorical: she did, in fact, care for this leprous scapegoat, whatever her occasional lapses or failures of understanding. That fact seems to Mrs Pickering to be 'the core' of 'it', the 'it' being Srinivas's death, though if 'it' also refers to the novel we have just finished reading, then there is clearly a much broader canvas on which the virtue of 'care' should be applied. Through his relationship with Mrs Pickering, Srinivas feels himself initially 'becoming more English than the English' (*NM*, 84), though he and we eventually appreciate the artificiality and destructiveness of this outmoded construction of nationality. The task the novel sets its readers is to abandon such archaic identifications and reach across the boundaries erected by class, and especially nation and race, with an ethos of care and with what the novel repeatedly characterises as a renewed sense of shame at empire's violent legacies. What form of conscious and voluntary affiliation might bring the people of 'England' together in the absence of the old, now thoroughly outworn, and malignant identifications? Mrs Fletcher, Fred's admirably honest and decent mother, disowns her son and resolves to assist Srinivas out of an impulse that emerges partly from their acquaintance and partly, we are given to understand, from some suppressed aspect of British culture that is only half-understood, though it is articulated with poignant candour:

> Affirming in quaking accents conclusions, scraped painfully out of experience and the overlaid core of her breed, which were to do with the intrinsic quality of human beings.
> 'You are my neighbour', Mrs Fletcher said.

As she would go on saying, as she was saying now, a straight statement which had taken on the aspects of an address of welcome, or it could even have been the format of a reborn world.

(*NM*, 313)

Auspiciously, the bonds of neighbourliness potentially trump those of family or race; propinquity is thicker than consanguinity.

Remember that it is very much the character of 'neighbourhoods', and therefore the category of 'neighbour', that was at issue in Powell's speech. 'Neighbour', Markandaya's narrator reminds us, is an Old English word meaning 'inhabitant'. According to the *OED*, a neighbour is 'a person who lives near or next to another' or, in 'echoes of biblical passages teaching responsibility, etc., towards others (such as *Matthew* 19:19): a fellow human'. This is perhaps the forgotten aspect of a specifically Christian heritage that the narrator is alluding to. The *OED*'s example of usage is from Chaucer's *Parson's Tale*: 'In the name of thy neighebor thou shalt understonde the name of thy brother.' *Matthew* 19:19 is, of course: 'Thou shalt love thy neighbour as thy self.' Neighbourliness and its opposite, ostracism, also call to mind the notorious campaign in the West Midlands seat of Smethwick at the 1964 general election. The victorious Tory candidate, Peter Griffiths, ran on slogans like 'If you want a n____ neighbour, vote Liberal or Labour', while his canvassers spread rumours that 'because most of the blacks have leprosy, they are building two secret leper hospitals in the town'.[48] Markandaya's novel clearly picks up on and explores the moral and political implications of this inflammatory vocabulary. It therefore intervenes explicitly in urgent political debates about the character of neighbourhoods and the responsibilities of neighbours. *The Nowhere Man* contrasts crude ostracisms on the basis of race with a much more inclusive ethos of neighbourliness. Bonds of responsibility, it suggests, can be formed by proximity. This ideal, of improvised ties of affection and obligation between people who just happen to inhabit the same place, may emerge 'out of experience' or out of the religious or cultural 'core' of Mrs Fletcher's 'breed'; either way, the ideal constitutes an emergent alternative to the moribund and cynically resuscitated identifications of nation and race.

The novel urges us to combat 'the stench of the ghetto' and exalt 'the webs of gentleness that still prevailed in the land, could still be found, obstinately clinging, their delicate fabric belying their strength and resisting all efforts of Fred and his henchmen to foul them' (*NM*, 337). This 'delicate fabric' would connect the inhabitants of an authentically postcolonial Britain on the basis of neighbourliness, care, and a clear-eyed understanding of shared history. *The Nowhere Man* could scarcely be more pressing in its defence of scapegoats violently expelled from the 'hostile climate' of group belonging or in its courageous determination to sketch 'the format of a reborn world'.

Raymond Williams's *Border Country* (1960) is a meditation on how the social tensions of post-war and post-imperial Britain are magnified by the frontier zone of the novel's Welsh–English border setting. In *Border Country*, echoes of political militancy from the 1926 General Strike, in addition to the divided loyalties of its protagonist, a working-class scholarship boy, disturb the apparently placid compromises of the post-war settlement. The novel's structure interweaves the present of the 1950s, in which Matthew Price, a London-based university lecturer in economic history, is visiting his family home after his father suffers a stroke, with the world of his childhood and also his parents' early years of marriage in the 1920s. The point seems to be that the tensions and incongruities felt by Harry Price are inherited by his son, albeit at a later and more conflicted stage of working-class history. The whole novel, in a sense, is Matthew's 'long dialogue with his father' about a predicament that is at once personal and historical – 'a dialogue of anxiety and allegiance, of deep separation and deep love'.[49] The young Matthew and his parents live in the literal borderland between Wales and England. Harry also resides in a social and economic border country between the class solidarity exemplified by the failed (or, the novel suggests, hastily suspended and therefore betrayed) General Strike of 1926 and the go-getting individualism of his former workmate Morgan Prosser. Harry is additionally squeezed between the sense of autonomy and locality represented by beekeeping and market gardening and the wider contacts and connections made possible by his work in the village's railway signal box. His son Matthew is a working-class scholarship boy, propelled by his own intelligence and by his class's appetite for education to Cambridge, London, and an academic career. He is thus fated to reproduce the various economic, social, cultural, political, and geographic tensions that characterised his father's life, his tortuous efforts to bring those intensifying tensions to some sort of conscious articulation on this unexpected visit home being the main subject of the novel. The younger Price is now caught between the margin and the centre; between his childhood home, where he is still familiarly called Will, and the more formal self-presentations of adulthood and the university, where he is known as Matthew or, presumably, Dr Price; and between the class- and place-based solidarities of the past and the more aspirational and classless post-war, but somewhat deracinated, present of the 1950s.

The great value of the book, as we see it, is its identification of a methodological problem or task that is explored in all of Williams's work: How do literary and other texts capture the full scale and complexity of a given culture, its characteristic tensions and conflicts, its various political aspirations, including its dominant, residual, and emergent modes?[50] *Border Country* anatomises the tensions and future possibilities of a distinctive but highly complex and conflicted working-class culture on one of the British nation's internal border zones. That is what Matthew is also trying to do in his academic study of 'population movements in the Welsh mining valleys in the middle decades of the nineteenth century' (*BC*, 5). He can make no headway with the project because he has not yet appreciated that the representation of any community, not just in a historical study but also in his own memories and reflections, and in the novel that is recording these, will be lifeless and inexact unless it presents that community as both multifarious and dynamic. Towards the end of the novel, Matthew therefore commits 'himself again, without conflict, to the work that gave meaning to this moving history. But in practice, in a different atmosphere, moving back necessarily into the long struggle with detail' (*BC*, 299). Both author and protagonist are trying to escape the 'detachment' of their academic training and its 'consistently abstracting and generalizing' language (*BC*, 79). We think the novel is most insightful and affecting where it struggles with detail, at the level of images, conversations, and tellingly unconcluded plots and subplots on the characteristic tensions and possibilities of post-war Britain's rapidly but contradictorily modernising borderlands.

How, Matthew the academic historian keeps wondering, do you 'measure' population movements with statistics? What form is required 'to write the history of a whole people being changed' (*BC*, 277)? The answer, he intuits, is by stepping outside the discipline and finding an idiom capable of evoking experience. By writing a novel, perhaps. How does one evoke a deracinated intellectual and farm worker's grandson's residual love of trees and wildflowers? Matthew notices beside his garden gate 'a laburnum, as he had learned to call it' (*BC*, 6). What is the attitude to 'learning' implied here? What sort of intimacy with place and nature is lost by the acquisition through a more formal system of education of an abstract Latin nomenclature and the consequent forfeiture of the familiar vernacular names imparted by other forms of erudition? To cite another example of the novel's detailed and very immediate depictions of the conflicted border country, the peripheral and even semi-colonial condition of Wales dawns on Matthew when, on a train, he notices a map of rail routes on which 'to the east the lines [were] running out and elongating, into England' (*BC*, 8), Wales being a country whose towns and cities are connected to parts of England rather than to each other.

The 'country between two cathedrals' (*BC*, 336) (presumably Hereford in England and Brecon in Wales) is, in fact, a 'living country' (*BC*, 65), as Matthew starts to appreciate. It bears the traces of a deep past in the border castles and the illegible fragments of a Saxon tomb in the porch of the Norman church at Glynmawr and traces of an unpromising present in the form of valleys 'blackened with pits and slag-heaps and mean grey terraces' (*BC*, 286). Economic, demographic, and even ecological change has left the border country's future radically uncertain. Farming methods are being 'modernised', and the rabbits are perishing horribly from myxomatosis. There are no more children playing in the lane, the station has been closed, and the road through the village is being straightened to allow thundering lorries to ferry agricultural produce to distant markets more quickly. The village is now, as Matthew discovers on his second return, after his father's death, a place of felled trees and grubbed-up hedges 'on the way to somewhere else, as almost everywhere in Britain was coming to be' (*BC*, 299). But at least back-breaking toil is a thing of the past, and for the first time, the village has a supply of potable water. The novel is full of such ambiguous changes, redolent images, unanswered questions, and open possibilities.

Culture in Williams's work is almost always a synonym for *democracy*; the term names spaces in which it is possible to negotiate and fight out the intentions, desires, and aspirations of different groups. That is exactly what *Border Country* tries to do, struggling its way towards a more precise and intimate register capable of evoking the complexities and conflicts of life in the borders in the midst of a process of rapid but contradictory modernisation. The novel dramatises in an intriguingly unfinished way the characteristic tensions of the post-war border country on Britain's under-represented margins, including those between belonging and individuality, class and classlessness, socialism and commerce, place and movement, past and future, the so-called 'regions' or 'provinces', such as the Welsh border country, and the ostensible centre that is London and England. The 'rhythm of the novel', as Dai Smith calls it, moving as *Border Country* does between these polarities without ever resolving them in a series of journeys, conversations, and meditations, makes visible the 'disputed ground' of post-war and post-imperial Britain's apparent peripheries.[51] One important tension that this novel barely hints at, by the way, is that between the received model for the lives of working-class women (wife, mother, helpmeet, service sector worker) and newer aspirations, though it is only fair to acknowledge that these questions are explored more purposefully in Williams's next novel, *Second Generation* (1964). These tensions are not only felt on the modernising British nation's frontier zones, of course, though they are magnified there. *Border Country* articulates some of the characteristic stresses we have been tracing in post-war British fiction and adds to them a sense of regional or, rather, national divergence that would only be spelt out as a full political programme in Nairn's *The Break-Up of Britain* in the late 1970s.

One novel that does express the new dissatisfaction of many working-class women with their status in post-war Britain and, specifically, post-war Wales is *The Awakening* (1956) by Kate Roberts. Roberts, a preeminent figure in twentieth-century Welsh-language writing, inverts the practice of using a female figure to personify an oppressed or insurgent nation by instead employing nationalist tropes (betrayal, solidarity, awakening) to explore the tentative break of a youngish woman, Lora Ffennig, from her neglectful husband and the social expectations of life in the fictional small town of Aberentryd in the Welsh-speaking, slate-quarrying region of Arfon. This significant but little-known novel deserves a much more thorough critical treatment than we can provide it with here. Let it suffice to say that the figure of Lora is significant because her growing confidence and self-awareness distance her not only from the expectations of the judgemental townsfolk but also from the conventional place of the female image in nationalist discourse. *Y Byw Sy'n Cysgu* is clearly, in some sense, an assertion of national and cultural, as well as, obviously, linguistic, particularity in the context of the construction in the 1950s of what Edgerton, as we have seen, calls 'the British nation'. But in this novel, women are emphatically not, as the poet Eavan Boland complains they often were in Irish nationalist discourse in the late nineteenth and the early twentieth century, largely silent and merely emblematic of a nation's beauty and purity.[52] Indeed, if it is symbolic of anything, Lora's beauty denotes her own pride and growing autonomy. In this realist novel, written from a distanced but compassionate third-person perspective, autonomy becomes a personal as well as cultural objective. In the final chapter, which moves into an appealingly reflective and expressive first-person voice in the form of an entry from her diary, Lora contrasts her former 'whitewashed happiness' in her marriage with her current excited 'dissatisfaction' after her feckless husband has departed.[53] She wonders whether writing itself is a catalyst for a kind of incomplete awakening, one that would amplify previously silenced or unconscious lives and voices like hers while forging imaginative connections with others:

> Now I must be awake, and though I'll be groping, I'll at least be groping with my eyes open.
>
> I also realise that we are able to keep our enthusiasm for life according to the amount of love we have for someone or something. I don't know what I now love, if not the burgeoning interest I now have in my own personality and through that in the personalities of others. Perhaps this is what makes people writers.[54]

This is a form of awakening that, in its uncertainty and inconclusiveness, in addition to its expansiveness and its proto-feminism, is radically unlike the belligerent divisions and exclusions characteristic of patriarchal nationalism. Post-war British fiction is a battleground on which the new, supposedly postcolonial British nation is challenged and contested. Britain is, in essence, an imperial construction, as we have been arguing. But even without an empire, there were political and cultural forces, most notably Enoch Powell's influential vision, that sought to hold Britain and its characteristic forms of political, economic, social, and especially racial identity together. Other projects sought to accelerate the break-up of the British nation. The novels analysed in this section articulate these rival possibilities.

The End of Empire in British Theatre

Our account of British drama also begins in 1948, the year of Windrush, and ends with the political ferment of the 1970s. In the established theatres of the West End, in the risk-taking Royal Court Theatre in Sloane Square (the home of the English Stage Company), in new civic theatres subsidised by the Arts Council, and in the new publicly funded institutions of the National Theatre and the RSC, post-war British theatre, at its best, dissected a heavily mythologised British nation. British theatre was not always radical during this period. For every daring play by a Harold Pinter or a Caryl Churchill addressing the exclusions and inequalities of post-war British society and democratising the medium by challenging the once-ingrained naturalism of British theatre, there were many more unadventurous farces, formulaic musicals, and plays by Noel Coward. Chapter 2 concludes, then, with a reflection on how British theatre dramatised the rival possibilities of post-war British culture and society. 'We don't live alone. We are members of one body. We are responsible for each other', the Inspector famously and rousingly declares in J. B. Priestley's *An Inspector Calls* (1945).[55] But who is that 'we'? Who gets to belong to that 'one body'? We begin with a play that, in our view, struggles to answer those questions. We do not mean *An Inspector Calls*, a play known in detail to generations of British schoolchildren due to its perennial place on school exam syllabuses, but Priestley's rarely staged and largely forgotten *Summer Day's Dream* (1948). This avowedly socialist play nonetheless demonstrates how the imagined community of a post-imperial Britain had to be drastically rethought in response to decolonisation, immigration, and new aspirations for social and gender equality. That rethinking would be a task discharged more consciously and enthusiastically, and often with more experimental forms and methods of staging, in the works of playwrights who came after Priestley.

Summer Day's Dream assembles a pastoral vision of the Sussex Downs in a future 1975 in order to denounce the madness of the nuclear arms race but also propound a dubious fantasy of a 'deep England'. The play was first performed at the St Martin's Theatre in the West End in 1949 and not revived until 2013, at the small Finborough Theatre in Earl's Court. The action is set over a few days at Larks Lea, an old country house on the South Downs in midsummer a few decades after a devastating third war. A 'fantastic comedy' according to Priestley's preface, the play contrasts the straitened and anxious state of Britain at the dawn of the nuclear age with a pastoral vision of a similarly impoverished but also post-imperial and seemingly post-capitalist, yet worryingly parochial, future England.

A helicopter carrying three agents of the new post-war order, Irina Shestova (a frosty Soviet apparatchik), Franklyn Heimer (a brash American business executive) and Dr Bahru (an Indian research chemist, a representative of Europe's newly independent and now non-aligned former colonies), has crash-landed in the vicinity of the picturesquely dilapidated Larks Lea. Eagerly accommodated there by the avuncular Stephen Dawlish, they are gradually seduced by the simplicity and beauty of Stephen's family's way of life in an obscure Atlantic island that turns out to have been designed by God, we are told, 'not for factories but for cattle-breeding'.[56] The English, it seems, do not belong to the first, second, or third worlds, having reverted to a sort of pre-industrial condition, a simple barter economy that employs horses rather than tractors and 'atomicars'. They are 'survivors from a wreck, from the war of split atoms and split minds' (*SDD*, 114), as Stephen neatly puts their situation. Stephen and his companions are not ingenuous yokels, however; they have intentionally renounced empire, money, export drives, and advanced technology. England is now, in Stephen's gleeful words, 'a little backwater of a country, no longer busy doing the world's work' (*SDD*, 39). This is in some ways a rather attractive projection of a country that refuses to be 'dragged in the dust behind the runaway chariot of commercial production' (*SDD*, 77), Stephen here, as elsewhere, sounding exactly like Priestley himself in his political writings.

The general slowdown is emphasised by the actors' deliberate movements and the slow scene transitions, both mandated in Priestley's detailed stage directions. This is a Wildean or Morrisian vision of the soul of man under a specifically English socialism, in which freedom from alienated labour leaves one free to indulge in earnest heart-to-hearts, brew beer and make cheese, compose music and poetry, or as some of the characters are doing, stage Shakespeare's *A Midsummer Night's Dream*, the play that Priestley's fantastic midsummer vision obviously references. There is a proto-ecological element to this fantasy. There is no petrol, for example: unlike tractors, horses help manure the soil, as Stephen explains to his visitors. And 'there are more flowers, more birds, than ever before', Stephen's grandson

Chris observes (*SDD*, 48), even plump bustards to be snared for dinner. It is capital and technology that have been renounced, however, not class or the national and racial ideologies that have always gone hand in hand with British capitalism. This socialist vision of a post-industrial and post-capitalist future harbours worryingly conservative assumptions about the nation's supposedly unchanging ethnic and cultural make-up. The things that seem to have changed in Priestley's near future do not include fixed and hierarchical gender identities, the thoughtless conflation of England with Britain, or hostility to immigration.

The political limitations of Priestley's play's utopian vision are starkly revealed when the characters get wind of their visitors' scheme to effectively colonise this English idyll to use the chalk in some new synthetic product. Heimer 'can't depend on the British' for hard work, so he hopes to transplant a 'mobile labour unit' of five to ten thousand Chinese workers to 'tear the guts out of these Downs'. Soon, according to Heimer, 'you won't know the place. Big plant, landing grounds, rows of hutments, bungalows for the technicians, cafes, dance halls. T-V-palaces, bright lights' (*SDD*, 58). The worst thing that might happen to England, it seems, is the arrival of foreign workers, a disappointing stance for the play to adopt in the year of Windrush and a thoroughly objectionable one when one bears in mind the little-known forcible repatriation of hundreds of Chinese seamen in the late 1940s by Clement Attlee's Labour government. England – indeed, the England of the post-war 'affluent society' that, in 1948, was just around the corner – is fatefully reimagined as a colony. The 'isle is full of noises' 'and sweet airs', Chris tells Dr Bahru as he quotes at length from *The Tempest*. Shakespeare's oeuvre is recruited here and by the play's title for a socialist utopia that is overtly national in orientation. But the isle in Shakespeare's play is not Britain, of course: 'This Caliban is presented as a victim of British imperialism' (*SDD*, 51), as the Soviet visitor Irina sagely points out, though Chris rejects this reading of Shakespeare's play. What gets repeatedly written out of Priestley's patriotic daydream of a deep England is, therefore, empire and its legacies. Even worse, in their horror of being invaded by immigrants, the English start to play the role not of imperialism's aggressors or beneficiaries but of its victims.

The end result of this way of thinking is the self-pitying resentment of the Brexit vote, where, in Fintan O'Toole's words, 'having appropriated everything else from its colonies, the dead empire appropriates the pain of those it has oppressed'[57] by self-pityingly reimagining itself as a colony assailed by immigrants and shadowy conspiracies of malevolent foreigners. Not only that, for on closer inspection, it is hard to see what is specifically socialist or democratic at all about Priestley's dream England. It is centred on an old country house owned by an irascible old paterfamilias. The name of the house is clearly highly significant. 'Larks Lea' perhaps alludes to Vaughan Williams's Romantic vision of a timeless England in 'The Lark Ascending' (in a much more laudatory mode than Selvon's *Moses Ascending*), while the literary and faintly archaic 'lea' (a term for an area of pastureland) conjures up a bucolic sense of both the pastoral and the past. Larks Lea even echoes Locksley, the Nottinghamshire village from which the original English freedom fighter Robin Hood is said by medieval chroniclers to hail. This is a somewhat conservative vision, therefore, though obviously not a Conservative one. The women are presented in the play as helpmeets and mystics or, else, as hard-working but clean-limbed and biddable girls. Irina, for example, goes from Soviet sourpuss to 'English rose', being reminded by Chris's creepy infatuation to 'start behaving like a woman' (*SDD*, 60). This English socialist utopia is therefore much more English than it is socialist or utopian and is characterised by important blind spots and exclusions.

It is surely significant that the resource for which a colonised England will be ruthlessly strip-mined in the play is chalk. This is the material that forms a large part of the geology of Southern England, of course, which here, as usual, stands in for the whole island of Britain. Chalk is associated with England's highly mythologised Southern borders. Indeed, the white cliffs of Dover are registered in England's high-flown poetic epithet 'Albion'. Southern England's striking, if friable and racially charged, Southern borders were further freighted with cultural meaning by the recent war as well. Priestley may have had in mind Alice Duer Miller's spectacularly successful 1940 verse novel *The White Cliffs* (made into a film by MGM in 1944) as well as Vera Lynn's patriotic, if ornithologically inaccurate, wartime song 'The White Cliffs of Dover'. What is being defended in *Summer Day's Dream* is not really a distinctively British socialist vision but a narrowly English and more specifically Southern English vision, one characterised by a disarmingly familiar class system and gender roles in addition to racially coded borders.

Priestley depicts an England that has survived an atomic war and reverted to what the play presents as its true bucolic self. This idea that the nation might simply renounce destructive technological developments has its merits. It resurfaces in Priestley's article in the *New Statesman* in October 1957, which called on the British people to show moral (rather than economic or military) world leadership by renouncing nuclear weapons; this speech led to the founding of the Campaign for Nuclear Disarmament.[58] Even here, though, the radical vision is tempered by a rather conservative sense of England's special role and virtue. *Summer Day's Dream* is an indication of the impoverished or at least highly restricted political imagination of many radical English writers in this period, where an ideal England is more often opposed to modernity itself rather than to capitalism or patriarchy, let alone to nationalism and imperialism and their racial dogmas. The play therefore anticipates the characteristic trajectory of national identity more widely after the war 'now that we're not a world power and nobody cares tuppence about us' (*SDD*, 75), as Stephen puts it. Even in the works of an avowed socialist like Priestley, an expansive but racialised and hierarchical idea of Britain as an empire morphs into a seductive but dubiously insular and backward-looking vision of an eternal England, much as it does in, say, J. R. R. Tolkien's portrait of 'the Shire' and the insular 'Shire-folk' in *The Lord of the Rings* (1955), or in Winston Smith's longing for a pastoral 'golden country' in George Orwell's *Nineteen Eighty-Four* (1949). It is a quasi-Powellite vision even before Powell himself had begun to formulate it. 'Send down your roots and lift your faces to the sun and stars' (*SDD*, 132), intones Priestley's mouthpiece at the end of the final act. The very serious drawbacks of a new ethic of rootedness, which were obvious enough to, say, Benjamin Britten's 1945 opera *Peter Grimes*, where the English village is a site of persecution, not redemption, would be demonstrated again in supposedly radical works in British theatre in the 1950s.[59]

John Osborne's *Look Back in Anger*, which opened at the Royal Court Theatre in May 1956, addresses developing ruptures and rifts in the British nation state in the year of the disastrous Suez invasion, the signal crisis of Britain's remaining imperial pretensions. That debacle, in which the British government was forced to abandon the occupation of the Suez Canal zone in response to American financial pressure, is then addressed more directly in Osborne's *The Entertainer*, which began its run at the Royal Court a year later. Despite their reputation for being watersheds in post-war British theatre, we do not think that either play does much more than gesture towards the deeper frustrations and radical possibilities germinating in British society in the 1950s. For a start, they are both formally rather conservative works. Notwithstanding the length and vituperativeness of Jimmy Porter's rants, *Look Back in Anger* is a naturalistic play with three acts and a decidedly sentimental ending; the fourth wall remains firmly in place. *The Entertainer* is more boldly structured like an evening in the music hall, with numbers, an overture, and intermissions. Its ending, too, though, is somewhat banal, as the ageing music hall entertainer Archie Rice, now eking out a living hosting nude reviews in a flea-bitten seaside resort, slowly leaves the spotlight as the music fades. Both plays express a kind of amorphous discontent with 'England' that was widely lauded at that time, not least by Kenneth Tynan, the influential theatre critic for *The Observer*. That discontent was, in fact, so amorphous and so limited that Osborne's later public persona after the 1970s, as a dyspeptic reactionary, can already be seen emerging in them, as can the later incarnation of Jimmy Porter in the play's misconceived 1992 sequel, *Déjàvu*, as a bibulous old Tory raving about gay people and the EEC.

Look Back in Anger is also, to be blunt, a work of unrestrained misogyny. Some audiences and readers might want to see Jimmy's increasingly obnoxious attacks on his partner, Alison, in act 1, while she does the ironing in the corner of the stage, as ironical or be inclined to read his furious denunciations of Alison's temporary replacement, Helena, in act 2 as almost self-subverting in their disturbed intensity. But the play's conventional ending, in which Helena leaves so that Jimmy and Alison can be reunited, simply returns us to the situation that greeted us when the curtain first rises, which will hopefully strike many latter-day audiences not as a hard-won affirmation of romantic love but as something much more unpromising and even disturbing. Furthermore, Jimmy's discontent is worryingly unfocused. He rails against national decline and 'the American Age'[60] while complaining famously that 'people of our generation aren't able to die for good causes any longer' because 'there aren't any good, brave causes left' (*LBA*, 83). It is worth pausing to observe what an odd statement this is in the seminal year of decolonisation, the Hungarian Uprising, and the foundation of CND. What sort of causes is Jimmy looking for? Alison's father, the Anglo-Indian Colonel, who is presented very sympathetically, eulogises the empire he served for 30 years before returning to England in 1947, the year of independence and partition.

> If only it could have gone on for ever. Those long, cool evenings up in the hills, everything purple and golden. Your mother and I were so happy then. It seemed as though we had everything we could ever want. I think the last day the sun shone was when that dirty little train steamed out of that crowded, suffocating Indian station, and the battalion band playing for all it was worth. I knew in my heart it was all over then. Everything.
>
> (*LBA*, 66)

This lament for imperial decline is worryingly similar to Jimmy's unfocused rants about the nation's falling-off.

The trouble with the play, as we see it, is that it works as invective but not as drama. The play struck a chord and remains memorable because of the sheer intensity of Jimmy's diatribes, especially in the context of the rather-stuffy protocols of British theatre in the 1950s, before the emergence of powerful new talents, and before the influence of European playwrights like Beckett, Ionesco, Brecht, and Artaud began 'to democratise the medium', as *The Guardian*'s theatre critic Michael Billington puts it in his survey of post-war British theatre.[61] The point of Jimmy's voice is that it is forceful but rambling and incoherent. The only alternative perspective is provided by Helena's reassertion of a kind of conservative morality when she leaves Jimmy to make way for the return of his wife in act 3.

The ease with which forceful discontent morphs in Osborne's work and career into reactionary grousing about the demise of 'England' tells us a great deal about the limitations of even ostensibly radical critiques in the 1950s. In these plays in particular, it is always 'England' that is at stake for Osborne. But England, Alex Niven has argued, as we saw in the introduction, is a 'geopolitical void'. What does it mean to lament England after the 1950s, an empire without colonies, a nation without a state, or rather, a state whose nation (Britain) was shrinking and falling apart? 'England' might, of course, be a convenient shorthand for the social order which these plays appear to be attacking, but in truth, the England whose demise they bewail is specifically the imperial 'England' elegised by the Colonel in *Look Back in Anger* and then epitomised by the moribund musical hall in *The Entertainer*.

Osborne's 'Note' to the latter play declares that the 'musical hall is dying, and, with it, a significant part of England. Some of the heart of England has gone; something that once belonged to everyone, for this was truly a folk art'.[62] The play uses 'some of the techniques of music hall', Osborne explains, including the use of 'numbers' rather than scenes, though the larger architecture of an overture and two intermissions looks like nothing so much as a conventional three-act structure. Archie's numbers are compelling in their verbal dexterity, but also rather pathetic, as Archie battles gamely against the implied indifference of his dwindling audiences. Given the number of pauses inserted into these routines, the ingratiating patter and the bad jokes clearly no longer work. What is dying reluctantly onstage is not only the entertainer himself but also 'England' and its empire, as Archie's songs make clear:

> Good old England, you're my cup of tea,
> But I don't want no drab equality.

Then, as the stage directions require the Union Jack to be dropped:

> Those bits of red still on the map
> We won't give up without a scrap.
> (*E*, 32–3)

The refrain of Archie's apparent signature tune, which he first sings in the seventh number, is 'Thank God I'm normal' (*E*, 60). This commitment to a kind of social and geopolitical, as well as presumably sexual, 'normality' may be ironical, as the spotlighting halfway through the ditty of '*a nude in Britannia's helmet and holding a bulldog and trident*' would suggest. 'For this was their finest shower' (*E*, 61), Archie warbles in the midst of the Suez invasion, a pun on Churchill's description of the Battle of Britain in 1940 as the empire's 'finest hour'. These numbers are poised somewhere between ironical destabilisation of patriotic clichés and a sincere elegy for the empire. The superannuated musical hall entertainer is, then, a metaphor for 'England', which is revealed to be similarly moribund by the humiliating debacle of the Suez invasion, which is unfolding offstage and in which Archie's son Mick is later killed. The crumbling Empire theatres of Glasgow, Liverpool, Hackney, and so on parallel Britain's similarly disintegrating territorial empire. Our view is that the use of a clapped-out musical hall artiste as a metaphor for a dying England does not do much, if anything, to illuminate the various issues of class, gender, empire, and so on that are spot-lit between Archie's vignettes by the bickering repartee of the increasingly inebriated Rice family.

This badinage is actually quite promising material for a 'state of the nation' drama. The play broaches some interesting conflicts and tensions, for example, between the elderly Billy's anti-immigrant chauvinism and his granddaughter Jean's vaguely signalled radicalism; she has been to a rally in Trafalgar Square, presumably against the invasion of Egypt. There is an intriguing contrast between Archie's callous philandering and the drunken self-pity of his second wife, Phoebe. But these conflicts are not really drawn out. Indeed, we think that *The Entertainer*'s central metaphor of a dying England, on which the light is extinguished at the end of the play, fails to do justice to these interesting tensions. The focus of the play is on Archie's vivid routines, as the title suggests; the play was, after all, written as a kind of star vehicle for Laurence Olivier. Instead of dramatic tensions that might help audiences explore the state of the nation, the play gives us a theatrical cliché (the tragic artiste) and a simplified metaphor (the musical hall artiste representing a dying England). That is the problem with the part of Archie (and perhaps with Olivier): he hogs the limelight. England's demise is exemplified not by the crises of class or gender or race that the play occasionally identifies but by the supposed humiliation of Suez. In a sense, it scarcely matters whether one reads Archie's patriotic paeans to empire and normality as ironical or sincere; they are clearly both, and the play alternates between moments of jocularity and high seriousness. Having said that, the family's placement of a Union Jack and Billy's hat and cane over Mick's coffin in the eleventh number to fading light and 'snatches of old tunes' (*E*, 83) does not strike us as ironical at all, though, of course, it depends on how the scene is played. Our point is that the play's preoccupation with a process of specifically *national* decline camouflages issues and questions that are, in fact, more directly social and political.

There is a telling relationship between disorder and order in *The Entertainer*, as there is in *Look Back in Anger*. In the first play, discontent is safely contained; Alison returns, the three-act structure and the sentimental ending reassert a very conventional idea of romantic love, and Jimmy's potentially incendiary dissatisfactions are ceaselessly channelled into an ineffectively conservative elegy for national decline. In the later play, the promising dramatic tensions that imply various political conflicts to do with class, generation, race and gender are again smothered by the central metaphor of national decline and by the conventional ending. The domestic numbers focus on Billy's hostility to the immigrants with whom he shares his bedsit; England is conceived of as 'a mad-house' filled with 'black fellow[s]' (*E*, 15) and 'bloody Poles and Irish' (*E*, 13). This potentially critical examination of the nature of British nationalism is overshadowed by Archie's numbers' greater commitment to striking tragic poses of national and imperial decline. *The Entertainer* shows how the nation's imperial identity might be performed sincerely or badly or even ironically; but it offers little indication of how the nation might assume a different part altogether. In Osborne's two celebrated and ostensibly radical plays of the mid-1950s, conservative forms are wedded to a fundamentally conservative account of the nation at the end of empire.

John McGrath's *The Cheviot, The Stag, and the Black, Black Oil* is a socialist and even overtly Marxist history of Scotland, first performed on a lengthy tour of schools, community centres, and dance halls in the Highlands and Islands in 1973. It is, more precisely, a dramatic history of 'the north of North Britain',[63] as Lady Phosphate of Runcorn, the trigger-happy wife of an English chemicals magnate, describes the Highlands and Islands while murdering scores of grouse with a machine gun. The destruction and enforced emigration of crofting communities as part of the Highland Clearances in the eighteenth and nineteenth centuries (to make way for the cheviot sheep) is linked by McGrath's play to the expansion of private estates dedicated to grouse shooting and deer stalking in the nineteenth century, and then in the 1970s the arrival of foreign-owned multi-nationals to exploit North Sea oil. The common denominator of Scottish history, the play contends, is capital and its depredations, including lowland capital, but especially English, and later American, capital. Scotland's story is one of, to borrow David Harvey's phrase, 'accumulation by dispossession' as well as by depopulation.[64] This is an anti-imperialist dramatic history, therefore, in addition to being an extremely radical anti-capitalist one. But as the play makes clear and as Graeme Macdonald acknowledges in a persuasive reflection on 'Postcolonialism and Scottish Studies', the Celtic margins of the British state have been both imperialism's victims and, intermittently, its beneficiaries. In Macdonald's words about the works of James Kelman, Alasdair Gray, Tom Leonard, Liz Lochhead, and Irvine Welsh, McGrath's play is

> postcolonial in the sense that [it] relate[s] indeterminate individual, social and psychological experiences to global patterns of trade, war, statelessness, labour transfer, dissidence, and displacement by an imperialist and capitalist system. Ultimately, [it] consider[s] the possibility of international alliance, communication and recognition – in short, of communality – between some Scots and those displaced and dispossessed in semi-dependent or newly independent nations – or those displaced and/or made anonymous by an overshadowing nation.[65]

It is not the case, therefore, that Scots have necessarily suffered *the same* processes of dispossession, exploitation, cultural alienation, transportation, and extermination as other subject peoples of the empire. Rather, as McGrath's play carefully delineates, Scots have been protagonists in the history of the British state and its depredations: 'neither fully coloniser nor fully colonised but both', in the historian Michael Fry's neat summation.[66] *The Cheviot, The Stag, and the Black, Black Oil* asks its audiences to contemplate the connections and similarities between Scotland's violent history and the unitary British state's other misadventures. In its revisionist account of Scottish history, and with its radically provocative techniques, the play provides audiences with opportunities to cultivate the forms of imaginative and practical connection required to surmount empire's legacies. It is a socialist play, sure enough, one that also envisages the break-up of the imperial British state.

The play grew out of McGrath's work with the radical 7:84 theatre company, a group dedicated to dramatising inequality; the name referred to 84% of Britain's wealth being held by 7% of the population. *The Cheviot* portrays the history of Scotland as a struggle between exploitation and organised resistance while trying constantly to provoke reflection and involvement from its audiences. This is Brechtian theatre in short, in which audience members are positioned as critics and collaborators, not as consumers, jolted in Brecht's own words 'from general passive acceptance' of the dominant order to a 'state of suspicious inquiry'.[67] Every effort is made to refute the sense that Scottish history is somehow innocuous or univocal, predetermined or resolved. To this end, audiences are treated to a veritable cavalcade of alienation or estrangement effects designed to discourage any passive acceptance of the official story of Scotland's incorporation into Britain (its reconstruction after the eighteenth century as *North* Britain) and steady material progress on the back of enclosure and empire. Songs in Gaelic lament the defeat at Culloden, but the emphasis throughout is on provocation and incitement rather than nostalgia or mourning for lost causes.

Readers and an MC frequently interrupt the dramatic action to remind the audience through statistics and stories culled from the company's extensive historical research that on the flip side of material progress, capital accumulation, and modern state formation can be found the sufferings and aspirations of real people. Other methods of defamiliarising both theatrical illusion and the official narratives of Scottish history include abrupt intrusions of didactic narration by the actors, multi-rolling, harsh lighting, freeze frames and tableaux, crash courses in Marxist economics, direct addresses to the audience, as well as often exaggerated, almost-vaudevillian forms of acting. The sets and props on the first tour were often minimal, with various settings being evoked by a sort of pop-up backdrop that could easily be transported from venue to venue in the back of a van. Actors sat at the side of the stage and could be seen changing costumes between scenes. Songs, to take one example, vividly personalise and humorously dramatise the deceptions and despoliations of landowners. The commodification of Scottish history and culture in the course of the nineteenth century into a series of romantic clichés, one ditty makes clear, did not alter the fundamental facts of exploitation, violence, and theft. As Lord Crask menacingly intones:

> But although we think you're quaint,
> Don't forget to pay your rent,
> And if you should want your land,
> We'll cut off your grasping hand.
> (*Ch*, 43)

By such theatrically innovative methods, *The Cheviot, The Stag, and the Black, Black Oil* showed Scottish history to be characterised by violence, exploitation, and struggle. The apparent aim of all these estrangement effects is to make audience members into participants rather than passive spectators of Scottish history, and even into a kind of nascent collective or political community. The play has no interval; it was, after all, agitprop theatre funded by the Scottish Arts Council, performed mostly in village halls rather than commercial theatres with well-stocked bars. Each performance then ended with the company 'trying to turn itself into a dance band', in McGrath's words, as the chairs and props were cleared, the floor swept, and a ceilidh held for several hours.[68] Here was an impressive use of the theatre to carve out the space as well as the time required for historical reflection and political engagement, deliberation, and collective enjoyment.

At one point, a 'Sturdy Highlander' compares the dispossession of First Nations peoples with the dispossession of Scottish Highlanders forced to immigrate to North America.

> But we came, more and more of us, from all over Europe, in the interests of a trade war between two lots of shareholders, and in time, the Red Indians were reduced to the same state as our fathers after Culloden – defeated, hunted, treated like the scum of the earth, their culture polluted and torn out with slow deliberation and their land no longer their own.
> (*Ch*, 29)

The Highlander is addressing the audience 'out of character' at this point, according to the stage directions, perhaps with the authority of this historically literate ensemble. The entire point of this play and, as we see it, the point of this extremely powerful declaration is to provoke reflection and disputation. We want to maintain that the violence of land clearances in Scotland was connected to but hardly 'the same' as the even greater violence of colonialism in North America. Indeed, the play later stresses Scots' complicity in empire, specifically the use of Highland Divisions 'to subdue other countries, whose natural resources were needed to feed the industrial machine of Great Britain' (*Ch*, 47). Indeed, this dual emphasis on Scots' complicity *in* and domination *by* the imperial British state also characterises one of the most popular and influential rewritings of Scottish history in this period, John Prebble's *The Highland Clearances* (1963), which we wager this historically literate ensemble must have read. In the nineteenth century, according to Prebble, Walter Scott and his imitators made the hitherto despised Highlander 'respectable enough to be a gun-bearer for an English sportsman, a servant to a Queen, or a bayonet-carrier for imperialism'.[69] But when the Duke of Sutherland's factor burned people from their cottages, left them to freeze and starve in exposed coastal settlements or perish in the coffin ships to distant lands, then he was, according to Prebble, 'as much a colonist as those of his contemporaries who were preparing to dispossess the aboriginals of America, Africa and Australia to make room for wheat, hide and wool on the hoof'.[70] Since Scotland has been at once a part and at the edges of the imperial British state, some Scots the state's prey and other Scots its accomplices, the final statement of McGrath's play, voiced by the entire company before they and the audience clear the hall and share a knees-up, is one of imaginative connection with former and current colonies. 'In other parts of the world – Bolivia, Panama, Guatemala, Brazil, Angola, Mozambique, Nigeria, Biafra, Muscat and Oman and many other countries – the same corporations have torn out the mineral wealth from the land' (*Ch*, 72). Disputation and collective solidarity are the play's principal themes, but also, hopefully, effects of its form. These are auspicious outcomes of a play that connects and also sometimes troublingly and provocatively conflates the historical dispossession of Scotland's poor with imperial depredations overseas. *The Cheviot*, thereby, reached into Scotland's past in order to open up possibilities for a transformed future outside the reach of the British state, but also beyond the structures of capital and empire. 'It's a story', the MC informs the audience at the start of the play, 'that has a beginning, a middle, but, as yet, no end' (*Ch*, 2).

Caryl Churchill's *Cloud Nine* explores one of the most important questions addressed by third-wave feminism: How are supposedly natural categories of sexuality and gender conditioned by society and culture? The play, which was first performed at Dartington College of Arts in Devon in 1979 before a run in London and several international tours, works to destabilise as well as historicise these categories within the context of British imperialism and the unfinished process of decolonisation. Gender, as the cultural theorist Judith Butler would later argue in the influential 1990 study *Gender Trouble: Feminism and the Subversion of Identity*, is 'performative', which is to say not voluntary but laboriously conditioned by powerful discourses and practices.[71] Gender identity is not simply given but made, in other words. For Butler, this insight ought to inspire feminist politics to go way beyond the defence and celebration of women's seemingly 'normal' or given identities and social roles. Politics should not be about what you are already or what the prevailing discourses and systems of power expect you to be but about what you might become. We see *Cloud Nine* as an appropriately theatrical exploration of how apparently natural sexual and gender roles, as well as (more problematically and less convincingly) racial identities, might be constructed differently and more freely. Importantly, it places these vital contemporary questions raised in the 1970s by feminist movements and intellectuals in the context of Britain's imperial history. The regulation of sexuality and gender is shown to be a legacy of imperialism. The utopian anti-identity politics envisioned by Butler is thereby revealed to be a radically anti-colonial project.

The first of *Cloud Nine*'s two acts takes place in an unnamed British settler colony in Africa in the nineteenth century; the second act, which features most of the same characters, takes place in London, in the play's present. It is the contingency and malleability of supposedly 'true' or fixed identities that are accentuated by the play's liberties with historical time, by its farcical misapprehensions and, most of all, by its use of cross-sex casting to visibly open up a gap between actor and character, what one is and the identity society obliges one to perform.[72] The great virtue of the play is that it destabilises identities in this way and does so in the context of empire, asking audiences to see dominant gender identities as obsolete legacies of colonial expansion. Its shortcomings, as we see them, include the play's more cursory attention to the vital imperialist ideology of whiteness. Furthermore, the theatrical trick of asking a female actor to play a male character (or vice versa) does not allow the play to explore more fluid forms of gender identity.

Just as the play was intensely workshopped with the company, so does it enlist its own audiences as collaborators in the production of its unmasking of identity's performative character; this is what Amelia Kritzer calls Churchill's 'theatre of empowerment'.[73] In act 1 of *Cloud Nine*, audiences are ceaselessly reminded that apparently fundamental social roles are, in fact, highly unnatural, mere conventions that might be made to seem strange and intolerable and therefore susceptible to radical political transformation. In the first act, the colonial administrator Clive's wife, Betty, is played by a man; their son, Edward, by a woman; and their Black servant, Joshua, by a white actor. The effect is to underline the absurdity and impossibility of, for example, Betty's painful conformity to a stereotype of femininity. She sings in rhyming couplets: 'The whole aim of my life, Is to be what he looks for in a wife. I am a man's creation as you see, And what men want is what I want to be.'[74] Joshua is similarly coerced into imitating a colonial norm: 'My skin is black but oh my soul is white. I hate my tribe. My master is my light, I only live for him. As you can see, What white men want is what I want to be' (*C9*, 2). Young Edward is shown to be unable and unwilling to conform to a masculine ideal: '"My son is young", says Clive. "I'm doing all I can To teach him to grow up to be a man", to which Edward's response is: "What father wants I'd dearly like to be. I find it rather hard as you can see"' (*C9*, 2). The same goes for the 4-year-old Cathy, who is played by a man in the second act. The emphasis there is on the considerable and, ultimately, futile effort required to interpellate children into conventional gender roles. Clive and Betty's daughter, Victoria, is played in the first act by a dummy, which emphasises the silence and violence inflicted on young women by a code of gender conformity.

The play, then, provides a graphic visual demonstration of the performative nature of identities and the lack of any easy correspondence between body and identity. The casting also points up the contrived quality of sexual roles and stereotypes. Betty (played by a man) and Betty's husband, Clive (also played by a man), may be a heterosexual or a homosexual couple, depending on whether one perceives Betty in terms of gender or biology. Clive tenderly embraces Betty but pulls away in disgust from the advances of Harry (who is also played by a man), which shows up the absurdity and arbitrariness of Victorian moral codes. There is also a comic contrast throughout the frantic action of act 1 between the physical and sexual vitality of the characters and their futile attempts to remain loyal to this rigid moral code. That code regulates, though not at all successfully, sex, sexuality, gender, and the racial identities enforced by imperialism. The possibility of sexual subversion, for example, is constantly shadowed by the possibility of anti-colonial insurrection. Clive, whose name, of course, recalls the once-celebrated Robert Clive of the British East India Company, is 'father to the natives here, And father to [the] family so dear' (*C9*, 1). The two systems intersect. As Clive says to his mother-in-law, Maud: 'I look after Her Majesty's domains. I think you can trust me to look after my wife' (*C9*, 7). Clive views both women and colonised people as objects of patriarchal power. Women's desires are, as Freud imagined them, a dark continent to be subdued, albeit one in a state of perpetual sedition: 'This whole continent is my enemy. . . . I sometimes feel it will break over me and swallow me up' (*C9*, 33); 'We must resist this dark female lust, Betty, or it will swallow us up' (*C9*, 34). Clive, who attributes the fall of Rome to homosexuality, urges his clearly gay friend Harry to get married for the sake of England. But even Clive lusts after the admirably self-possessed widow Mrs Saunders, who disdains the institution of marriage. And the sly civility his servant, Joshua, shows Clive is clearly belied by Joshua's defiance and rebelliousness. In short, the same capitalist-imperialist system that requires the subordination of women also requires the subordination of subject populations as well as the repression of dissident sexual energies. The iniquity, and especially the absurdity, in addition to the ultimate impossibility of maintaining this system in the face of the characters' ebullient desires and their visible but unofficial identities, is what the play demonstrates. Joshua's raising of a gun at the end of act 1 obviously signifies the downfall of the colonial system.

There is an impressive discontinuity between the colonial past and the postcolonial present of act 2, with many of the same characters, such as Edward and Betty, finding new freedoms of personal expression and new forms of social and sexual connection in the relatively liberated context of the late 1970s. The dramatic styles of the two acts are quite different, with the artificial and oratorical speeches of the first act replaced by the relative informality and the more blunt language of the second. There are some new characters, but the retention of key figures from act 1 tells us that the play is most interested in the possibility of transcending the ideological legacies of a still-powerful colonial past. In act 1, space is divided sharply between inside and outside; activity in which conventional roles are complicated and transgressed takes place on the veranda beneath the Union Jack or in the grounds of the compound. The house is a site of control; at one point, the women are restricted to an enclosed room with the blinds drawn while the men flog the servants. These kinds of segregation are clearly being loosened in the exterior setting of the urban park in act 2. In act 1, the characters lack the vocabulary with which to articulate their desires. Betty, for example, can only express her desire for Harry indirectly by placing herself as a passive object of desire ('Please want me' (*C9*, 14)), while the lesbian governess Ellen's desire for Betty is almost unintelligible to both Betty and Clive. There is a greater emphasis in the second half of the play on choice and sexual freedom. Lin and Victoria become lovers. Edward adjusts to Gerry's abandonment of their monogamous relationship and even gets involved in a ménage à trois with Lin and Victoria. Martin adjusts to his separation from his wife and helps take care of the children. All kinds of queer families and kinship relations are being forged outside of monogamy and the contractual relationship of heterosexual marriage; this is shown to be a difficult and sometimes painful but also exhilarating task. Betty is divorced from Clive and learns to appreciate and value her independence. Accents and speech are less formal, while the dialogue is more vernacular and reflective. The action is altogether less frantic as characters are seeking deliberately to overcome limitations and stereotypes.

This is not quite a utopia or Cloud Nine of sexual liberation, however. 'Churchill challenges notions of fixed identity and normative sexual identifications', as Janelle Reinelt argues, 'but in her juxtaposition of Victorian and contemporary moments, she is also vigilant to represent how the legacy of the past makes differentiation in the present complex and extremely difficult'.[75] The unmastered legacies of the Victorian and colonial past are still felt through the second act: ghosts from act 1 admonish Betty, and the invocation of the mythical goddess in the park leads to Lin seeing her brother, who has been killed serving in the army in Northern Ireland. In the absence of the authority of Clive and of paternal authority generally (Lin's father will not speak to her because she went on a Troops Out march), there is hesitation and uncertainty. The formation of new values and relationships is an exciting but difficult work in progress, for as Betty says, 'if there isn't a right way to do things you have to invent one' (*C9*, 86).

Clive reappears at the end of the play to express his disapproval of Betty's frank conversation with her son's former boyfriend about sex and sexuality. Does his final reappearance at the end of the play demonstrate the longevity of the forms of imperial and patriarchal power that he personifies, or their ridiculousness and obsolescence?

> You are not that sort of woman, Betty. I can't believe you are. I can't feel the same about you as I did. And Africa is to be communist I suppose. I used to be proud to be British. There was a high ideal. I came out onto the veranda and looked at the stars.
>
> (*C9*, 87)

Is this elegy for Britishness and its attendant ideologies of sex, sexuality, gender, and race now simply ridiculous? Resigned? Or in the late 1970s, is Britishness somehow reconstituting itself, a still powerful and eloquent revenant from an unmastered imperial past? Is the ending threatening and menacing, therefore? The audience is invited to assess this uncertain conclusion and to carry out the final liberation from stereotype and convention which the play has not quite felt able to anticipate.

Indeed, we think the limitations of the play's own method prevent it from portraying an achieved vision of emancipation. The cross-sex casting succeeds in destabilising gender by flaunting the gap between actor and character or between the self and the self's social presentation. In the play, it is also desire, mainly sexual desire, but also political desire for various forms of personal and even collective independence, that pushes the characters beyond established identities and social appearances. But while the play seeks to expose patriarchal and colonial structures and the identities that underpin them, there are many relationships and identities, in particular, trans relationships and identities, that might not be made visible by simple inversions and reversals, as J. M. Harding has argued.[76] Moreover, the play is clearly more committed to the subversion of gender than it is to the subversion of race. The only subversion of dominant racial identities is a white actor in a Black character's role in act 1, which we see as a failure to interrogate the construction of whiteness. There are no Black actors in white roles. Indeed, there are no non-white characters at all in act 2's semi-liberated London of 1979. The play definitely fails, in our view, to countenance what, in an American context, the historian David Roediger has called the 'abolition of whiteness'.[77] As Mary Luckhurst has suggested, 'Cloud Nine is long overdue for creative reinvention by directors who want to experiment with cross-racial casting'.[78] Such performances would help audiences explore more consistently the connections between compulsory heterosexuality, patriarchy, and imperialism, as well as envision alternatives.[79] *Cloud Nine*, therefore, represents a forceful but incomplete revision of the conventional assumptions about race, gender and sexuality, that underpin Britishness. It connects various forms of domination and defamiliarises the seemingly natural identities that underpin them. It asks questions about the possibility of unfixing and transforming identities in Butler's sense. But it offers no glib celebrations or definitive answers. Indeed, we view post-war British theatre, as we viewed post-war British fiction, as a space in which the supposedly postcolonial British nation was fought out. Even where dissident energies are powerfully articulated, in the splenetic force and the post-imperial visions of Osborne, in the socialist daydreaming of Priestley, and in the anti-colonial histories and theatrical innovations of Churchill and McGrath, the ghosts of empire proved exceedingly hard to exorcise.

Conclusion

In her afterword to an informative collection of essays on the end of empire and the English novel, Elleke Boehmer suggests that 'the predominant mode through which the post-1945 English novel has registered the British imperial experience as well as the retreat from world dominance, more specifically, is melancholic'.[80] We are not so sure about that. It is true that the English frequently looked like a sad and disoriented bunch in the decades after the war. 'Poor loves', as Connie Sachs, the eccentric and hard-drinking former researcher for British intelligence, calls them in John le Carré's *Tinker Tailor Soldier Spy* (1974): 'Trained to Empire, trained to rule the waves. All gone. All taken away. Bye-bye world.'[81] But we have been trying to trace in post-war British fiction and in post-war British drama what are often surreptitious and necessarily tentative or embryonic alternatives to the atmosphere of post-imperial melancholia. What Boehmer says of English fiction is not true of British writing more broadly during this period. Arguments that British writing was sinking or shrinking or just in need of urgent rethinking do not even capture, as Matt Whittle's persuasive study of English fiction after the war has shown, the complexities and contradictions of apparently formally and politically conservative works by white male writers, such as Anthony Burgess, William Golding, Colin MacInnes, and Graham Greene. Whittle dissects a 'self-conscious literature of transition' in the 1950s that is committed 'to a new conception of Britishness that does not rely on static ideas about national or racial superiority'.[82] Despite the clear presence of significant trace elements of these things in, for example, Burgess's *Malayan Trilogy* (1956–1959) or MacInnes's *City of Spades* (1957) and *Absolute Beginners* (1959), these works also offer a 'challenge to dominant ideas about British imperial identity based on racial and cultural superiority' and actually anticipate the more expansively postcolonial concerns of writers after the 1970s.[83] Critical preconceptions about the prevailing melancholia of post-war British writing certainly do not account for the work that we have been looking at by, say, Markandaya, Churchill, and Selvon, writers who do seek to process either the trauma of imperial loss or the infinitely greater traumas undergone by the empire's victims and legatees, especially where these latter categories include immigrants to Britain or the various groups that empire otherwise displaced or disenfranchised. These writers take stock of empire and explore different kinds of future.

Our narrative of British writing in the three decades or so after the war and during the processes of large-scale immigration and imperial contraction owes much to Jed Esty's ingenious account in *A Shrinking Island: Modernism and National Culture in England* of 'a major literary culture caught in the act of becoming minor' after the 1930s.[84] Esty does not quite argue that the formal innovations and the cosmopolitan sensibilities of high modernism in, say, T. S. Eliot's 'The Waste Land' (1922) or Virginia Woolf's *Mrs Dalloway* (1924) and then the more urgently political and often explicitly anti-fascist objectives of late modernism in, to stick with the same writers, *Four Quartets* (1943) and *Between the Acts* (1941) gave way, in the aftermath of war and imperial retreat, to a sort of formal and political parochialism in British writing. The island was not 'sinking' into economic and literary decline, as that apostle of high modernism Hugh Kenner contended in *A Sinking Island*, the book to which Esty's title alludes.[85] The 1940s, 1950s, and 1960s were not, we hope to have shown, a sort of pre-postmodern desert of incorrigibly parochial melancholics. Esty is correct, in our view, to point to an 'anthropological turn' after the war in which writers looked more analytically and judgementally in their work at the new national rather than imperial culture and society that emerged in these years. 'England', he argues, became an object of knowledge and a focus of representation and dissection for fields as diverse as Keynesian economics, the new formation of cultural studies led by figures like Raymond Williams, Stuart Hall, and Richard Hoggart, conservative modernists like Eliot, liberal modernists like E. M. Forster, and what Esty characterises as the new writing of the emerging multicultural England of the 1950s exemplified for him by Doris Lessing and George Lamming. The turn towards England or Britain might be integrative and tribal or it might be, as Whittle is more prepared to spell out than Esty, and as we have been trying to trace in this chapter over a period from the late 1940s to the late 1970s, profoundly critical and subversive as well as determined to explore the possibility of post-imperial *and* post-British sensibilities. What take shape in many of the texts discussed in this chapter are general ethical commitments to new forms of social and intimate connection, neighbourhood and community.

David Edgar's play *Destiny*, which was first performed by the RSC at Stratford in 1976, shows what was at stake in the struggle to radicalise or partly reverse the tentatively postcolonial formation of the post-war 'British nation'. It is another work that traces the political convulsions of that decade to the unprocessed or, to use the German term, *unbewältigte* – that is, unmastered – legacies of imperialism. This didactic, if very powerful, play opens in India at the moment of Indian independence as disgruntled officers reluctantly set down the 'White Man's Burden'. The rest of the play follows a by-election in the 1970s in a West Midlands constituency that resembles Enoch Powell's former seat in Wolverhampton. The seat is eventually lost to the Tories by an ideologically muddled Labour Party when a new fascist movement called Nation Forward (which shares the initials and platform of the fascist National Front) eats into Labour's support. This is the period, as a lone guitarist sings at the end of a Nation Forward rally, in the words of Rudyard Kipling's wartime poem 'The Beginnings', 'that the English began to hate', when the assured imperial pretence of noblesse oblige gives way to a kind of crabbed anti-immigrant paranoia.[86] The strike by Asian workers at a local factory, which is joined by Khera, the harassed factotum in British India from act 1, recalls the seminal dispute at the Grunwick film processing laboratory led by Asian women workers that began during the play's first run. Nation Forward emerges from the kind of sinister conflabs between reactionary tycoons, retired generals, and rogue branches of the secret service that were a notorious feature of the mid-1970s. 'We are at war', as the ultra-reactionary former army officer Rolfe harangues the audience at the end of act 2, histrionically clutching a crumpled Union Jack as he collects the dead body of his son from army HQ in Lisburn, Northern Ireland. 'In Belfast. Bradford. Bristol, Birmingham, the one we lost in Bombay thirty years ago' (*D*, 377).

But what is so alarming about the play and so painfully prescient is not its portrait of a possible fascist insurgency by Hitlerite groups on the far right. Rather, *Destiny* shows how the compromises and concessions made by supposedly mainstream political parties lead to the legitimisation of the far right's rhetoric and programme. Something like fascism becomes the nation's destiny almost by default in the absence of some more democratic, egalitarian, and inclusive vision of the future. As the cunning former Nazi Maxwell suggests, this will be a form of racism and nationalism appropriate for an ostensibly democratic society in which 'you can't, now, operate a show on Nordic runes and Wagner' (*D*, 374). The only option, the play suggests as the curtain falls on a recording of Hitler himself describing how Nazism might have been 'smashed' (*D*, 405) when it first appeared, is militant resistance, typified in the play by organised solidarity between white workers and workers of colour.

We have tried in this chapter, therefore, to show how, even in the apparently settled and consensual atmosphere of post-war reconstruction and imperial retreat, there is a centripetal, 'break-up of Britain' logic to British writing. The British Empire became in this period a British nation state. But texts continued to explore the constitutive contradictions of that nation: between the state's enduring commitment to whiteness and the presence of large numbers of non-white British citizens, between the perennially centralised nature of the British state and devolutionary energies in the regions and nations, in addition to a growing recognition that the carapace of Britishness belied all kinds of social, gender, racial, and sexual identities craving expression. Chapter 3 shows how writers continued after 1980 to interrogate Britain and Britishness even as the state fought to hold them in place.

Notes

1 David Edgerton, *The Rise and Fall of the British Nation: A Twentieth-Century History*, Harmondsworth: Penguin, 2019, p. xxiii.
2 Edgerton, *The Rise and Fall of the British Nation*, p. 262.
3 Peter Hennessy, *Having it so Good: Britain in the Fifties*, Harmondsworth: Penguin, 2007, p. 24.
4 Anthony Sampson, *Anatomy of Britain*, London: Hodder and Stoughton, 1962, pp. 637–8.
5 C. P. Snow, *The Two Cultures and the Scientific Revolution*, Cambridge: Cambridge University Press, 1959.
6 'What sort of an island do we want to be? ... A lotus island of easy tolerant ways, bathed in the golden glow of an imperial sunset, shielded from discontent by a threadbare welfare state and an acceptance of genteel poverty? Or the tough dynamic race we have been in the past, striving always to better ourselves, seeking new worlds to conquer in place of those we have lost, ready to accept growing pains as the price of growth?' Michael Shanks, *The Stagnant Society*, Revised edition, Harmondsworth: Penguin, 1972 [1961], p. 232.
7 Alan Sinfield, *Literature, Politics and Culture in Postwar Britain*, London: Continuum, 2004, p. 10.
8 Tom Hazeldine, *The Northern Question: A History of a Divided Country*, London: Verso, 2020, pp. 115–36.
9 Perry Anderson, 'Edgerton's Britain', *New Left Review*, 132 (2021), 41–52: 49.
10 See John Medhurst, *That Option No Longer Exists: Britain 1974–1976*, Winchester: Zero Books, 2014.
11 David Olusoga, *Black and British: A Forgotten History*, London: Pan Books, 2017, p. 14.
12 Olusoga, *Black and British*, p. 12.
13 Olusoga, *Black and British*, p. 15.
14 Camilla Schofield, *Enoch Powell and the Making of Postcolonial Britain*, Cambridge: Cambridge University Press, 2013, p. 3.
15 Schofield, *Enoch Powell and the Making of Postcolonial Britain*, p. 246.

16 Paul Gilroy, *There Ain't No Black in the Union Jack: The Cultural Politics of Race and Nation*, London: Routledge, 2002 [1987], pp. 45–7.
17 Paul Foot, *The Rise of Enoch Powell: An Examination of Enoch Powell's Attitude to Immigration and Race*, Harmondsworth: Penguin, 1969.
18 Peter Fryer, *Staying Power: The History of Black People in Britain*, London: Pluto Press, 1984, p. 381.
19 'In other words, the structures of social difference which had once ordered British rule were beginning to unravel. Through all this, Powell retained a profound belief in the imperatives of patriarchy and dramatically committed himself to the 'survival' of the nation, against (post) imperial international concerns and, later, against the transnational commitments of both the New Left and postcolonial, diaspora communities in Britain.' Schofield, *Enoch Powell and the Making of Postcolonial Britain*, pp. 11–2.
20 Maya Goodfellow, *Hostile Environment: How Immigrants Became Scapegoats*, London: Verso, 2019, p. 78.
21 Ian Sanjay Patel, *We're Here Because You Were There: Immigration and the End of Empire*, London: Verso, 2021, p. 7.
22 Ralph Miliband, *Class War Conservatism and Other Essays*, London: Verso, 2015.
23 Quinn Slobodian, *Globalists: The End of Empire and the Birth of Neoliberalism*, Cambridge, MA: Harvard University Press, 2018, p. 3. The classic account of neoliberalism as a project of bourgeois class power is David Harvey's *A Brief History of Neoliberalism*, Oxford: Oxford University Press, 2007.
24 Paul Arnott, *Windrush: A Ship Through Time*, Stroud: The History Press, 2019, p. 169.
25 Nick Bentley, 'Form and Language in Sam Selvon's *The Lonely Londoners*', *Ariel*, 36:3–4 (2005), 67–84: 68.
26 Jed Esty, *A Shrinking Island: Modernism and National Culture in England*, Princeton: Princeton University Press, 2004, pp. 200–1.
27 Sam Selvon, *The Lonely Londoners*, Harmondsworth: Penguin, 2006 [1956], p. 1. Subsequent references are given in the main text after *LL*.
28 'The purpose of art is to impart the sensation of things as they are perceived and not as they are known. The technique of art is to make objects "unfamiliar".' Victor Shklovsky, 'Art as Technique' (1917), *Literary Theory: An Anthology*, Revised edition, eds. Julie Rivkin and Michael Ryan, Oxford: Blackwell, 1998, pp. 17–23: 18.
29 Krishnan Kumar, *The Making of English National Identity*, Cambridge: Cambridge University Press, 2010, pp. 16–7.
30 See Christine L. Corton, *London Fog: The Biography*, Cambridge, MA: Harvard University Press, 2015.
31 T. S. Eliot, 'The Waste Land', in *Collected Poems, 1909–1962*, London: Faber & Faber, 1974, p. 65.
32 Charles Dickens, *Bleak House*, ed. Norman Page, Harmondsworth: Penguin, 1971 [1853], p. 49.
33 Quoted in Bentley, 'Form and Language', p. 68.
34 John McLeod, *Postcolonial London: Rewriting the Metropolis*, London: Routledge, 2004, p. 39.
35 Graham MacPhee, *Postwar British Literature and Postcolonial Studies*, Edinburgh: Edinburgh University Press, 2011, p. 125.
36 Paul Mendez, 'I Going England Tomorrow', *London Review of Books*, 44:13 (17 July 2022), 31–4: 32.
37 The voices, discourses, and embodied practices of Black British Caribbean women and how they shaped decolonial and feminist projects are the subject of Denise Noble's outstanding *Decolonizing and Feminizing Freedom: A Caribbean Genealogy*, Basingstoke: Palgrave, 2016.
38 Sam Selvon, *Moses Ascending*, Harmondsworth: Penguin, 2020 [1975], p. 10. Subsequent references are given in the main text after *MA*.

Post-War Unsettlement, 1948–1980   133

39 Hari Kunzru, 'Introduction', in Selvon, *Moses Ascending*, Harmondsworth: Penguin, 2020, pp. vii–xvii: xiv.
40 Sam Selvon, *Moses Migrating: A Novel*, London: Lynne Rienner, 2009 [1983], p. 45. Subsequent references are given in parentheses in the main text after *MM*.
41 *The Nowhere Man* is published by Small Axes, an imprint of HopeRoad, which aims to publish new and classic but neglected voices from Asia, Africa, and the Caribbean.
42 Kamala Markandaya, *The Nowhere Man*, London: Small Axes, 2019 [1972], p. 348. Subsequent references are given in the main text after *NM*.
43 British fascism partly switched during the 1950s from the anti-Semitism of the British Union of Fascists before it was proscribed in 1939 to a new emphasis on racist hostility to immigration and a kind of post-imperial resentment about loss of national status. Moseley stood as a candidate in Kensington at the 1959 election after the attacks on West Indian immigrants by white mobs the year before.
44 Dominic Sandbrook, *Seasons in the Sun: The Battle for Britain, 1974–1979*, London: Allen Lane, 2012, p. 593.
45 Hannah Arendt's emphasis on the links between European imperialism and European fascism is one of her most important insights. 'When a European mob discovered what a "lovely virtue" a white skin could be in Africa, when the English conqueror in India became an administrator who no longer believed in the universal validity of law, but was convinced of his own innate capacity to rule and dominate. . . . The stage seemed to be set for all possible horrors. Lying under anybody's nose were many of the elements which gathered together could create a totalitarian government on the basis of racism.' Hannah Arendt, *The Origins of Totalitarianism*, New York: Harvest, 1968, p. 221.
46 Goodfellow, *Hostile Environment*, p. 7.
47 Stuart Hall et al., *Policing the Crisis: Mugging, the State, and Law and Order*, London: Macmillan, 1978, p. 244.
48 Dominic Sandbrook, *White Heat: A History of Britain in the Swinging Sixties*, London: Abacus, 2007, p. 669. When Griffiths made it to the House of Commons, he was denounced by the new Labour prime minister, Harold Wilson, interestingly, as a 'Parliamentary leper'. See Ben Pimlott, *Harold Wilson*, London: William Collins, 2016, p. 355.
49 Raymond Williams, *Border Country*, Cardigan: Parthian Library of Wales, 2006 [1960], p. 18. Subsequent references are given in the main text after *BC*.
50 Williams sets out his theory that a given culture has dominant, residual, and emergent elements in *Marxism and Literature*, Oxford: Oxford University Press, 1977, pp. 121–7.
51 Dai Smith, 'Relating to Wales', in *Raymond Williams: Critical Perspectives*, ed. Terry Eagleton, Boston: Northeastern University Press, 1989, pp. 34–53: 45.
52 Eavan Boland, *Object Lessons: The Life of the Woman and the Poet in Our Time*, Manchester: Carcanet Press, 1995.
53 Kate Roberts, *The Awakening*, trans. Siân James, Bridgend: Seren, 2006 [1956], p. 227.
54 Roberts, *The Awakening*, p. 228.
55 J. B. Priestley, 'An Inspector Calls', in *Six Plays*, London: Heinemann, 1979, p. 337.
56 J. B. Priestley, *Summer Day's Dream*, London: Oberon Books, 2013, p. 34. Subsequent references are given in the main text after *SDD*.
57 Fintan O'Toole, *Heroic Failure: Brexit and the Politics of Pain*, London: Head of Zeus, 2018, p. 21.
58 J. B. Priestley, 'Britain and the Nuclear Bombs', *New Statesman*, 2 November 1957.
59 In Alex Ross's persuasive account, Britten's opera, which opened at Sadler's Wells in June 1945 before the end of the war, transcends the inherited forms of opera. It also, in our view, transcends or at least questions the dominant form of English nationalism emerging in this period. 'This is opera that presses constantly at the borders of the genre, whether high or low: it bursts with folk song, operetta and vaudeville tunes, and the vernacular punch of the American musical, and, at the same time, it erupts in twentieth

134 *British Writing from Empire to Brexit*

      century dissonances. In many ways, Grimes is an English *Wozzeck*, extending sympathy to an ugly man, using his crimes to indict the society that sired him.' Alex Ross, *The Rest is Noise: Listening to the Twentieth Century*, London: Harper Perennial, 2009, p. 460.
60 John Osborne, 'Look Back in Anger', in *Plays One*, London: Faber & Faber, 1996, p. 13. Subsequent references are given in parentheses in the main text after *LBA*.
61 Michael Billington, *State of the Nation: British Theatre since 1945*, London: Faber & Faber, 2007, p. 83.
62 John Osborne, 'Note', in *The Entertainer*, London: Faber & Faber, 1957, p. 7. Subsequent references are given in parentheses in the main text after *E*.
63 John McGrath, *The Cheviot, the Stag and the Black, Black Oil*, London: Methuen, 1981, p. 40. Subsequent references are given in the main text in brackets after *Ch*.
64 David Harvey, *The New Imperialism*, Oxford: Oxford University Press, 2003, pp. 137–82.
65 Graeme Macdonald, 'Postcolonialism and Scottish Studies', *New Formations*, 59 (2006), 116–31: 122.
66 Michael Fry, *The Scottish Empire*, Edinburgh: Birlinn, 2002, p. 498.
67 Bertolt Brecht, 'A Short Organum for the Theatre', in *Brecht on Theatre: The Development of an Aesthetic*, ed. John Willett, London: Methuen, 1978 [1948], pp. 192–3.
68 John McGrath, 'The Year of the Cheviot', in *The Cheviot, the Stag and the Black, Black Oil*, London: Methuen, 1981, pp. v–xxviii: xi.
69 John Prebble, *The Highland Clearances*, Harmondsworth: Penguin, 1969 [1963], p. 16.
70 Prebble, *The Highland Clearances*, p. 304.
71 Judith Butler, *Gender Trouble: Feminism and the Subversion of Identity*, New York: Routledge, 1990.
72 On the way the play employs 'farce as politics', see Susan Bennett, 'Growing Up On *Cloud Nine*: Gender, Sexuality, and Farce', in *Essays on Caryl Churchill: Contemporary Representations*, ed. Sheila Rabillard, Winnipeg: Blizzard Publishing, 1998, pp. 29–40: 29.
73 Amelia Howe Kritzer, *The Plays of Caryl Churchill: Theatre of Empowerment*, Basingstoke: Macmillan, 1991.
74 Caryl Churchill, *Cloud Nine*, London: Nick Hern Books, 1989, p. 1. Subsequent references are given in parentheses in the main text after *C9*.
75 Janelle Reinelt, 'On Feminist and Sexual Politics', in *The Cambridge Companion to Caryl Churchill*, eds. Elaine Aston and Elin Diamond, Cambridge: Cambridge University Press, 2010, pp. 18–35: 29.
76 J. M. Harding, 'Cloud Cover: (Re)Dressing Desire and Comfortable Subversions in Caryl Churchill's *Cloud Nine*', *PMLA*, 113(2) (1998), 258–71.
77 David R. Roediger, *Towards the Abolition of Whiteness: Essays on Race, Politics, and Working Class History*, London: Verso, 1994.
78 Mary Luckhurst, *Caryl Churchill*, London: Routledge, 2015, p. 81.
79 A sceptical reading of the play's efforts to explore post-imperial identities is provided by Apollo Amoko, 'Casting Aside Colonial Occupation: Intersections of Race, Sex and Gender in *Cloud Nine* and *Cloud Nine* Criticism', *Modern Drama*, 42(1) (1999), 45–54.
80 Elleke Boehmer, 'Afterword: The English Novel and the World', in *End of Empire and the English Novel since 1945*, eds. Rachael Gilmour and Bill Schwarz, Manchester: Manchester University Press, 2011, pp. 238–43: 239.
81 John le Carré, *Tinker Tailor Soldier Spy*, London: Hodder and Stoughton, 1974, p. 113.
82 Matthew Whittle, *Post-War British Literature and the 'End of Empire'*, London: Palgrave, 2016, p. 2.
83 Whittle, *Post-War British Literature and the 'End of Empire'*, p. 15.
84 Esty, *A Shrinking Island: Modernism and National Culture in England*, p. 3.
85 Hugh Kenner, *A Sinking Island: The Modern English Writers*, London: Barrie & Jenkins, 1987.
86 David Edgar, 'Destiny', in *Plays: One*, London: Methuen, 1982, p. 356. Subsequent references are given in parentheses in the main text after *D*.

3 'We Have Been Made Again', 1980–2016

Where Chapter 2 addressed the 'precarious refinement of a Britishness focused on the national rather than the imperial' [135], it also sought to contextualise this in the nation's 'continuing commitment to imperial structures' [135] enacted internationally and domestically. The chapter aimed to 'show how writers and their texts portrayed Britishness in the three decades or so after the war, its tensions and exclusions, and the emergent possibilities taking shape in opposition' [135]. These emergent possibilities proceeded to evolve over the following decades as writers continued to 'interrogate Britain and Britishness even as the state fought to hold them in place' [135]. In this developing political and cultural context, the frameworks for understanding, managing, and challenging forms of belonging and exclusion took on the shape of categories such as multiculturalism, integration, and assimilation. These categories were tested, extended, and expanded to incorporate a consideration of new socio-economic realities of established but now newly politicised communities of migrants, refugees, and asylum seekers. This, in turn, and over time, as we argue, collided with the state's growing concerns with radicalism and, by extension, a newly developed grouping of emerging fears and anxieties that came under the label of 'terrorism' and 'security'. Brexit, a culmination or *resurrection* of the convergence of multiple lines of arguments around perceived threats to national integrity, forced a reckoning to many who had laboured to foreground how writing critiques but also shapes imaginative futures beyond the narrow confines of geographical borders.

An examination of how these categories are experienced socially, domestically, and materially in the literature often points to the productive ways in which writing engages with political, social, and cultural legacies. We may want to call some of this work postcolonial in that the writing we engage with could be said to be contributing to a broad definition of *decolonisation* in the sense that we understand the project of colonialism to have found a new home both in the socio-political rhetoric that frames the rejection of multiculturalism and also in the discourses that contributed to the popularisation of the idea of an inhospitable environment. Writing here acts as a gesture in that it points to the exclusionary violence behind this rhetoric at the same time as it acts as an invitation to complicate it and to continually provide nuance and perspective on this legacy.

DOI: 10.4324/9781003230816-4

We are interested in looking closely at a particular selection of authors, some of whom became outspoken figures who sought to use their reputations to bring attention and awareness to the material and social conditions of contemporary Britain. Their works, we argue, creatively reconsidered the numerous historical power structures that actively shaped and still shape politics and policy today. Those who centralised imperialism and colonialism in this way engineered a discursive landscape that could then make room for a representation and critique of the inheritance of this vast history. Through actively resisting historical amnesia, they instead examined, in various forms and styles, the enmeshment of the past with the present. Aware of the vast literary inheritance that had grappled with the socio-economic, political, and cultural conditions of the pre- and post-war era (as we discussed in Chapters 1 and 2), writers from the 1980s onward were producing material in the context of a growth in the discipline of postcolonial studies that prioritised the necessity of the establishment of a set of questions and, subsequently, a frame that would act as a live rebuttal to the social and political apparatuses enjoined to reject and deny the continued influence and legacy of empire. Britain, intellectually poised to creatively consider these questions, would, however, eventually pursue a much more convoluted approach mired in myopic national self-interest, party politics, reactionary policies, fear, and finally, populism.

In *Beginning Postcolonialism*, John McLeod points to the 'material and imaginative legacies of both colonialism and decolonisation' that 'remain fundamentally important constitutive elements in a variety of contemporary domains, such as anthropology, economics, art, global politics, international capitalism, the mass-media and . . . literature'.[1] The emphasis on the global here points to the impossibility (as argued in earlier chapters) of somehow detaching a discussion of contemporary British identity from global politics. In fact, it is the ways in which colonialism and decolonisation *remain* constitutive elements in the social and political structures established to sustain a particular nationalist rhetoric and how these elements shape-shift to suit misguided policies that affect individuals and communities in the local and global contexts that most interest the authors that we examine in this chapter. In order to do this equitably, we examine texts that engage in the broader understanding of *Britishness* as a concept that contains within it a continued negotiation of empire as well as texts set *within* Britain that reflect on the changing dynamics of what underpins and constitutes a changing and diverse nationalist sentiment. We want to firstly show how certain realisations dramatised by postcolonial writers such as Salman Rushdie impacted and influenced our understanding of how ideas engage with and travel across space and time. In other words, many of the ideas around the expression of nationhood, nationalism, and how writing can articulate complex affective and material realities in contemporary writing gestated in contexts that reflected on the colonial relationship and its correlation to the colonial centre in a material sense. For this reason, this chapter examines texts written from the 1980s onward that explicitly engage with continuing debates around nation and belonging and the various social and political contexts that contributed to their development. We are interested here in exploring how writers both expanded and contracted their understanding and representation of belonging and the relationship of that belonging to a changing definition of Britishness. The works that we look at in this chapter continue to be interested in the possibilities of narrative form and how this can contribute to making visible the sharp contradictions between the ideal national image of continued and in-good-faith attempts at cohesion and the often-cruel manifestations of its failure. Within those two extremes, we have stories that engage with loss, desire, nostalgia, hope, despair, and everything in between. Through looking closely at the work of Arundhati Roy, Zadie Smith, Monica Ali, Abdulrazak Gurnah, Nikita Lalwani, Kamila Shamsie, and Salman Rushdie, we begin to make sense of how these emerging realities take shape and address these growing concerns against a backdrop of a deeply instructive but often publicly unacknowledged history.

Our critical thinking is informed by many historical, theoretical, and political paradigms. In a sense, the critical framework here is as instructive as the literature in the sense that it is situational and manifests as the specific need of each interpretive act makes itself known. For example, we may have started out by imagining that the work of Homi Bhabha on mimicry and hybridity would constitute a frame within which we might understand the usefulness and potential salutary aspects of a burgeoning multicultural policy. Though understood to extend what Mary Louise Pratt termed the 'contact zone',[2] Bhabha's articulation of a dynamic hybridity leant a more animated potential to the colonial encounter and, thus, to a postcolonial framework. Rather than reinscribe the always-already established and inflexible racial and national hierarchy at the heart of all colonial encounters, the frame of hybridity imagined an alternative to this relation. In *The Location of Culture*, Bhabha articulated the concept of a third space imagined as an 'international culture, based not on the exoticism of multiculturalism or the whereas diversity of cultures, but on the inscription and articulation of culture's hybridity',[3] whereas our aim here was to consider hybridity as the *starting* point of *any* culture. An acknowledgement of this inscription (and one that we have found to be a major stumbling block in the resurgence of ideas around national and ethnic purity) that then informs the building blocks of an imagined international culture seems both unimaginably radical and profoundly necessary. We read authors such as Monica Ali and Zadie Smith in order to better inhabit the complex and thoughtful ways in which they navigated the terrain of the 'in-between spaces' that are borne out of the historical and cultural specificities in which they found themselves and about which they chose to write. The concept of a universal hybridity sees its inheritor in a political and social multiculturalism that, however, wavers between a celebration of difference and a corrosive re-interpretation and application of hierarchical structures that undermine not only the more celebratory ambitions of a hybrid culture but also the potential cultural aspirations of a multicultural society. In essence, we see the space of the multicultural as a place of possibility at the same time as it presents a risk of exclusion. As Salman Rushdie writes in *The Satanic Verses*:

> We are here to change things. I concede at once that we shall ourselves be changed; African, Caribbean, Indian, Pakistani, Bangladeshi, Cypriot, Chinese, we are other than what we would have been if we had not crossed the oceans . . . we have been made again: but I say that we shall also be the ones to remake this society, to shape it from the bottom to the top.[4]

To remake and to reshape drive much of the fiction in this chapter as authors retain a curious outlook towards what this refashioning will look like in the context of developing social and political ideologies adapted to suit a particular idea of a contemporary Britain within a globalised world.

Concepts that appear dry and uninspiring in the political sphere, such as 'integration' and 'assimilation', take on a very different life in the writing of authors such as Abdulrazak Gurnah, Monica Ali, and Kamila Shamsie. Inter-racial relations and the complexities of attending directly to the consequences of the long history of colonial exploitation bring us up against a postcolonial landscape that is itself experienced at both the intimate and the civic levels. The writing that we engage with reflects in various ways on the representation of governmental structures and national institutions that seek to routinely impose parameters to the experience of inclusion, integration, and assimilation at the same time as they hail these initiatives as progressive. The writers that we examine question the limited assumption that national identity can somehow be owned by those seen to be deserving of it by accident of birth – as if this advantage ensures an imagined cohesive continuity uninterrupted by historical contingency. Changing political, cultural, and economic priorities put pressure on the ways in which individuals and communities imagine their boundaries.

This chapter spans a significant time period as it tries to capture a wide array of experiences associated with Britain's charged relationship with its colonial past in the context of a public discourse that seeks to manage this complex legacy. By encouraging the principle of multiculturalism, political policies in the early eighties spawned reactions ranging from outright denial to clumsy forms of engagement. Whilst these policies, both formally and informally, were attempting to open up definitions of *belonging*, they often worked to set up divisions that showed up cultures as different in opposition to a coherent British identity that was to be aspired to or that had been lost. The writing we examine considers this tension through the depiction of the experience of this belonging, often finding the price of entry too high, the sacrifice too extensive. As Salman Rushdie writes in *Imaginary Homelands*, what 'racial harmony ... meant in practice was that blacks should be persuaded to live peaceably with whites, in spite of all the injustices done to them every day'.[5] The authors we focus on show up the complex negotiation entailed in moving through this changing landscape, seeking solidarity and new modes of inclusion. The writing also works to bring a rich texture to a more complex society that is both shaped and limited by exclusionary political structures but that also produces individuals, communities, and experiences that question such limitations in a variety of ways. Belonging, and the route to it, retains its value, even as it routinely needs to be questioned. As Zadie Smith articulates in *White Teeth* (2000), where would we be without it?

> And then you begin to give up the *very idea* of belonging. Suddenly this thing, this *belonging*, it seems like some long, dirty lie ... and I begin to believe that birthplaces are accidents, that everything is an *accident*. But if you believe that, where do you go? What do you do? What does anything matter?[6]

In different but exciting ways, all the writers we examine experiment with forms of community building against an intransigent vision of the however often elusive qualities needed to belong. Following Nick Bentley's invitation to see how novels such as *White Teeth* involve 'a negotiation, rather than rejection, of more established constructions of Englishness', we look to see how this negotiation takes place.[7] They complicate any idea of a fixed space that can claim the rights over national unity, opting, instead, to depict the strong force of the imagination and the alternative existences that this allows for, sometimes removing characters from any fixed notion of place altogether (Monica Ali, for example, does this most persuasively), showing up the often illusionary certainty that often binds physical place to notions of belonging. Paul Gilroy's 'convivial culture'[8] was hard to find in these texts, though characters kept up the search. What we did find was a restless reflection on what might constitute a shared culture. Characters often embraced this reflective mode only to find that the idylls that British culture promised were constantly redefined, always remaining *just* out of reach. The ways in which race, ethnicity, gender, and class intersect in space and place often gave rise to fresh contexts that were difficult to navigate and that required the imagining of alternatives to restriction and regulation. The (imagined) rights of citizens to shape their own destiny loom large in the writing we look at, and sometimes this can bring with it an all-too-quick impulse to ignore Gilroy's warnings against 'revisionist accounts of imperial and colonial life'[9] that may seek to erase the past. This attitude may appear to be putting the past to rest in the interests of an imagined shared future, but it compounds the issues brought to the surface by that history. The texts we examine here reveal the multiple ways in which revisionism, often a tool in the arsenal of communities attempting to place value in their agreed-upon version of their interpretation of the historical record at the expense of another's, can produce fear and distrust. Some of the work exhibits what Wiktoria Tuńska has recently termed feanxiety: 'a critical concept that brings together literary representations of fear and anxiety'.[10] For Tuńska, this is 'one of the fundamental components of Brexit's emotional tenor' that has 'naturally been a pivotal element of Brexit fiction, too',[11] and a concern that we shall return to later on in this chapter.

As Roger Hewitt argues in *White Backlash*, 'during the 1990s increasing hostility to multiculturalism in its various forms was apparent both nationally and internationally'.[12] Speaking in particular around the publication of *The Stephen Lawrence Inquiry Report* and the Macpherson Inquiry Report, Hewitt makes a case for why, even though public 'repugnance at racial violence was widely expressed and a broad proforma consensus existed over the need to make multicultural societies work, there was also conflict over what multiculturalism meant and how or if it worked in practice'.[13] How we understand the evolving nature of multiculturalism 'continues to influence contemporary struggles over race and justice, migration and settlement and the national policies designed to address them'.[14] What Hewitt terms a 'backlash' to multiculturalism is often taken as a challenge by the authors we examine. Living and thriving in the context of backlash presents unique opportunities, as narratives contend with the tension created by both the lingering promises of multiculturalism *and* the challenges to that model. Importantly, remembering what Hewitt calls the 'two distinct streams'[15] of multiculturalism can frame what it is that writers are trying to balance. On the one hand, we have the 'domestic contexts' that look to the historical and intellectual framework within which the multicultural project resides. This is set alongside the 'international framework' that is 'less susceptible to sudden changes of circumstance and is closely tied to global issues concerning migration, settlement and rights'.[16] Importantly, this second stream is best understood and experienced as part of a broader rights and minority-based discourse[17] that has its political foundations in international institutions, such as the UN. It is what occurs at the intersection of the domestic and the international that becomes relevant when we look to Abdulrazak Gurnah's *By the Sea* (2001).[18] The ways in which 'multiculturalism' is invoked in transnational spaces have also impacted the longevity of the category long after it has eroded and succumbed to fracturing and critique in local and national politics. Domestically, we also need to consider how a multicultural agenda, in seeking to celebrate and find space for community identity, might have also constituted new barriers for cross-community allegiances. For our purposes it is useful to mobilise Lasse Thomassen's understanding of *multiculturalism* as 'a representational space, or a discursive terrain'.[19] An engaged literature does not map the beginning and end of this or that policy; instead, it is in dialogue with the long-lasting residue of social, political, and cultural ideas regardless of their policy use-by-date. In fact, 'multiculturalism' is not a *coherent* representational space.

Within this space there exist a number of competing articulations of the ideas and practices said to define British multiculturalism.[20] That an ethos of multiculturalism might still be pervasive even as it struggles to compete with the fallout of assimilationist political strategies points to its more salutary qualities. Kamila Shamsie's *Home Fire* engages with the complexity of powerful competing ideologies of belonging struggling to gain prominence, whilst Zadie Smith's *White Teeth* both mocks and embraces the possibilities of stretching the category of multiculturalism to its limits. In Monica Ali's *Brick Lane*, it is clear that multiculturalism is a privilege that migrants must aspire to and work hard towards, rather than one into which they are welcomed, in which they will thrive, and to which they can contribute. On the contrary, multiculturalism is often experienced as a tool of separateness. A variegated understanding of liberalism also further complicates the co-option and performance of a multicultural discourse, as it seeks to untether the individual from the multi-layered ties that may bind them at certain moments to a community or communitarian values. We see this in Nikita Lalwani's *Gifted*, where a desire for the migrant family to get ahead and utilise advantages and opportunities made available does not always sit well with the impulse to sit quietly with the comfort of the memory of a violent past and sometimes refuse to participate in any civic gestures of unity. Participation, understood here as a public-facing performance of belonging, is a strain on the characters we encounter in *Brick Lane*, *Gifted*, *By the Sea*, and *Home Fire*. Non-participation can sometimes be seen as a form of resistance to any requirement to have to comply to any spoken or unspoken set of rules constructed to produce visibility around the already-nebulous, but somehow politically quantifiable, category of the multicultural. In other words, characters find themselves in positions where they have to prove allegiances in spaces and institutions designated to discipline them and bring them in line. Airports in *By the Sea* and *Home Fire* perform such functions, as do schools in *Gifted* and *White Teeth*, and even other well-meaning fellow migrants, such as those in *Brick Lane*. Together, institutions and immediate surroundings police the quality of these allegiances and perform the role of the panopticon state.

In their article 'British Multiculturalism after Empire: Immigration, Nationality and Citizenship', Richard T. Ashcroft and Mark Bevir argue that once in power:

> New Labour 'drew on a communitarianism that valorized shared values and an "active citizenship" comprised of both rights and duties. And whereas Thatcher attacked the economic "dependency" engendered by the welfare state, New Labour drew on both new institutional and communitarian conceptions of social capital in order to reduce exclusion.[21]

This active citizenship, then, was the price to pay for an open invitation to the multicultural family. In Zadie Smith's *White Teeth*, the characters' reliving of their participation in the Second World War from the margins of empire is seen as almost a duty. Men and women from minority backgrounds must perform their right to be included in a 'Western' framework through exposing their social capital – to belong in these texts is to be aware of the obligation to position oneself on an axis populated by unquestioned shared signifiers. The acquisition of such social capital and the labour required to transpose it accurately is always gruelling and rarely successful. Monica Ali's *Brick Lane* (2003)[22] makes clear the deep disappointment at the heart of actions designed to showcase the subtle moves of cultural and social capital that somehow seem to miss their mark. The 2000 Commission on the Future of Multi-ethnic Britain, termed 'the "high-water mark" of postwar British multiculturalism',[23] had a 'remit to analyse the current [1990s] state of multi-ethnic Britain and to propose ways of countering racial discrimination and disadvantage and making Britain a confident and vibrant multicultural society at ease with its rich diversity'.[24] The literature that we examine is at pains to reveal the richness of individual and communities though struggles to always reflect a 'vibrant multicultural society' *at ease* with this richness. The first of the six tasks identified by the commission was that of 'rethinking the national story and national identity'.[25] Unsurprisingly, perhaps, the report cites the Nigerian British author Ben Okri on the question of the stories we tell ourselves:

> Many of the current dominant stories in Britain need to be rethought, for they omit large sections of the population. Britain is a recent creation, not ancient, and colonialism and empire were integral to its making. Therefor virtually all

current citizens are part of a single story – though their ancestors, of course, engaged with it in a range of different ways.[26]

Of course, this issue of citizenship as precursor to engagement with the nation and its history is also questioned in Gurnah's *By the Sea* and Shamsie's *Home Fire* (2017).[27] Citizenship as conferred by the state enables certain forms of engagements and bestows certain rights. When this is refused or removed via the use of laws that, as Shamsie notes, 'make migrants feel perpetually insecure',[28] then the relationship to this thing called 'Britain' is up for re-evaluation. This insecurity was exacerbated in particular from the 2000s onward, first during the North of England race riots in 2001, followed by local and global events, such as 9/11 and the War on Terror, 'to which the government responded with a more strident emphasis on the need for immigrant and minority communities to assimilate British values and traditions'.[29] Legal changes extended to a 'tightening of immigration and asylum law and draconian anti-terrorism legislation'[30] also took hold. Writing that turns to the experience of refugees, migrants, and the displaced makes evident how important the earlier discourses are in shaping the various forms of nationalist ideology. The work of Abdulrazak Gurnah brings into sharp relief the difficulty of convincingly articulating the multifaceted and idealistic landscape of what Giorgio Agamben points to as 'the dissolution of the nation-state and its sovereignty'.[31] Though we may be tempted to hold up the refugee and the asylum seeker as the emblem of all that is dysfunctional about the discourse on sovereignty, and although this does allow us to reposition the refugee's agency as something ideological and even practical, the material effects of displacement as articulated in, for example, *By the Sea* are unknowable in their totality.

This complicates the instrumentalisation of the figure of the refugee for future-thinking post-national paradigms. The refugee and asylum seeker in this context may give shape to this imagined dissolution of the nation state or endow it with different values, but it also reminds us of the power of nation states and their continued desirability and, by extension, the sacrifices made to attain a place within them. 'Refugee.... Asylum', says Saleh Omar, Abdulrazak's protagonist in *By the Sea*, on arrival to Gatwick Airport (*BTS*, 9). The image of the border is an important one that embodies these fears and aspirations at the same time as it highlights the profound injustices that lead to such circumstances. In the words of Mohsin Hamid, the response of states, to 'simply hardening borders and watching refugees drown offshore or bleed to death on razor wire'[32] cannot endure as it impacts what we might want to call 'national character'. Britain (and other nations across the globe) will need to decide whether they wish to 'become the sorts of societies that are capable of taking the steps that will be required to stop the flow of migration'.[33] As Kristin Shaw has pointed out, 'asylum seekers and refugees complicate (and force a reconceptualization of) unconditional hospitality, revealing the stark limitations of cosmopolitan discourses when discussing issues of national belonging, humanitarian intervention, and openness to otherness'.[34] In the context of Brexit, these issues become even starker, as those campaigning in its favour sought to undermine any redeeming qualities of a looser but no less constructive multiculturalism. In targeting the category without qualification or nuance, the baby was effectively thrown out with the bathwater. As Ashcroft and Bevir note:

> Brexit was driven by conflicting evaluations of multiculturalism, national identity, and the worth of multiple citizenships. Resistance to immigrant multiculturalism was a substantial factor in the Leave vote. Immigration, multiculturalism, race, and security were frequently conflated in public discourse during the campaign. . . . This played into the narrative that *multiculturalism has damaged social cohesion*, making Brexit part of a broader contest over national identity.[35]

As Anne Marie Fortier argues in *Multicultural Horizons*, after the events in London of 7/7, 'debates around the benefits and failures of multiculturalism were reanimated . . . blaming it for fostering national *disunity* and for being the root cause of the attacks in London because of its benevolence and soft-touch approach to cultural difference'.[36] The consequence of this prolonged debate permeated and, to some extent, dominated the British political discourse around multiculturalism in the years preceding the Brexit vote. The consequences of this were anticipated by writers such as Kamila Shamsie, who, in *Home Fire*, imagined an Asian-born Home Secretary eager to double down on the rights to citizenship. His exclusionary rhetoric reshapes the parameters of national belonging and citizenship, reframing these as gifts bestowed by a benevolent state that can, when angered, revoke such rights. *Home Fire* goes on to explore the pressure points that make up the context of imagined radicalisation and gives space to the various alternative violent narratives of belonging that can, in certain circumstances, become attractive (and no less intense) as they purport to give back dignity and purpose to individuals. *Home Fire* does not shy away from articulating the immense privileges available to those who find themselves profiting from their positions as protectors of an insular and inward-looking state, keen to protect citizens it deems worth protecting from home-grown 'radicalisation' at the same time as it ignores the deteriorating social conditions to which communities are forced to acclimatise and which might, in time, produce some of the insupportable social and economic circumstances where radical rhetoric might indeed flourish. When inflammatory rhetoric replaces the slow graft of solidarity and cohesion, the results are different forms of extremism, whether it be extreme obedience to a cruel state or fanatical belief in alternative forms of governance. Where the 'multiculture', as Fortier terms it, could be 'put to work . . . mobilised to produce desires, identities, anxieties . . . in the reconfiguration of what connects inhabitants of the national space to one another, as well as to the nation itself',[37] the destructive version of this highlights the equally seductive spaces of disconnection and betrayal that might fuel alternative visions of solidarity.

As Susheila Nasta argues:

> The more visible presence of a substantial black and Asian population in Britain during the years following the Second World War has not only

challenged embedded conceptions of 'Englishness', an imagined homeland built on ideas of purity, rootedness and cultural dominance, but also brought into closer view some of the less palatable realities underlying the ancient myth of England as a green and pleasant land.[38]

This visibility engendered the cultural and political category of the multicultural – a category that found itself having to somehow coordinate the complexity of diversity and mobilise political strategies around it, all the while experiencing what Corinne Fowler has recently termed this 'green *unpleasant* land'[39](my emphasis). This chapter looks at the work of those writers who capture the growing unease around national identity in the context of what Fortier has called 'cultural and ethno-racial pluralism'.[40]

The texts discussed here boldly rethink the parameters and boundaries within which identity and belonging are formed. They are all, in different ways, innovative, both thematically and formally, as they seek to question and complicate a stable or authoritative idea of Britishness. As the authors of Britishness beyond the New Britain argue, 'conviviality in Britain is challenged from within and without, as discourses about new forms of migration, fundamentalism, surveillance, regionalism and British-European relations suggest'.[41] Simon Featherstone notes in his reflection of the work and legacy of C. L. R James that postcolonial writers and thinkers are to be engaged with from their vantage point of 'participating in the construction of new nations and intellectual traditions'.[42] Their works, we argue, open up fresh ways of considering the complexities of belonging. Furthermore, as John McLeod has argued, and we would be inclined to agree, given the analyses to come, 'postcolonial fiction anticipated, apprehended, and critically explored the political and cultural milieu which facilitated the outcome of the 2016 European Union (EU) referendum'.[43] Writing specifically of authors such as John Lanchester's 2012 *Capital*, Caryl Phillips's 2004 *A Distant Shore*, and Zadie Smith's 2012 *NW*, McLeod posits that:

> There has been gathering for quite some time in literary fiction the signposting and critique of the political, social, and cultural entanglements that have directly contributed to the Brexit imbroglio. Postcolonial writers have contributed significantly to this activity, and over many years, not least by exposing and exploring the calcification of prejudice, the intensification of malevolence, and the growing disparities of wealth and impoverishment that have characterized Britain's hostile environment since at least the turn of the century – to the extent that the result of the referendum should not have come as a great surprise to readers who had been paying attention. To be blunt: we were warned.[44]

We would agree that the warning signs had been there for quite some time but that, within the context of a series of attempted policies and ideologies aimed at various attempts or formulations towards the enactment of a convivial culture, these signs were perhaps masked. In addition to this, and supporting many of the argumentative claims we put forward in Chapter 2, McLeod reminds us how, for a moment in the post-war era, the end of empire served as a premise from which to imagine a *new* post-empire British identity. Reflecting on Matthew Whittle's inspiring work, McLeod points to how 'such post-war endeavours were part of an important critical re-imagining of Britishness firmly in the light of decolonisation in Asia, Africa and the Caribbean'.[45] McLeod argues that it was

> precisely this critical trajectory, one that has also helped open a space for subsequent postcolonial literary explorations of the metropolis towards the end of the last century, that Brexit has hoped to stymie by determinedly remodulating conceptions of both British imperial identity and the legacy of World War II to serve reactionary not radical ends.[46]

These legacies, then, can also be said to have always been, in a way, residing behind attempts to fully explore alternatives and have never quite quit the scene (manifesting in various forms as either a discursive/performative nostalgia at best or one that fed into right-wing populist politics at worst). It is useful to keep in mind that imperial nostalgia was at its height in the early 1980s with the release of the films *Gandhi* (1981), *Heat and Dust* (1983), *The Jewel in the Crown* (1984), and *White Mischief* (1987).

For postcolonialists interested in the enduring creation and mythologisation of nation and the enabling but also destructive ideologies of belonging that came in its wake, Salman Rushdie's *Midnight's Children* (1981) provided a blueprint. As Cathy Cundy notes, 'one of the chief achievements of *Midnight's Children* is the way in which is serves as a testament to the importance of memory in the recreation of history and the constitution of the individual's identity' (Cundy, 32). If *Midnight's Children* acts as a type of record of the birth of a nation, then the structures that give shape to that nation immediately set to work reconstructing and recreating history in order to catch up with the present moment. This temporal problem, the one of myth-making as a nation constructs itself, also refashions memory. 'Rushdie admits that the act of reclaiming the past is subject to the vagaries of the memory on which its reconstruction relies' (Cundy, 33). The stories of all nations, we could argue, to a degree, also depend on the 'vagaries' of memories. *Midnight's Children* acknowledges this whilst also revealing how authorial control manipulates memory and 'truth', showing them to be contingent on the needs and desires of national narratives. The reliability of the historian is brought into question, but the wonder of narrative is dramatised as the certainty often attributed to historical accounts is rendered farcical in *how* Rushdie writes events. Nicole Thiara notes Rushdie's 'unorthodox history-writing, without proper explanation or referencing',[47] and points to his erratic and improvised, chaotic, and elliptical narrative, which is, in turn, confusing and shocking, but also points towards the risk of considering the story of imperial history as *anything other* than chaotic.

Midnight's Children articulates *how* national narratives are made. It highlights the often-arbitrary nature of inclusionary and exclusionary tactics that shape these national narratives and, over time, fuel identity politics. Rushdie's writing as a method for rethinking cultural hierarchies helped shape our understanding of the trajectory of contemporary postcolonial literature in the sense that it centred the loss of empire and the project of decolonisation as an unfinished process now playing out in multicultural Britain. Texts such as *Midnight's Children* re-embedded the long history of empire and challenged us to rethink disparities and dependencies in different ways. Where *Midnight's Children* provided a frame for the reconsideration of empire as a stable and somewhat noble founding myth, Salman Rushdie's *The Satanic Verses* (1988) was disruptive in a very different way. For Anne-Marie Fortier, 'the Rushdie affair of the late 1980s was a key moment in shifting the focus onto religious faith within political debates about multiculture'.[48] In *From Fatwa to Jihad: How the World Changed*, Kenan Malik argued that:

> The Rushdie affair was the moment at which a new Islam dramatically announced itself as a major political issue in Western society. It was also the moment when Britain realized it was facing a new kind of social conflict. . . . It was the first major *cultural* conflict, a controversy quite unlike anything that Britain had previously experienced.[49]

The challenge of the aftermath of 'the Rushdie affair' was to understand how such a cultural conflict had gone unnoticed for so long in the mainstream. We had to consider whether the affair later legitimised the focus on religious otherness and the ensuing political parameters set up to control and manage this or whether it revealed the depth of ignorance at the heart of the multicultural enterprise. As Dobbernack, Meer, and Modood note in their article 'Muslim Political Agency in British Politics', in the context of how multiple 'misrecognitions' have directed 'negative responses to the Muslim presence in British politics':[50]

> It has been suggested that the experience of stigmatization, in the aftermath of the *Satanic Verses* and exacerbated after 9/11, has led to political orientations that are primarily reactive and articulate grievances. There is a risk of reductionism in such accounts. British Muslim politics is characterized by diversity and, although the concern to defeat stigmas may be widely shared, political objectives differ in line with different religious, strategic, and ideological commitments and follow distinct grammars of political agency.[51]

This assumption that the Rushdie affair somehow legitimised the public expression of social grievance is one that *Home Fire* communicates. What *Home Fire* also articulates, however, is this complex and 'distinct grammar' of the differing experiences of Muslims in Britain across a vast array of characters and events. Moving away from an emphasis on 'grievances' opens up a space for 'the proliferation of alternative sites of Muslim civil society', and in our view, cultural engagement, such as that offered by *Home Fire*, permits a 'political pluralisation of the public sphere'.[52] As Claire Forbes argues in her work on the political and social consequences of the 2001 onwards media focus on Muslims, 'if the increased coverage of Muslims in the UK press has generated greater awareness of Islam among the public, it has also served to highlight Muslims' political as well as religious identity'.[53] Citing Poole, Forbes emphasises how 'a continual association of Muslims with immigration, sometimes as illegal immigrants or those seeking unwarranted asylum, positions them as a drain on resources, as importing alien values and practices to the UK and, therefore, a threat to mainstream British values'.[54] The literature we examine positions Muslims in Britain as strident creators of their own identity politics, able to offer robust responses to generalised accusations who also understand their vulnerability as individuals and community as recipients of a coarse discourse based on what Forbes describes as 'mediatisation': where 'social interaction, within the respective institutions, between institutions and in society at large, takes place via the media'.[55] *Home Fire* is particularly interested in the consequences of prolonged mediatisation, and this is an issue we explore in depth in what follows.

If particular communities and their vulnerability to changing national discourses are the focus of *Home Fire*, then Zadie Smith's *White Teeth* rehearsed different but nevertheless equally crucial social and cultural experiences that consolidated the critique of empire as a continued, legitimate, and unfinished ambition for fiction. *White Teeth* pursued, played with, and tested notions of purity, origin, and wholeness in ways that queried the defining premise of all nationalist projects. It problematised at the same time as it demonstrated what Dominic Head termed 'the process of national redefinition' that came with rethinking 'post-war Britain facing the challenges of Empire'.[56] In her analysis of intergenerational trauma in the work of Zadie Smith, Perez Zapata argues how the novel 'presents readers with the need to redefine the understanding of trauma through the concept of "original trauma"', which has, in turn, revealed the 'need of Britain, as a nation, to remember its colonial past and face the grave consequences of historical amnesia in postcolonial times'.[57] Perez Zapata extends the understanding of trauma (a term used in the novel) to include

> the erasure of one's origins and the complete assimilation, rather than integration, into English culture and the adoption of preconceived identifications with the dominant culture are a response to the unbelonging caused by ethnicity and, more acutely in this case, by class and place.[58]

Seen in particular in the Iqbal family in *White Teeth*, marginalisation here is understood to be a space where 'shameful histories' reside.[59] Events in the Iqbal family, and in particular the character Magid's desire to step away from any sign of his Bangladeshi Muslim heritage, lead him to imagine himself as Mark Smith, with all the attending characteristics that make up his narrow vision of 'English' culture. Perez Zapata notes:

> Magid's trauma of origins is thus intrinsically connected with class difference and it is his desire to belong to the ordinary, middle-class English population, to the 'everybody', that drives him to reject and subsequently erase any trace of his Muslim, Bangladeshi origin. Assimilation seems the only possible route to belonging.[60]

This brings us up against the very problem of such categorisations that Smith is also keen to question in a broader sense in the context of a political and cultural multiculturalism. The novel does not so much champion multiculturalism as it, instead, gives shape to how such a concept might materialise and what obstacles it might come up against in the context of assimilationist and integrationist discourses. Incredibly, Ulrike Tancke reminds us of a time when the novel was considered to have engaged in a 'facile take on the contemporary multicultural reality'.[61] We recognise the position that Smith's 'novel seemed to tie in with the prevailing cheerfully positive vision of multicultural Britain in the early Blair years',[62] and we did read *White Teeth* within the political context of the emerging optimistic discourses on multiculturalism. As Graham MacPhee argues, Andrea Levy's *Small Island*, Smith's *White Teeth*, and Monica Ali's *Brick Lane* perhaps present 'more optimist endings' than 'other recent novels that consider muti-cultural British society'.[63] For MacPhee, *Small Island*, in its ending, engages more deeply with 'an ominous picture of the racism of postwar Britain' and imagines the shape of worst things to come. For all its perceived optimism, however, *White Teeth* does engage fully with the diversity of what a British post-imperial identity might look like when both the legacy of imperialism and the consequences of this on identity are being questioned. As Fortier argues, we might understand '"multiculture" as a key site where the politics and culture of the nation and its limits are embattled'.[64] This productive proposition allows us to also view multicultural articulations as moments that attempt to anticipate the sense of an inevitable *embattled* landscape, working desperately to provide alternative viable solutions for what, in all cases, must mean some form of compromise. Fortier's position influenced our thinking around the role of writing in supporting to establish 'what national issues are at stake in celebrating, questioning, or dispensing with multiculturalism'.[65] Here, we viewed *multiculturalism* as a set of ideas that helped shape how discourses of belonging were formed in reaction to the changing boundaries of the national imaginary rather than as an end product of some form of forced or coercive edict or, indeed, some depoliticised clarion call for us all to come together and live in harmony. For us, the question was not whether the multiculture failed or succeeded but how it was instrumentalised in the service of arguing the very meaning of national expansion and inclusion and, ultimately, transformation. To take into account that this was, indeed, embattled is productive in that it reveals the very material consideration that multiculturalism sought to address. The Commission on the Future of Multi-Ethnic Britain's October 2000 report moved the debate to the

> new ground of re-imagining Britain not only as a multicultural society or a multi-national state, but as a multicultural *nation* in the sense that Britishness is conceived as a unifying *identity* and *community* characterized by a long history of diversity and mixing.[66]

This retrospective challenge was perhaps too ambitious, and *White Teeth* undoubtedly experimented with this thought at the same time as it reflected on the often 'painful effects of ethnic mixing and the blurring of racial and cultural boundaries'.[67] Tancke prefers to focus on the novel's 'critique of fashionable multicultural

'We Have Been Made Again', 1980–2016   149

discourse and the multicultural reality' and notes that 'underneath its surface comedy, *White Teeth* presents uncomfortable truths not just about British multicultural society, but also about the human condition at large'.[68] This long history of diversity and mixing was memorably visualised by the family tree in the second half of Zadie Smith's *White Teeth*.

It is not possible to look at this tree and not laugh at how it challenges the idealism that often underpins narratives of purity. In one deft move, Smith complicates any idea of certainty around origins and, in the process, disturbs the possibility that such certainty might even exist. What is important here is the fabrication of discourses around origins as stable markers of authenticity. The subsequent social and cultural ideologies that might arise from these are here shown to be based on very shaky ground, indeed. And yet rather than move in the direction of cultural despondency on how this uncertainty may only evolve into radicalism (though this does also happen in the novel with the future mouse team), *White Teeth* explores

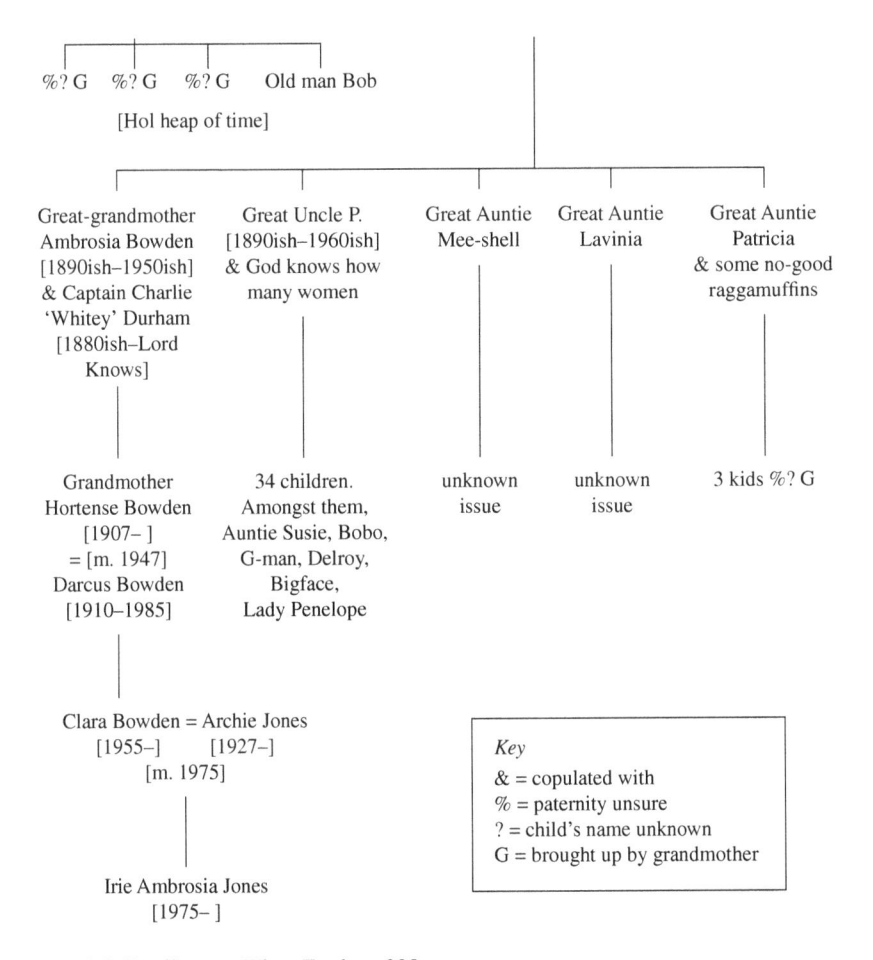

```
    %? G    %? G    %? G    Old man Bob

         [Hol heap of time]


Great-grandmother    Great Uncle P.         Great Auntie    Great Auntie    Great Auntie
Ambrosia Bowden      [1890ish–1960ish]      Mee-shell       Lavinia         Patricia
[1890ish–1950ish]    & God knows how                                        & some no-good
& Captain Charlie    many women                                             raggamuffins
'Whitey' Durham
[1880ish–Lord
   Knows]


Grandmother          34 children.            unknown         unknown         3 kids %? G
Hortense Bowden      Amongst them,           issue           issue
[1907– ]             Auntie Susie, Bobo,
= [m. 1947]          G-man, Delroy,
Darcus Bowden        Bigface,
[1910–1985]          Lady Penelope


Clara Bowden = Archie Jones         ┌─────────────────────────────┐
[1955– ]       [1927– ]             │ Key                         │
       [m. 1975]                    │ & = copulated with          │
                                    │ % = paternity unsure        │
                                    │ ? = child's name unknown    │
                                    │ G = brought up by grandmother│
                                    └─────────────────────────────┘
Irie Ambrosia Jones
     [1975– ]
```

Figure 3.1 Family tree, *White Teeth*, p. 338.

the possibilities that might arise in the context where this very uncertainty is used to challenge any form of social exclusion based on ethnic, racial, or national grounds. This seemed to be a broader and more engaging way to come at *White Teeth* rather than to view it as somehow uncovering 'hybrid multicultural identities'.[69] In fact, the family tree seems, in our view, to be mocking the expectation of certainty around the issue of origins and roots whilst still highlighting the investment that individuals and community might have towards these categories, depending on historical, cultural, and political needs.

In other words, a consequence of the uncertain 'origins' of a single family or the partial certainty obscured by the admired structures of record-keeping and the subsequent undermining of the privilege of origin *itself* might form the blueprint for a more inclusive society and, indeed, a redefinition of inclusion that is far from a one-way top-down process. Smith's horticultural analysis also provides many different ways of thinking about how change comes about and the pitfalls of celebrating an outmoded idea of purity as a legacy of the Second World War and the clear historical dangers in doing so. As Perez Zapata argues, looking closely at the 'transgenerational trauma in the Bowden and Iqbal families reveals new facets of original trauma and exposes how the particularities of each family's traumas are entangled in broader cultural and historical ones'.[70] The context of imperialism and the Second World War, where all manner of identities was put to the test, extolls a particular kind of pressure of identification. For example, the character Samad 'struggles with class, race, and the anxieties that arise out of his double colonial identification as both Bengali and British', and it is in his participation in the war where he has the realisation that 'colonialism has split his identity' – fighting for the British army in India and becoming confused about where he belongs and whether it matters.[71] Perez Zapata argues that Smith 'seems to suggest that that it is not the trauma of war, or rather the trauma of surviving war, but colonialism that has wounded Samad's psyche and generated a sense of abandonment and unbelonging prior to the experience of war'.[72] This makes MacPhee's assertion all the more potent when he points out that we need to consider how '*all* postwar British literature needs to be read with a consciousness of the continuing relevance of that imperial legacy'.[73] *White Teeth*'s rehearsing of some of the questions that linger on from the Second World War makes clear the extent to which postcolonial subjects enact their positions through making explicit the imbrication of British identity with the unfinished project of colonialism. One aspect of this legacy is the unearthing of the seductive and somewhat comforting nature of the origin myth (to be embraced as part of a myth of nation) – to this Smith responds with a narrative that both performs and, at the same time, questions forms of identity formations and complicates any enduring usefulness of origin myths.

White Teeth can also be read as a response to Gilroy's persuasive argument on melancholia and convivial culture, which acts as a warning against complacency in the face of social and cultural impediments to the possibility of a functioning multiculturalism. Where Gilroy is concerned that certain arguments may

> salve the national conscience . . . they [also] compound the marginality of colonial history, spurn its substantive lessons, and obstruct the development of

multiculturalism by making the formative experience of empire less profound and less potent in shaping the life of colonizing powers than it actually was.[74]

White Teeth attempts to both give shape to these substantive lessons at the same time as it wants to reanimate a multicultural project, with all its flaws. The formative experience that Gilroy speaks of is one that must and does haunt the text as the legacy of colonialism permeates the process of a political and social multiculturalism. Smith attempts to somewhat temper the power of origin myths and instead engages thoroughly with the linear and comforting illusion of purity (whether in nature or engineered via mutation) and juxtaposes this with the chaotic nature of people and their lives. However many attempts at control are made via any means available, be it cultural, scientific, or political, to shift narratives in one direction, the element of *chance* is always there to thwart any neat configurations. This contingency is what most influenced our consideration of Smith's contribution to broader questions around writing and its role in the formation and reflection of nation and identity.[75]

Smith's evocations of how events are vulnerable to chance,[76] gaps, inconsistencies, and haphazard connections all reflect, and perhaps even expose, the dangers of attaching too much value to anything that appears to present solutions and certainty. If this is a prelude to thinking about the possibilities of a multicultural society, then this, too, had its detractors. In thinking about Samad's crisis of belonging, I am reminded of Rushdie's essay 'The New Empire Within Britain', where he bemoans 'the call for a "racial harmony"' as 'simply an invitation to shut up and smile while nothing was done about our grievances'.[77] For Rushdie, writing in the early 1990s, multiculturalism was 'the last token gesture towards British blacks', and he argued for it to be 'exposed, like "integration" and "racial harmony", for the "sham" it was'.[78] Smith attempted to envision the political and social complexities of the work of a multicultural discourse, but *White Teeth* also critiqued any attempt to render this move benign. What Smith termed 'Happy Multicultural Land' . . . was not clear in its offerings – it was certainly not the 'green and pleasant libertarian land of the free', and neither was it 'neutral'. What *White Teeth* allowed us to see was that, in practice, whatever 'baggage' was expected to be given up in favour of some idealised national harmony was too much (and could be seen as one of the sources of that original trauma). Of immigrants and their desires, Smith noted that 'they cannot escape their history any more than you yourself can lose your shadow' (*WT*, 466). Dominic Head also saw the novel as treading a fine line in representing what work a particular vision of multiculturalism might do.[79] This was perhaps to celebrate some part of the multicultural project against an image of it that had developed that instead supported a performance of what Fortier calls 'legitimate and illegitimate patriotisms along the lines of pride and shame', and how these might have led to social and political moves that would seek to erase 'certain histories, and to sanitize Britishness under a veneer of tolerance'.[80] In other words, *White Teeth* experimented with the cost of pursuing the image of the 'greenandpleasantlibertarianlandofthefree', where embattled histories had still to run their course.[81] What is interesting for scholars and readers alike here, of course, is that although there was a time when multiculturalism was discussed as a political project and its ostensible demise in terms of a series of failed policies, questions that arose as part of that project were profound. Take Tony Blair's speech 'Multiculturalism and Integration', given at 10 Downing Street in December 2006, the year of the London 7/7 bombing, for example, which reveals how durable (though contingent) the concept was:

> When it comes to our essential values, the belief in democracy, the rule of law, tolerance, equal treatment for all, respect for this country and its shared heritage – then that is where we come together, it is what gives us what we hold in common; it is what gives the right to call ourselves British. . . . The right to be in a multicultural society was always implicitly balanced by a duty to integrate, to be part of Britain, to be British and Asian, British and black, British and white.[82]

It is not clear what was here meant by 'shared heritage' (which also includes a history of violence against Asian and Black communities) insofar as the various components to be shared often told a history of intolerance and oppression rather than tolerance and equal treatment. To reverse-engineer a shared past as a platform upon which to build a duty to nevertheless integrate in the *present* was paradoxical and clearly confusing. For what need for integration in the face of a shared heritage? What we understand here instead is that this was, in fact, a call for a collective *forgetting* of a painful shared heritage, that of imperialism and colonialism, in the service of a new world order where Britishness was associated with the rule of law, and integration enacted through the sharing of (certain) values and a reconfiguration of heritage. In *Decolonizing Colonial Heritage*, Britta Timm Knudsen et al. argue that although 'heritage is notoriously difficult to define, resting as it does alongside words and ideas like culture, tradition and identity', what really is at stake, beyond what 'form of material relics' heritage takes, is 'heritage considered as a discourse in which each present constructs its own past (whether for strategic political reasons or through preservation policies)', or in other words, 'heritage as a renewable resource that is transformed in any given present'.[83]

This new shared 'heritage' would now need to be re-established in a way that best countered perceived current threats and presented in such a way as to remain recognisable as a 'shared' one. In other words, what was being asked of the nation was participation in a collective act of amnesia, one vehemently rejected in narratives from Monica Ali's *Brick Lane* to Abdulrazak Gurnah's *By the Sea*, Nikita Lalwani's *Gifted*, and Kamila Shamsie's *Home Fire*, among others. This harsh and often aggressive aspect of ongoing nation formation was here exposed as a process built on the sacrifices or silences of others. As Tancke reminds us,

> beyond its commentary on contemporary multiculturalism, what *White Teeth* promotes is a set of unsettling truths: the inescapability of roots and history in human lives, the impact of biology and the body on our sense of self, and the violence intrinsic to human affairs.[84]

Whilst articulation of a national heritage my seek to impose a version of the past that serves contemporary needs, writers such as Smith show that 'under close scrutiny, nothing is ever pure or simple, all roots are entangled, all binary structures open to dismantling'.[85] In *White Teeth*, even the characters seemingly most wedded to proclaiming their fundamentalist beliefs are subject to mockery by Smith, and her deliberate mixing and matching reveal how 'these irreverent genealogies underscore the hybrid nature of religious identity'.[86] Genealogy continues to work in the novel to poke fun at any category or action that seeks to present certainty as its structuring motif, and as Magdalena Maczynska notes, overall, *White Teeth* shows up a 'preference for heterodox solutions and identities'.[87]

Integration, how we might understand it and critique it as a thought experiment, policy, and lived reality, frames our reading of Monica Ali's *Brick Lane*. The context of the events of the summer of 2001 and the later attacks on 7/7 gave rise to vehement critiques on how 'multiculturalism had encouraged Muslims to separate themselves and live by their own values, resulting in extremism and, ultimately, the fostering of a mortal home-grown terrorist threat'.[88] Keeping separate was, however, very narrowly conceived as reactive rather than as a means of protection and guardianship. Muslims became too visible, and the ensuing debates around immigration were often uncritically folded in. Writing in 2007, Arun Kundnani reminds us how, after 2001, 'existing right-wing critics of multiculturalism . . . found allies from the centre and left of the political spectrum [and] all agree[d] that "managing" cultural diversity [was] at the root of many of the key problems facing British society'.[89] A commitment to the idea of the tolerance of difference and diversity gave way to new 'integrationism', which redefined integration as, effectively, assimilation to British values rather than, as Roy Jenkins had stated in 1966, 'equal opportunity accompanied by cultural diversity, in an atmosphere of mutual tolerance'.[90]

We consider Ali's *Brick Lane* as a work that addresses the tensions that underpin a performative uncritical embracing of heritage within the context of multiculturalism (for we argue that there is never an uncritical acceptance of top-down policies aimed at social engineering). In addition to this, we look at the conceptualisation of the figure of the migrant in order to better understand how their representation contributes to an alternative way of thinking about a national rhetoric trying to backtrack from a seemingly tolerant discourse around ethnic and cultural diversity. In other words, unfolding events in *Brick Lane* consider the sacrifices made across the spectrum and, in particular, identify the extent of pain and suffering in the face of unimaginable experiences of loneliness and shame. *Brick Lane* is sensitive to the everyday humiliations that arise in the most unexpected of places but that incrementally reveal a hostile environment in the making. In particular, Ali pays attention to how fear can also breed a particular kind of insularity: an insularity that can be read as reactionary. The novel was written in the political climate post-2001, that 'focused on the need to integrate Muslims', where 'individual and institutional racisms, which remained the principle barriers to the creation of a genuinely cohesive society, received little attention'.[91] In light of this, it is perhaps not surprising to have come up against critics of Ali's novel that take issue with its representation of unapologetic individualism and liberalism.[92] However, 'while many postcolonial critics are loath to admit it, their relativistic defence of cultural differences is not free of problems', argues Ali Rezaie,[93] and might unwittingly sideline Ali's political project to 'show how liberalism better ensures the autonomy and equality of women in non-Western societies and cultures than relativistic discourses such as postcolonialism and multiculturalism'.[94]

The protagonist Nazneen's relationship to her husband, Chanu, and Chanu's particular brand of disappointment in the trajectory of his London life is particularly interesting to us. The Tower Hamlets of 1985 London are the backdrop to the action. The novel performs a neat trick, however – by limiting most of Nazneem's space to Brick Lane and to her home and expanding her inner life via her sister's letters, we are made aware of the vast and largely unknowable landscapes largely unavailable to integrationist discourses but nevertheless representing a risk to them. Zadie Smith's *inescapable history* cannot be contained and finds expression. This dynamic comes up against Tony Blair's idea of the 'common', for any commonality in this context is almost always imaginary, as is the fantasy of a 'shared heritage'. The expansive inner lives of first-generation migrants nourished by memories challenge any undermining of the labour required for a particular form of integration. Critics have convincingly defended a reading of *Brick Lane* that sees Nazneen's transformation from 'passivity to agency'[95] in particular, as it is contrasted with the endlessly difficult life of her sister, Hasina, in Bangladesh. However, Nazneen's 'journey' is not a swift one, and the stages of her adaption are painful and full of sorrow. *Brick Lane* formulates an allegiance to another home community and its values and positions these as very real adversaries – another complex heritage – to integrationist politics that might be cruel and unforgiving. Chanu also uses his memories of Bangladesh to support his bitter disappointment in the context of a political rhetoric aimed to further exclude him as a Muslim.

Nazneen's initial physical limitation, contained as she is to her flat and her immediate geographical surroundings, is in direct antithesis to her expansive *inner* life, where new connections are made and allegiances reaffirmed. As Nick Bentley points out, 'the technique of defamiliarization [in the novel] is useful here for describing the experience of the newly arrived migrant'.[96] It is also, however, a technique that is just as useful in disrupting the idea that familiarity with any place is not, in any case, always socially and culturally constituted. The Bangladesh of Nazneem's past is not fixed, somewhere to return to that is somehow congealed in the past. It is a place brimming with action and change and, in fact, requires a process of refamiliarisation and renewal via, among other things, her sister's letters. The interaction here is complex and rich, and though it may seem safe, it is also a space of tension and worry for Nazneen. Nostalgia is, indeed, laborious, as it requires engagement with multiple perspectives. We are indebted to Stephen Morton's expansive interpretation of Nazneem's actions in the text and build on his articulation of how simply viewing 'Nazneen's narrative as multicultural bildungsroman' takes away from how we might see the novel as one that instead questions how 'liberal discourses of women's empowerment have been increasingly subordinated to the economic rationality of neoliberalism'.[97] That this empowerment, in our view, forms in very small and localised domestic spaces can be seen as an even more substantial threat to the mirage of neoliberal productivity and the performance of public labour. 'Against the promise of happiness associated with the lures of diaspora', Morton suggests that *Brick Lane* 'helps to illuminate the ways in which late liberal discourses of multiculturalism are increasingly subordinated to the economic norms and values of neoliberalism'.[98] In other words, time spent in reverie about home, and time spent *at home*, where labour is not visible, is potentially time wasted, as are other forms of labour that do not connect outwards towards the visible marketplace. Monica Ali's insistence, and, as we shall see, Nikita Lalwani's too, on depicting these spaces of the imagination where other affective dimensions are formed, functions as a response to any position that might want to link migration to productivity and to quantify engagement through measurable forms. We might, indeed, see *Brick Lane* as a novel that dramatises the intersection of multiple diaspora experiences, interior and exterior, as characters navigate, whether consciously or unconsciously, multicultural idealism (which would expect visible labour) and neoliberal materiality (which assumes that economic advancement always already underlines migrant agency). This is also visible in Lalwani's *Gifted*,[99] where the teenage protagonist, Rumi, is singled out at her school for her mathematical talent. Her father, Mahesh, believes that the 'the term "gifted" was meaningless to them as a family' and, when invited by a media interview to comment on his daughter's success, is surprised when asked about 'the Indian immigrant's particularly intense drive to achieve' (*Gifted*, 181–182). His surprise does, however, indicate his lack of loyalty to this particular narrative on migrant (economic and academic) success. What the question does point to, however, is the expectation of success that belies a fear of failure. When Rumi forgoes her predicted brilliant career in mathematics and runs away from her Oxford exams, the media response is to, however, *own* her achievements as British: 'Police are searching the entire country for one of *Britain's* brainiest girls' (my emphasis) (*Gifted*, 271).

Monica Ali is also sensitive to the performance of the well-intentioned migrant, hypervigilant to forms of surveillance that shape how actions are perceived. *Brick Lane* points to the essential unknowability of the migrant's past through drawing on the vast landscape of interiority shaped by multiple, often unknowable, forces. Ali's depictions of Nazneen's husband Chanu's broken dreams of migration are poignant, beholden as he is to the measures of success that are out of his control:

> When I came I was a young man. I had ambitions. Big dreams. When I got off the aeroplane, I had my degree certificate in my suitcase and a few pounds in my pocket. I thought that there would be a red carpet laid out for me. I was going to join the Civil Service and become Private Secretary to the Prime Minister. . . . That was my plan. And then I found things were a bit different.

> These people here didn't know the difference between me, who stepped off an aeroplane with a degree certificate, and the peasants who jumped off the boat possessing only the lice on their heads. . . . I did this and that. Whatever I could. So much hard work. . . . All the begging letters from home I burned.
>
> (*BL*, 26)

Chanu's deep desire to be 'seen' as a worthy colonial subject travelling to the imperial centre is thwarted. All the effort that he has put in to act as mediator between the two worlds is both exhausting and disappointing, as it affords Chanu no particular leverage or advantage in public life. In fact, so disappointing is the reality that awaits him that Chanu cuts off all ties to home, ashamed to admit his failures. Chanu then transfers this deep disappointment to his wife, whom he chastises for not mastering English. Ali astutely dramatises the ways in which different requirements around cultural adaptation sometimes open up new fissures in family dynamics. Linguistic proficiency and its associated cultural mastery are here for Chanu intrinsically tied to survival. His 'conquering' of English is a small victory that enables him to work and provide for his family and, in turn, justify the sacrifices he has made and the aggression he has endured. It does not, however, adequately compensate for the feelings of inadequacy he experiences and the lack of respect he has to confront. His education in Bangladesh, which has enabled him to quote from 'Chaucer or Dickens or Hardy' is rendered worthless (*BL*, 29). These accomplishments offer no route to intellectual recognition – neither have they facilitated acculturation. Gauri Viswanathan's now-seminal work on the centrality of the promotion of English literature as part of the project of empire pointed in particular to the role of the Bildungsroman and how it prioritised 'personality development' with the explicit purpose of 'inserting the mature individual into the accepted social spaces of the modern nation-state'.[100] In the context of migration, knowledges gleaned and experiences formed in the former colonial context might be expected to have transformative effects in the postcolonial centre, acting as shorthand and making room for individuals new to social spaces. Echoing Bhabha's ambivalent formulation of the mimic man, Chanu, however, finds that this education does not afford him the cultural currency he had hoped for and that it instead leaves him half-formed, neither here nor there, unable to seek validation from either space.

Brick Lane works to reveal how specific experiences inform migrant contexts. In particular, the novel reflects on how inclusion is constructed. From citizenship classes to new courses for migrants on living in Britain, these structures emphasise an ideal political and cultural vision that somehow migrants must actualise. Eschewing the much called-for multicultural ideal, such structures reinstate a single point of reference for inclusion – an imaginary Britain. Through the figure of Chanu in *Brick Lane*, we witness the high cost of trying to be the 'same': failure. *Brick Lane* here attempts to incorporate a messier way forward and to literalise a perhaps more honest understanding of the experience of loss as also *lost*. When Nazneen leaves her flat on her own for the first time, she is finally hit with the full force of her isolation – although she, at first, experiences invisibility, this is soon overridden by her feelings of helplessness – and as she finds herself unable to return home, the reality of her detachment from her surroundings is evident and unmistakable. Nazneen is not seen but also cannot situate herself. Inhabiting this space, though fraught and terrifying, constitutes a more powerful realisation of the migrant experience and a better understanding of sacrifices made. Chanu's silent rejection of Nazneen's desire to go to college and learn English not only reveals his controlling attitude towards his wife but, more interestingly, also reveals his uncertainty over how her experience of English and England may be *different* to his and how this will affect the way that they maintain their Bengali values within their household.

Whilst desperate to engage with the world outside of his home, Chanu is keen to retain the values of his other home, Bangladesh, within the four walls of the flat. Rather than understand this space as a refuge, we argue that the value of home and belonging needs to be reinstated and often re-learned. Chanu's laborious task of re-learning his own history comes about as a result of his disappointment with his lack of success in the Britain of his imagination. This leads him to reinvent himself: 'If you have a history, you see, you have a pride. . . . In the Sixteenth Century, Bengal was called the Paradise of Nations. . . . These people here do not show our nation in its true light' (*BL*, 151). 'A loss of pride', Chanu says, 'is a terrible thing' (*BL*, 153). Re-integrating himself into a history that he can claim as his own acts as a bulwark against shattered dreams (we see this narrative move in Lalwani's *Gifted* as well). Chanu's ultimate return home is testimony to the inability to reconcile this deep disappointment, whereas Nazneen's more fraught yet active negotiation of her place in this new cultural and social framework may make her ultimately more resilient. In particular, Nazneen's reading of the evolving nature of the migrant experience and her ability to stand outside of herself and witness this are crucial. Towards the end of the novel, when she rejects both the opportunity to leave her husband and the offer to marry the younger activist Karim, she notes that Karim sees her as 'the real thing. . . . A Bengali wife. A Bengali mother. An idea of home. An idea of himself that he found in her' (*BL*, 380). Nazneen's rejection of this identity suggests more formative ways of negotiating belonging away from tired expressions of automatic behaviours that seek to reproduce an ideal home away from home. Neither fully there nor fully here presents a challenge, but one that is worth taking up. This is made even clearer in the figure of the refugee in Abdulrazak Gurnah's novel *By the Sea*.

In 2000, Gurnah wrote about the 'inattentiveness of postcolonial analysis to particularities of the fragmentations within colonised cultures', and to perhaps the overemphasis, in criticism and literature, on the encounter with European colonialism in a more uncomplicated way that placed more importance on oppositions rather than depth of context. *By the Sea*, we suggest, addresses this complexity through the narration of *multiple* stories and, through them, the layered histories of what Gurnah calls 'Little Zanzibar' and elsewhere. In *By the Sea*, what appear to be simple categories belie complex histories, and so terms such as 'refugee' and 'asylum seeker', imposed onto characters, are soon revealed as limiting categories structured around the ethno-political needs of nations at any given time and beholden to shifting cultural and economic ideologies. Unpredictable and cruel policies (see Chapter 2 for a fuller appreciation of the context of these policies) framing the reception of refugees and those seeking asylum are enacted in *By the Sea* by robotic agents of the state or well-intentioned but often insensitive and harried social workers. The experience of these conditions or states of being, mediated through heavily boundaried institutions, such as border force, controlled housing, and crushing bureaucracy, activates an expanded interiority that works to furnish characters with the resources to endure and, in some cases, flourish. Memory, whether therapeutic, generative, or nostalgic, serves to ensure that experiential value is not only derived from observable action and that agency is not contingent on external affirmation. Expanding in various directions into the past, *By the Sea* functions to make visible the long roots of colonial influence, buried as they are in layered material, economic, personal, and collective experiences. The expansion of the category of the refugee in the book works to embrace a totality of experience where memory plays a vital role. In her work *Nostalgia: When are we Ever at Home*, Barbara Cassin contemplates nostalgia in the context of hospitality and how this experience can shape space and time in very particular ways.[101] For example, in *Making Sense of Contemporary British Muslim Novels*, Claire Chambers argues for a focus on a 'haptic sensibility'.[102] In her discussion of Monica Ali's *Brick Lane* and Nadeem Aslam's *Maps for Lost Lovers*, Chambers argues that one of the ways that the authors 'explore multiculturalism is through the depictions of the sense of smell'.[103] Chambers points to how 'the cartographic aspect' of the author's 'sensory mapping' helps bridge unfathomable distances.[104] At the start of *By the Sea*, the protagonist, Saleh Omar, who has stolen an old adversary's identity and is using it to seek refuge, is challenged at UK immigration for seeking asylum. Unpacking Saleh Omar's few belongings, the immigration officer unearths what he believes to be 'a kind of incense'.[105] Saleh Omar sets off on an imaginative journey that spans almost *17 pages* in the novel, telling the story of this 'incense' in sensory detail:

> So I didn't tell him that it was ud-al-qamari of the best quality, all that remained of a consignment I had acquired more than thirty years ago.... Ud-al-qamari: its fragrance comes back to me at odd times, unexpectedly, like a fragment of a voice or the memory of my beloved's arm on my neck. Every Idd I used to prepare an incense-burner and walk around my house with it, waving clouds of perfume into its deepest corners.... The man I obtained the ud-al-qamari from was a Persian trader from Bahrain who had come to our parts of the world with the musim, the winds of the monsoons, he and thousands of other traders from Arabia, the Gulf, India and Sind, and the horn of Africa. They had been doing this every year for at least a thousand years.
>
> (*BTS*, pp. 13–14)

As Chambers notes, 'migrants, and Muslim migrants in particular, are especially vulnerable to cognitive dissonance, since they have strong "home" values connected to religion and culture'.[106] In her reading of these contexts, it is cultural 'translation and transculturation'[107] which is developed internally – both as a retreat to a detailed past and also as a means through which to embed this past in the present moment. We can contrast this with the blunt instrument of the state: the immigration officer in *By the Sea*, who proclaims that '[they'll] need to get this [the incense] tested' (*BTS*, p. 14), against the description of the complex and capacious trade patterns that have enabled the ud-al-qamari to travel across to Tanzania for a thousand years. Such a description of broad exchange jars against national and international institutions that seek to constrain and ration the movement of people. Here, man-made laws silence other routes dictated by, in Saleh Omar's story, the winds that 'blow steadily across the Indian Ocean towards the coast of Africa, where the currents obligingly provide a channel to harbour' (*BTS*, 14). Attuned to centuries of trade and colonial development, Gurnah nevertheless allows for an expansion of place and space by describing in detail the movement of people, their gods, their needs, their desires, and their ways of life. Alert to how this movement of travellers, migrants, refugees, and colonists changes the very nature of a place, the texts contrasts this with the definition put forward by the United Nations High Commission for Refugees, which requires asylum seekers to speak their fear.[108] The injunction for Saleh Omar, the refugee seeking asylum, to rehearse a historical injustice and inhabit the status of victim ensures a somewhat one-dimensional existence. What Saleh Omar's memories instead show us is the almost-infinite landscape of his experience. Those seeking refuge of any kind are not made worthy or bound by a singular experience intelligible to officials, untethered from kin, politics, and economics.

National asylum systems exist to decide which asylum seekers qualify for protection. Those judged through state-sanctioned procedures not to be refugees and therefore not entitled to international protection can legally be sent back to their home countries.[109] The mass movements of refugees often occur as a result of conflicts with long histories of (often unacknowledged colonial) violence, though the detail is often sidelined in the context of competing nationalist needs and the perception of limited resources. Thus, Saleh Omar in *By the Sea* is rebuked not only for wanting to seek asylum (a sign of his neediness) but also for seeking it in Britain (thus stirring up memories of an imperial past). Memories of the various trade routes and colonial and nationalist enterprises that graced the shores of Tanzania points to the existence of multiple means of engagement with land and communities beyond the categories of citizenship that are now being elicited by nation states. The citizenship/nation model so revered by nation states (as well as the particular historiography that accompanies it) is presented in the novel as only one of many relational frames that organise and manage access to rights and resources. Where the border officer in the UK wants to know the provenance of the incense and to have it tested, for Saleh Omar, the incense holds within it another world altogether. Rather than the ud-al-qamari acting as an indicator of a fixed location and provenance, it *expands* the frame of reference. This expansion is, of course, much more strikingly evident in Nikita Lalwani's *Gifted*, which we focus on in the next section. In his interview with Carin Klaesson of the Nobel Prize Museum in 2023,[110] Abdulrazak Gurnah makes explicit how certain stories never appear to enter the frame of colonial narratives. The vastness and complexity of experience to him are absent from the debate of even the most well-intentioned postcolonial critiques. Gurnah uses the term 'incomplete' when considering the overall narrative of colonialism and, by implication, suggests that the processing of this legacy is also incomplete. *By the Sea*, in its emphasis on false identities, stories within stories, and chance encounters, espouses a rather more frantic and sprawling series of lives and locations, none of them *reducible* in any way to a particular organising principle through which communities are imagined or, indeed, managed. This is most evident in a memorable set of scenes where it transpires that an interpreter has been sourced to help Saleh Omar with his asylum case. The interpreter is deemed to be qualified for this role as an 'expert' of a culture that requires interpretation in order to be intelligible (we might think of this as another form of border force). Shocked at this idea that he may be someone who can be *interpreted*, Saleh Omar mulls over what this might mean in practice:

> An expert in my area, someone who has written books about me no doubt, who knows all about me, more than I know about myself. He will have visited all the places of interest and significance in *my area*, and will know their historical and cultural context when I will be certain never to have seen them and will only have heard vague myths and popular tales about them. He will have slipped in and out of *my area* for decades, studying me and noting me down, explaining me and summarising me, and I would have been unaware of his busy existence.
>
> (*BTS*, 65)

Expertise here masks a longer history of oftentimes violent extractivism and exploitation (both material and intellectual). Confronted with the possibility that he could somehow be deciphered and his existence plotted and studied, Saleh Omar operationalises the phrase 'I prefer not to', borrowed from Herman Melville's 'Bartleby the Scrivener', in order to cease engagement in a process that he intuits is arranged to humiliate him and reinforce his difference (or to somehow find him lacking). For, as he notes:

> She [Rachel, his assigned social worker] did not have to listen in silence while stories were told about her, only ring a couple of organisations to see if they had an interpreter for a client who spoke a language she could not name and was too ignorant of the cultural geography of the world to make a guess. It was not even ignorance but an assurance that in the scheme of things it did not matter very much what language I spoke, since my needs and desires could be predicted, and sooner or later I would learn to make myself intelligible.
>
> (*BTS*, 66)

Here, Saleh Omar uses the experience of being interpolated as an opportunity to, in Bill Ashcroft's words, '[resist] the forces designed to shape [him] as "other"'.[111]

Ashcroft's articulation of this relational approach helps us better situate Omar's response in a broader postcolonial frame:

> Interpolation describes the access such 'interpellated' subjects have to a counter-discursive agency. This strategy involves the capacity to interpose, to intervene, to interject a wide range of counter-discursive tactics into the dominant discourse. . . . When we view the ways in which dominant discourse may operate to keep oppositional discourses located, defined and marginal, we see the strategic importance of a form of intervention which operates within the dominant system but refuses to leave it intact. Fundamentally [this is the] process of insertion, interruption, interjection.[112]

This frame of a counter-discursive agency is productive, as it expands our understanding and appreciation of Saleh Omar's response to a series of interpretive incursions over time. Gurnah's narrative makes us consider the contextual hierarchy of certain forms of knowledge: where it can be put to use and where it remains hidden. Saleh Omar's political, geographical, historical, and literary frames of references are abundant. During a particularly detailed conversation with the 'expert' academic Latif Mahmud, who, we come to learn, is known to Omar from his life in Tanzania, a particularly poignant conversation reveals the unexpected sources of knowledge. During a conversation about Melville's Bartleby, Mahmud notes how he loved 'the impassive authority of that man's defeat, the noble futility of his life' (*BTS*, 156). Curious to know how Omar came by the story, he asks him if he had ever studied it. 'I just read it' (*BTS*, 156), Omar offers up, going on to detail how he came across it and how, as part of his work buying up the contents of departing colonial administrators, he had managed to build up an impressive book collection made up of

> poetry anthologies and colonial adventures . . . Rudyard Kipling and Rider Haggard and G. A. Henty . . . and *Origin of Species* . . . *The History of the World*, that kind of thing, and some old atlases. . . . But among these books [he] found the short stories of Herman Melville. [He] had never heard of him . . .
>
> (*BTS*, 157)

These all form a background to a counter-discursive logic, feeding into a knowledge base from which to better understand the formation of colonial discourse, but also using it as a means to stand against it. This contrasts sharply with the social worker Rachel, who does not *need* to know where Omar is from, is not *required* to have any knowledge of his heritage, is not *expected* to have any idea what language he speaks. Her access to resources (a phone, a list of names) allows her to bypass this deeper 'cultural geography' that would instead constitute her presence within Omar's frame differently. Although we certainly do witness a duty of care, this care is structured organisationally. Lucinda Newns posits the term 'non-home' to

162 *British Writing from Empire to Brexit*

indicate spaces that might formally qualify as home but do not provide *care* in any sense.[113] Newns argues:

> The kernel of this non-home can be found within the judicial concept of 'asylum' itself. The term 'asylum' implies the notion of sanctuary, a temporary shelter from harm, but one that is not meant to provide a sense of permanence required to make a home.[114]

Newns's engagement with Sarah Gibson's work on the asylum hotel debate shows up how the current process of accommodating asylum seekers intersects with wider conversations around hospitality, which Gibson argues has been politicised.[115] In his article on hospitality in *By the Sea*, David Farrier argues for how 'hospitality is equated with recognition' and yet goes on to outline how the 'formerly sacrosanct category of "refugee" has since the early 1990s suffered significant erosion', as it has moved away from 'the definitions laid down in the 1951 Refugee Convention'.[116] Farrier's nuanced outlook on how terms matter (how they matter to Gurnah) and how 'asylum seeker' has, in some cases, come to replace 'refugee' points to an 'atrophy of a schedule of rights previously afforded to the refugee by the host nation'.[117] In this context, we can see the limits of hospitality echoed in what Farrier terms 'the current vocabulary of asylum and immigration' that has, over time, coalesced to turn into a 'complex terminology of *unbelonging*, within which the potential of a particular term to confer legitimacy is always impermanent and increasingly limited'.[118] Farrier's reach here extends outwards to ways in which we might better understand the political frameworks that operate to delimit zones of exclusion and inclusion. Gurnah's text is alert to this at the same time as it broadens its geographical and temporal scope by evoking what Edward Said called 'the voyage in', thus making visible the conscious effort to 'enter into the discourses of Europe and the West, to mix with it, transform it, to make it acknowledge marginalised or suppressed or forgotten histories'.[119]

In *By the Sea*, Saleh Omar takes the voyage in and, in so doing, disrupts the stable national genealogies that he encounters. Sissy Helff has called these multiple encounters 'dialogic contact zones'.[120] Borrowing the well-known term from Mary Louise Pratt, Helff explores the contact zone in migrant literature and notes that 'Gurnah's case is special because his stories draw a vast collective panorama of cultural encounters' as interested in East African history as it is in European history.[121] This also serves the purpose of ensuring that we do not limit the category of the refugee to a particular cultural and historical moment but also work to show how this category recomposes political and cultural border zones and, in so doing, unmoors specific communities (host nations) from collective responsibility. People or groups who inhabit the category of refugees, we argue, are not social problems or political inconveniences – they are the result of socio-political and historical realities, and there is a responsibility here to represent this causality. Categorisation occurs as a result of myopic processes that seek to rally around particular articulations of state or nation that are discursively sewn together and then sectioned off. As Gurnah's text amplifies, the alternative, to tell another story, is to dismantle the one that came before it. What *By the Sea* reveals is the extent to which sovereignty, citizenship, and rights are contingent on the expulsion or prohibition of communities not permitted to inhabit those categories (and whose understanding of those categories, in any case, would diverge and be impacted by alternative histories and political discourses).[122] Giorgio Agamben's challenge, to come around to a view where 'the refugee should be considered for what he is, that is, nothing less than a border concept that radically calls into question the principles of the nation-state and, at the same time, helps clear the field for a no-longer-delayable renewal of categories',[123] is reflected in the drawing up of this complex figure in *By the Sea*.

What is the place of the refugee, then, within nationalist discourse? What space can be constructed for the refugee within the boundaries of the nation state? Does the refugee anticipate the uncoupling of citizenship from the nation, and what uncomfortable questions does the figure of the refugee raise about national belonging and rights? We looked to *By the Sea* to complicate thinking around the representation of the category of refugees, of asylum-seeking, of leaving home, but also of carrying the history of that home with you. Gurnah's aim is not to humanise, by which I mean to make us empathise with the refugee – not at all. If this were the case, the story would not be one of so many surprises and shocks; rather, it is to render the refugee multiple, with faults, quirks, complex, and sometimes hiding a dirty past, but nevertheless someone with rights to an opportunity for a dignified future. 'My life has been at risk for a long time', says Saleh Omar to his social worker, Rachel. 'It is only a worthless life now, *but it matters to me*. Perhaps it was always worthless though it mattered even more before' (*BTS*, 67–68, my emphasis).

What home is and how it is defined, what boundaries are and how they are set up and maintained, are a recurring theme in *By the Sea*. Indeed, the claims of the refugee are linked intimately to the ironies and consequences of colonial history:

> Kevin Edelman, the bawab of Europe, and the gatekeeper to the orchards in the family courtyard, the same gate which had released the hordes that went out to consume the world and to which we have come sliming up to beg admittance. Refugee. Asylum-seeker. Mercy.
>
> (*BTS*, 31)

Admittance is a theme tackled in Lalwani's 2007 novel *Gifted*, a novel that fully engages the complexities involved in managing the tensions at the centre of the diaspora experience. In *British Multicultural Literature and Superdiversity*, Ulla Rahbek leans on Steven Vertovec's conceptualisation of 'superdiversity as a multidimensional perspective on contemporary social and cultural diversity that moves beyond a focus on the ethnic group ... and provides commentators with a new language to approach social complexity, especially in Britain's *urban* areas'[124] (original emphasis). Whilst the critical focus here is on the various forms of isolationism brought about by a fractured multicultural landscape, *Gifted* does offer alternative overarching frameworks within which we can navigate political and social spaces that are complex and in flux. The book opens with an epigraph from 'My Back Pages' by Bob Dylan. This is a song that speaks of, among other things, idealism and political activism and how, in looking back at a younger self, one's actions seem so assured and certain in the face of what can be quite uncertain and precarious moments. Before moving to the broader categories that the book might be inviting us to entertain, this opening also suggests how spaces evolve and how experiences that seem solid may be looked back on differently from an alternative vantage point. We were therefore interested in how different forms of *anchoring* take place in the novel as characters struggle to participate in challenging contexts as they attempt to bridge current lives in the multicultural space with memories and expectations of a life left behind. What gripped our interest in *Gifted* was the richness of the depiction of the background landscape of the main characters and the curiosity that this ignited. Rahbek does point to the potential of novels like Lalwani's to contribute to a project of 'promoting *intercultural literacy* and of fostering civic virtues such as tolerance and open-mindedness . . . that do not shy away from representations of the complexities of living multicultural lives'[125] (my emphasis). This concept of intercultural literacy is certainly an experience towards which literature can productively contribute.

We are not saying here that we read books to learn about other cultures, but rather that we engage with texts in order to bear witness, even when we may not fully understand the multiple signifiers at play, to a diverse range of cultural, linguistic, and historical references that make evident the often-unacknowledged daily microimaginaries required for daily survival. The circumstances of the family in *Gifted* make them vulnerable to a particular type of diaspora experience. Here we leant on the work of diaspora theorists who mapped the particular dynamic of diaspora and its expression in the context of assimilationist expectations. Intergenerational experiences were also an interesting locus of investigation, and the children, in particular, the young 14-year-old daughter, Rumi, in the novel, being primed for Oxford, dramatise the tensions across multiple demands.

It was important for us to understand how this sense of frequent re-acclimatising and re-adapting to *multiple* spaces at the same time (as we saw in *Brick Lane*) informs and colours daily interaction. In particular, we wanted to better configure how these often-visceral diasporic links were experienced first-hand by parents and then second-hand by the younger generation. We found that the often-conflicting accumulation of cultural and social capital had to be continually re-oriented to suit the receiving culture. It was rare that the new home environment, in this case Cardiff, welcomed or was hospitable to the opportunity to bear witness to otherness. *Gifted* is particularly inspiring in the way that it allows these moments to unfold – often painfully, but always candidly and patiently. Here we want to focus on the ways in which the novel imaginatively conceives of the price for this constant re-orientation, understanding it as a fundamental component of the constant pressures of adaptation to a new culture.

Rahbek rightly notes the compartmentalisation that takes place for the children and, in particular, the daughter Rumi.[126] Parents Mahesh and Shreene, however, do not police their feelings to such an extent and, given the vast imaginative resources at their disposal, live a life that is much more permeable than compartmentalisation would suggest, though no less painful. This 'background noise' that at all times coexists in characters' lives and thoughts provides a foil against daily humiliations and intrusions. The family in *Gifted* is one that has kept itself isolated, far from other migrant communities. Mahesh and Shreene shape their new lives at the same time as they continually envelop and refer to historical, cultural, and contextual moments, memories, and histories that serve to keep their past alive in the present. This attachment and its performance are a burden of sorts. In *Diaspora Criticism*, Sudesh Mishra points to several ethno-cultural articulations of the experience of migration and diaspora. In his questioning of one of the more popular understandings of how diaspora communities may experience place, that of the scene of dual territoriality,[127] Mishra instead suggests a different way of thinking about this that might better reflect a set of experiences that constitute a direct challenge to any assimilationist or integrationist agenda: what he calls 'situational laterality'.[128] Here, what constitutes loyalty is an important factor that often determines the extent to which a nationalist agenda is made visible. With reference to a little-known diaspora thinker, Walter P. Zenner, whose focus is on diaspora Jewish identities, Mishra notes that 'Zenner's view of Jewish culture as a transmission without origins[129] or unidirectional territorial ends offers an early alternative to the bipolar territorial framework for describing disaggregated ethno-national entities'.[130] Mishra also points to the work of Paul Gilroy and specifically to how his trans-historical exploration of Black culture actively dismantles the comfort of the assumption of linear experience, focusing instead on a 'non-linear circulation of "black" Atlantic cultures, ideas, politics, commodities, iconographies and peoples which actively contributed to the emergence of that temporal regime called *western* modernity'.[131] Mishra goes on to argue how this contribution has been repressed in the history of development and left out of a particular understanding of modernity. With this in mind, Mishra looks out at the diaspora landscape and sees something else: 'exponents of the dual territorial approach guardedly repeat an ideological ploy in representing diasporas as self-marking ethnic minorities sundered from a homeland entity and residing in a host territory belonging *self-evidently* to a dominant ethno-national identity.'[132] The problem with this, according to Mishra, is that this does not sufficiently take into account how temporality and location feature in the construction of identity away from any fixed understanding of ethno-nationalist categories both at the point of (in any case, mythic) origin and in the host nation, itself mired in ongoing ethno-nationalist debates. This concept of situational laterality helps complicate Ullbeck's call for us to surrender to the invitation for intercultural literacy. In other words, the very intercultural literacy that readers are exposed to is itself contingent on the particular forms of knowledge and experience being presented by the author through their particular characters. What we cannot fall back on in our reading is any sense of a reducible and thus fully intelligible set of national markers that fix a particular ethnic group (in either direction). In other words, to use *Gifted* as a specific example, there is no fixed idea of 'India' that a reader can hold on to that can help frame the Vasi family's past. India is reconstituted and reconfigured within and against the needs of the present by each individual family member, who also experiences their present lives in individual and discrete ways.

Appreciating this can also help expand our definition of a multicultural framework that is not dependent on certainty and that is in flux.[133]

We are drawn to these instances, available to writers and readers in the literature we examine, that make clear the shifting allegiances that make any singular reading of loyalty (to any one location) possible. In this case, it is also important to consider the direction of locality (skewed towards the homeland, toward other migrant/diaspora communities?). As Avtar Brah notes, 'the identity of the diasporic imagined community is far from fixed or pregiven. It is constituted *within* the crucible of the *materiality* of everyday life; in the everyday stories we tell ourselves individually and collectively'.[134] In looking both inward and outward, therefore, migrant diaspora communities are constituted spatially and temporally. In *Gifted*, the young father Mahesh is confronted by the latent racism that his daughter is experiencing at school. Whilst processing this, he recalls his own activist upbringing, when he and his comrades were political firebrands 'chewing betel, relishing the bitter stain on their lips and debating whether class was compatible with non-violence' (*Gifted*, 4). As 'Gandhian Communists', Mahesh and his friends' participation in the social and cultural movements of their time anchors Mahesh and also expands his activist past. This works in multiple ways in the text: it affords a vision of political agency and control, it functions to remind us of the significance and reach of Gandhian politics to this particular family, and it also points to the broader back story/history of the South Asian diaspora, which can easily become forgotten and diluted in the pressures of the everyday (experienced here by the daughter as latent racism).

Gifted also reveals tensions often located at the site of the diaspora experience: home, work, community. *Gifted* afforded us the opportunity to look closely at the diasporic negotiation of place and the extent to which expectations shape behaviour and identity. In many ways, this continues the work that we have been doing across the book and allows us to introduce further complexities encountered in our understanding of how identity and nation correspond in particular circumstances. For example, one of the main concepts explored in *Gifted* is that of *home* differently to *By the Sea*. As the novel is largely interested in the experience of a family that negotiates its belonging to a South Asian diaspora, first generation, in Britain, it seems apt to reflect on Susheila Nasta's understanding of home as a place where one begins.[135] Part of this family (the parents) starts *again* in Britain, while another part (the children) starts in Britain. For all of them, however, and throughout the novel, there is another presence: that of another place that plays a significant role in their lives. And there is also the presence of another time (as we experience in *Brick Lane* and *By the Sea*). In other words, there is a consciousness that resides both in the here and now of Wales and of the moment of leaving India, the life left behind there, the memories of there that shape the present, as well as the future nostalgia that is ever present are marked in the novel and present a challenge to the present.

The novel incorporates a confrontation of sorts, a polite one that takes place externally, while internal arguments rage wildly. Lalwani exposes the labour involved, both mentally and physically, in the negotiation of such spaces. The Vasis are visited by a well-meaning Mrs Gold from Rumi's school, who insists that Rumi is a gifted mathematician and suggests enrolment in Mensa and further nurturing of her talents. '"Have you heard of a place called Mensa" asks Mrs Gold' (*Gifted*, 7). Mahesh, a skilled mathematician who has encouraged his daughter's skill, is frustrated by this line of questioning that assumes a one-dimensional existence:

> What preconceptions did she bring with her. . . . He was not going to make a grand statement. . . . But, if he could, he would tell her everything. He'd tell her he'd got into all their universities. . . . They had wanted him here, a foreigner with no more than five pounds in his pocket.
>
> (*Gifted*, 8)

Having differentiated himself from more disadvantaged groups, Mahesh is quick to further differentiate himself from Asian refugees and to thus place himself in a different category that emphasises his skill and entitlement:

> He had not been among the thirty thousand Asians haemorrhaging out of the ugly scar in Uganda's belly that same year, seeping into the dark spaces of Britain . . . the crawling masses who had fallen into the pockets of Leicester and Wembley. He was not going to be dissolved into the rivers of blood.
>
> (*Gifted*, 8)

This is also, we argue, a form of identity-making. On the one hand, as an instance of intercultural literacy, the novel takes the bold move to reflect how British Asian diaspora communities may actively differentiate between *one another*, particularly when under any form of threat. In so doing, the novel also begins to contribute to a broader definition of contemporary British culture in unearthing these constituted histories and breathing life into them. The 1972 Ugandan political crisis saw the 'expulsion of all Asians from Uganda. Just over 28,000 men, women and children came to the UK, making them one of the largest groups of displaced people to enter the country'.[136] Mahesh's distancing from this history of Asian migration speaks to Brah's claim that 'at the heart of the very notion of diaspora is the image of a journey',[137] though importantly this is not the *same* journey for everyone, as Mahesh is at pains to articulate.

'We're never going back, are we?' asked Shreene soon after her marriage to Mahesh and their move back to Wales. We might want to extend the question, then, to who travels, *when*, *how*, and under *what* circumstances. And if the circumstances of leaving are important, so, too, are those of arrival and settling down. In addition to this, the stories we learn in the novel are a complex web of memory, fantasy, and nostalgia and serve particular functions that are not easy to compartmentalise, as their effects are unpredictable. In an often-cruel context of everyday casual racism and reminders of being other, Rumi dreams of going back to India, where she might recapture a modicum of acceptance. These dreams are based on a mythologisation of what is recalled in the family as the 'India trip'. Looking back at Rumi's accessing of her memories of the trip to India, the narration of this is a wonderfully evocative exercise into how recollection is a combination of purposefully called-up moments that come to represent more than they were ever intended to and to bridge challenging experiences:

> Rumi's main memory of the India Trip was linked inextricably with the mythology of the Vasi household. Even her father, usually so suspicious of his wife's growing flirtation with superstition and emotional recall, was influential in nurturing the story's development. . . . Rumi had been eight years old when she made the trip, which had begun with the funeral of Shreene's father; the intervening two years since had accentuated its mystique. . . . Sometimes when she went to sleep *she worried she might forget it*, that it would turn into a dream and disappear, *leaving her at the start, having to begin all over again*.
>
> (*Gifted*, 125)

Lalwani insightfully sketches out the often-mechanical way in which memory is organised and subsequently automated, often to make it easier, as Rumi notes, for her to 'live up to the memory so that when Nibu [her younger brother] was older she could pass it on to him' (*Gifted*, 125). Lalwani is also sensitive, however, to the ethereal qualities of memory and to the world that underpins it that requires activation and validation in order to remain relevant. This notion of *living up* to the memory is of particular significance here as it suggests that remembering the experience is detached from those who have had it and that somehow the memory performs the labour of direct experience. This extends our understanding and concern over the question of loyalty mentioned earlier, beyond a specific place and into the realm of shared memory. In the introduction to her book on radical nostalgia, Anindya Raychaudhuri writes that 'the year 2016 had been a big one for nostalgia', referring to the Brexit referendum as one long journey down various forms of 'conservative nostalgia', taking care not to reify this experience and reminding us of the publication that same year of Owen Hatherley's *The Ministry of Nostalgia*, where he 'identifies the emotional attachment on the part of both the British Right and the British Left to particular moments in its national history' as forms of participation in a selective history that ensure the exclusion of the long legacy of colonialism.[138] In this context, Raychaudhuri asks if it is 'possible to also think of a counter-hegemonic progressive nostalgia that celebrates and helps *sustain* the marginalized'.[139] In addition, we also wanted to explore whether nostalgia may be even more disruptive in that it can threaten to instil a near-constant and dynamic comparative approach to other political systems, beliefs, and social structures that operate differently. Raychaudhuri sees nostalgia as a 'diverse set of processes and discourse that represent a particular use of the past in order to re-create an imaginary, imaginative version of it in the present'.[140] Specifically, she notes that:

> When cultural memory leads to particular narratives of home and homeliness, when these narratives can be said to be attempting a reimagining and reconstruction, then these acts of memory can be described as nostalgic.[141]

As well as participating in reimagining and reconstruction, we are also keen to emphasise that nostalgia is also 'fundamentally counter-hegemonic because it is always attempting to change the contemporary status quo'.[142] See Rumi's recollection of the story of the trip to India and how Lalwani sets it up into four parts:

1. The Arrival (and the biscuits)
2. The Palm Reader (and the prediction)
3. The Train Journey (and escaping death)
4. The Mountain Top (and the wish that came true)

(*Gifted*, p. 25)

Memory as episodic and formulaic ensures its longevity – the earlier example articulates how collective memory works to link moments to each other in such a way that creates knowledge. As Anh Hua notes, 'memory is distorted by needs, desires, interests and fantasies', and 'an understanding of how memory works within diaspora studies . . . can help us rewrite oblivion. Forgetting is more active than we think'.[143] Indeed, as Vijay Agnew argues:

> The diasporic individual often has a double consciousness, a private knowledge and perspective that is consonant with postmodernity and globalization. The dual or paradoxical nature of diasporic consciousness is one that is caught between 'here' and 'there,' or between those who share roots, and is shaped through multilocality. The consciousness and identity of diasporic individuals may focus on their attachment to the symbols of their ethnicity, and they may continue to feel emotionally invested in the 'homeland.' Yet such attachments and sentiments are experienced simultaneously with their involvement and participation in the social, economic, cultural, and political allegiances to their homes in the diaspora.[144]

What role memory and forgetting play in these attachments also impacts the present. For Shreene, arriving in India for her father's funeral after a nine-year absence is bittersweet. Smelling her surroundings, Shreene, Lalwani writes,

> breathed it in, captured it in her gut and tried to solidify it to stem the hunger. Because even though she was there, she still craved it for the imminent future. She knew her arrival home meant only one thing: that she would have to leave.

(*Gifted*, 41)

This aspect of the text exemplifies the work of a future-facing nostalgia. The lived experience of diaspora, in Brah's words, '*embodies* a subtext of "home"'.[145] What we might want to ask is: What are the implications of this subtext? In other words, how and why does 'home' become so integral to the diasporic condition, and what are the implications of this powerful nostalgia in the host nation? More importantly, we wondered what the impact was of multiple variations of home residing in one psyche. The 'processes of multi-locationality across geographical, cultural and psychic boundaries',[146] or situational laterality, to use Mishra's term, all complicate any fixed notion of a diasporic migrant community participating in a broader multicultural space and contributing to it in any stable or predetermined way. Our sense was that what Lalwani captures so evocatively in *Gifted* are the moments when the feeling of what has been left behind catches the characters by surprise – it is often a physical reaction, removed from any logical process. This is different than the 'uncritical nostalgia found in some diasporic narratives about the home country'.[147] Recall the scene where Shreene, rushing to get Rumi back home from the shops one afternoon, is caught out when it looks like a warm rain might soon begin:

> Then it swamped her. Monsoon. She froze, feeling her body betray her. It was the sudden desolation that often overtook her without warning, come back to ruin her on the way home, bleaching her surroundings with white cold, licking every street, house and passer-by into numb caricatures of their incarnations just thirty seconds previously. Although she was used to this feeling, right now it caused her immense strain; it was as if her heart would pop in the silence. They walked past a telephone box and Shreene diverted into it, taking Rumi inside.
>
> (*Gifted*, 43)

This action very much articulates the dangers inherent in diaspora articulations of home that can, in some cases, 'subvert nation states because diasporic identification can exist *outside of and in opposition to modern citizenship*'[148] (my emphasis). This challenge can disrupt the political project of assimilation and integration as it seeks buy-in from a committed membership that is, however, in many cases, powerless to give up the condition of fluctuating divided loyalties.

Film plays a significant role in *Gifted*, as it works to provide what Rajinder Dudrah has called the 'haptic ethnoscape' formed through cinema. Dudrah describes this as

> the availability of . . . sounds and images for diasporic ethnic groups in centres of the developed world that help create a diasporic imaginary, one that enables diasporic subjects to imagine and represent themselves further against rigid configurations of race and nation and ensuing identities.[149]

Cinema is one of the experiences, then, that helps reframe 'relationships with countries of origin and countries of settlement as informing each other to produce new sensibilities of being and belonging'.[150] When Mahesh takes his family to see Richard Attenborough's 1982 film *Gandhi*, the children fall asleep, but Rumi is confronted with her parents' visceral reaction to events in the film:

> When she woke, towards the end, the first thing she noticed was Shreene's tears, wept heavily into a cotton handkerchief embroidered with green triangles. Even Mahesh's eyes had a swollen gleam, visible beneath the rich sheen of light superimposed on the lenses of his glasses.
>
> (*Gifted*, 57)

'We Have Been Made Again', 1980–2016   171

Although Dudrah is primarily focused on the role of popular Hindi cinema in the context of diaspora, we might here also read the popularisation of important historical moments in Indian history to have a similar effect. Not long after the trip to the cinema, and in an emotional conversation with an old friend about the relative merits of the film, Mahesh finds himself defending the film's ambitions. Caught up in the film's various historical inaccuracies and selective representation, Mahesh's friend Mark Whitefoot is not sensitive to Mahesh's affective relationship to the wider significance of the film. '"You are forgetting," Mahesh tells him, "that I was there at the time. This film you are discussing is more than just a – a playground for your usual cynicism. This film is about my life, Mark, and Shreene's too"' (*Gifted*, 64). Mark, however, seems unable to edge into this frame of reference. Assuming that Mahesh has taken offence to his less-than-charitable view of Gandhi, he offers platitudes to try to diffuse the growing discomfort. Frustrated beyond reason, Mahesh makes his position clear:

> 'OK, look,' said Mahesh, meeting Whitefoot's eyes sternly. 'This is how it is.' He cleared his throat violently, the sound filling the air. 'Basically what do you want me to say? That I was four years old when the whole thing [partition] happened? That my mother, pregnant with my sister, carried me over the border in a suitcase . . . that we lived in a refugee camp in Gurgaon? You enjoy the sound of the word "refugee", it has an honest ring for you. I know that appeals.'
>
> (*Gifted*, 65–66)

In this instance, the film works to validate a particular experience and to provide the context of its articulation. In his scathing critique of Attenborough's *Gandhi* in *Imaginary Homelands*, Rushdie bemoans the popularity of the figure of Ghandi represented in the film: as 'guru', 'dedicated to ideals of poverty and simplicity' and revolution via 'submission, and self-sacrifice, and non-violence'.[151] Pointing to the lack of a focus on Tagore and Subhas Bose,[152] Rushdie posits an intellectual and academic response to the limitation of the film. For Lalwani's Mahesh, however, the film stands in as evidence of a paucity of cultural literacy. More importantly, it seems to enable participation in Dudrah's haptic ethnolandscape, where the sounds and images in the film recreate a moment that is otherwise invisible to the community that the Vasis reside in. Where Rushdie is caught up in the (lack of) attention to detail in the film, claiming that '*Gandhi* presents false portraits of most of the leaders of the independence struggle',[153] Mahesh makes clear that he understands very well the artistic license practiced by the film but nevertheless appreciates its engagement with the events of partition as part of *his* political and experiential past. More importantly, this defence is also one of the personalisation and ownership of the mechanics of nostalgia. Whereas for Whitefoot the exchange constitutes intellectual banter, for Mahesh, the film is one of many nostalgic hauntings that produce a multi-layered and complex past. This provides access to another place and pushes against the unspoken jealous demands and requirements of a demanding nation state.

In our conclusion from *Empire to Brexit*, we look to thinking more broadly about these demands and requirements and consider what a literature that might *convey a sense of the life that Britain contains*, against and within enduring dominant national imaginings that came to the fore most forcefully during the years leading up to the Brexit campaign, might look like. We also consider various examples of what shape a literature that is 'provisional' and 'inclusive' and able to tackle the many complexities of contemporary societies might take. Where our conclusion references directly some of these works, we here want in the last part of this chapter to offer some thoughts on how Kamila Shamsie's *Home Fire* articulates some of the concerns that constituted the political and cultural landscape leading up to the Brexit referendum.

In a 2019 interview, Kamila Shamsie gave an unambiguous view of the parameters for her novel *Home Fire*, wanting it to question how far we had come as a society in allowing for diversity and multiplicity to underpin a variegated understanding of belonging and nation. Shamsie, it seemed to us, had here laid a trap, and a clever one at that:

> *KS*: So actually one of my points of interest with the book is not just how you construct your identity, but *how other people see that and how it affects you*. You know, one thing I was very clear about the novel was, I didn't at any point want any of the characters to not be British, or to not think of themselves as British, but because Britain itself was so confused about quite what it might mean to be British Pakistani Muslim. What does that mean and how much value does it have and am I an equally regarded member of the state.[154]

Shamsie achieves this not only via a complex schema of characters across a wide social spectrum but also via a multimodal text that incorporates fragments, news reports, trending hashtags, Twitter statistics, tabloid news, poems, and televisual information that come together to form a broad canvas (or chorus) upon which the experience of identity can be chronicled, critiqued, and debated. One of the challenges of fiction is to articulate the presence and influence of various forms of communication. Belonging can now be said to be negotiated across a wide variety of locations, which is not to say that this has brought with it a democratisation of values and views. *Home Fire* plays with form and theme, representing multiple configurations of media in order to give voice to how a fast-growing populism might take shape alongside an even faster articulation of radicalism and extremist nationalism. Forced to sometimes make quick decisions around complex themes and issues, characters find themselves reacting to soundbites and headline news, stating firm opinions built on shaky ground, and taking up positions stripped of any historical or contextual nuance and bolstered by unsubstantiated fears.

Not only does *Home Fire* reflect on the meaning of home and belonging across a wide spectrum; it also lands on themes that came to occupy the years leading up to the Brexit referendum: radicalisation, fears around security, and a growing public debate over what might constitute betrayal or loyalty towards family and nation. Using Sophocles's 'Antigone' as a framing device, Shamsie prophetically intuited a future need to construct a broad-based alliance against injustices committed in the form of state-sanctioned slow violence engineered to gradually corrode faith in government and redirect accountability towards individuals unable to comprehend, let alone tackle, complex educational, health, and welfare systems.

Here, citizens would instead come to fear the power of the state and its ability to dismantle their very visibility. For Rob Nixon, one of the most destructive types of violence and change is that which 'is decoupled from its original causes by the workings of time'.[155] This form of slow-moving structural violence is so insidious because it is not possible to discern the consequence over time of any action that does not have immediate and visible effect. This type of violence is designed to distribute its effect so widely to the extent that its origin is obscured. *Home Fire* invites us to consider *this* form of distributed violence in action by looking at the volatile context sitting as it does at the cusp of a very divisive period in British and European politics. The events in the novel mark a specific take on, for instance, the multicultural project, watered down through the gradual weaponisation of politics around integration and assimilation, now overtaken by a politics of exclusion based on unfounded arguments around, for example, limited resources. New boundaries are drawn around ethnic, economic, social, and even *generational* lines in order to put forward fresh reasons that permit new forms of minoritisation. These discourses all find expression in *Home Fire*, which dramatises both a vehement and misguided patriotism underpinned by socially inequitable and discriminatory policies contributing to a radicalised landscape that is then branded as unpatriotic and un-British. 'There is nothing this country won't allow you to achieve' (*HF*, 87), says Karamat Lone, Muslim Conservative MP and wannabe Home Secretary, in a speech to a Muslim school in Bradford stuffed with what Robert Spencer has termed 'retro-certainties . . . about some sort of normative ideal of Britishness':[156]

> Olympic medals, captaincy of the cricket team, pop stardom, reality TV crowns. And if none of that works, you can settle for being Home Secretary. You are, we are, British. Britain accepts this. So do most of you. But for those of you who are in doubt about it, let me say this: don't set yourselves apart in the way you dress, the way you think, the outdated codes of behaviour you cling to, the ideologies to which you attach your loyalties. Because if you do, you will be treated differently – not because of racism, though that does still exist, but because you insist on your difference from everyone else in this multi-ethnic, multi-religious, multitudinous United Kingdom of ours. And look at all you miss out because of it.
>
> (*HF*, 87–88)

What, one might ask, remains of the multi-ethnic, multi-religious, or multitudinous United Kingdom if difference is not *insisted* upon? Insisting on one's difference is here seen as a scourge, or even barnacle, on the smooth continued narrative of integration and on an idea of success and hard work centred on sports and celebrity status. In other words, it is through an allegiance to these new forms of identity that citizens can perform loyalty. In the essay 'Brexlit', Kristian Shaw reminds us that:

> The years leading up to the EU referendum witnessed a sudden and violent shift towards right-wing populism, hostility towards supranational forms of cosmopolitical democracy and global interdependence, extensive opposition

to open border policies, discontent with the cultural implications of globalisation, and a xenophobic resistance to both immigrants and transnational mobility in general.[157]

This shift went against the complex articulation of various forms of experience functioning within the nation state and redefining it: from multicultural citizens, migrants, refugees, and asylum seekers to diaspora communities finding ways to navigate new definitions of being at home but open to what these new forms might eventually allow for (an open and truer articulation of where we are). The backdrop to the Brexit referendum, illustrated by Shaw, points to the sharper end of these experiences. *Home Fire* forces a reckoning of sorts in not permitting a retreat from the consequences of these distributed effects, consequences that housed a growing resentment to forms of exclusion that had themselves been bolstered by fears around the threat of a growing global terrorism and the unwarranted connection to a perceived unfettered mass migration movement. The inability of a national voice to effectively frame these fears constructively within broader global geopolitical crises as reactions to declining standards of living, increased economic precarity, destabilising global conflicts, and civil unrest led to a poorly conceived and ultimately damaging standpoint. The failure to promote a culture of accountability to these issues both within and outside Britain and to incorporate any meaningful cultural literacy into educational curricula and national debates also paved the way for a 'perceived spread of Islamic ideology beyond the nation's perimeter and the growing demands for devolution and independence within provoked populist responses and a renewed effort to preserve established *national traditions and values*'[158] (my emphasis). In her article on *Home Fire*, Rehana Ahmed notes how 'the novel's emphasis on performance and surveillance highlights the role of the visual in shaping or entrenching perceptions of others, and thereby entrenching barriers between cultural groups, or impeding communication across them'.[159] In an ill-timed interview at border control, the character Issa, who wears a hijab, is questioned about 'her thoughts on Shias, homosexuals, the Queen, democracy, the *Great British Bake Off*, the invasion of Iraq, Israel, suicide bombers, dating websites' (*HF*, 5) in order to ascertain whether she considers herself to be *British*. Like Karamat Lone earlier, border force profiling seeks to homogenise the engagement with citizenship in order to distil national loyalty to prerequisites arranged on a predetermined axis.

In the novel, Issa's younger brother Parvaiz is approached and eventually drawn into a group practising extreme political and social ideologies with a view to recruiting members to support the establishment of the caliphate in Syria. Farooq, the most persuasive of these recruiters, manipulates Parvaiz's loyalty to more locally inflected, though no less vital, battles: in this instance, saving the neighbourhood library from closure by the local London council. Here, Parvaiz's actions are significant as they stand in for continued community participation, care for local cohesion, and commitment to forms of civic belonging. As he distributes leaflets, attends meetings, organises campaigns and fundraisers, and helps 'transport books local residents donated, volunteer[s] at the library every Sunday', he engages with intimate forms of belonging in areas where he might be able to bring about change (*HF*, 142–143). Confused as to whether any of these actions resonate and remain worthy in a 'world ablaze with injustice' (*HF*, 143), Farooq is there to assure him that these acts are worthy:

> 'The library . . . of course it matters. Same as what they're doing to the NHS, welfare benefits, all the rest of it. You know this country used to be great.'
> 'When was that?'
> 'Not so long ago. When it understood that a welfare state was something you built up instead of tearing down, when it saw immigrants as people to be welcomed, not turned away. Imagine what it would be like to live in such a nation.'
>
> (*HF*, 144)

As Nivedita Majumdar argues, 'by situating . . . Parvaiz' turn to radicalism, within a broader context of racial history and, especially, the conservative politics of economic austerity, Shamsie calls for a shared responsibility for the emergence of radicalism of different kinds'.[160]

It is in the context of what Majumdar terms 'the harshest cuts in public funding'[161] that Farooq entices Parvaiz by painting a picture of a successful nation attentive to the contribution of its citizens: 'a place where migrants coming in to join are treated like kings . . . a place where skin colour doesn't matter. Where schools and hospitals are free, and rich and poor have the same facilities' (*HF*, 144). This description of a paradisial caliphate echoes the aspirations of a socially minded welfare state, aspiring to justice and equality – a multicultural ideal that imagines a renewed blueprint for a just and fair society. In sympathising with Parvaiz's despair at the loss of the library, Farooq manipulates the loss of 'belonging and community' that comes from the erosion and 'slow disappearance of resources like public libraries which serve everyone equally'.[162] He understands how these callous and short-sighted institutional decisions contribute to humiliating individuals, as they limit opportunities and produce cultures of shame. Vulnerable young adults such as Parvaiz are sensitised to an ill-defined sense of injustice and taken in by arguments that sound convincing because they contain grains of truth: '"How can you live in this mirage of democracy and freedom" Farooq asks Parvaiz' (*HF*, 148).

Home Fire is at its most visionary when it draws attention to the voracious consumption of the image in contemporary culture: controlling the narrative and story is made palpable through the splicing of news stories with trending hashtags alongside interviews and tabloid journalism. The text gives shape to the speed at which opinions and reactions render all experiences as sensational and vacuous all at once. It is no laughing matter that Parvaiz is hired by the caliphate in order to ensure the professional quality of their *media* output. The tactics are the same, though the motivations may differ. What is missing in these swiftly produced and consumed representations, however, are slow and deliberate considerations of the fabric of contemporary British society in a globalised world. *Home Fire* represents a political context that reflects the culmination of several decades of competing forms of national identities vying for attention. This politically engaged set of authors whom we have engaged in this chapter all understand well the risks involved in making loud and public claims about the long legacy of empire and the continued traces of the unfinished business of colonialism in the developing frameworks enacted and often legislated to either produce conditions for inclusion or, and often at the same time, set up structures for exclusion from full participation in national politics. The authors that we have focused on here do not shy away from interrogating these structures and insist on a more nuanced approach that understands the risks associated with trying to redefine and give new energy to a thriving and inclusive state and its citizens. This chapter has captured the various ways in which writing has contributed to providing a fuller sense of what it means to experience fractured lives in a fractured nation. The conclusion to this book ponders how narrative might help us navigate a new cultural moment. As Alsana reminds us in *White Teeth*, 'you go back and back and back and it's still easier to find the right hoover bag than to find one pure person, one pure faith, on the globe. Do you think anybody is English? Really English? It's a fairy tale' (*WT*, 209).

Note

1 John McLeod, *Beginning Postcolonialism*, London: Routledge, 2007, p. 7.
2 Mary Louise Pratt, *Imperial Eyes: Travel Writing and Transculturation*, 2nd edition, London: Routledge, 2008.
3 Homi K. Bhabha, *The Location of Culture*, London: Routledge, 1994, p. 38.
4 Salman Rushdie, *The Satanic Verses*, New York: Random House, 1988, pp. 413–4.
5 Salman Rushdie, 'The New Empire Within Britain', in *Imaginary Homelands: Essays and Criticism, 1981–1991*, London: Granta Books, 1991 [1982], pp. 133–6.
6 Zadie Smith, *White Teeth*, London: Penguin, 2000, pp. 407–8. Subsequent references are given in the main text after *WT*.
7 Nick Bentley, 'Re-writing Englishness: Imagining the Nation in Julian Barnes's *England, England* and Zadie Smith's *White Teeth*', *Textual Practice*, 21:3 (2007), 483–504: 498.
8 Paul Gilroy, *After Empire: Melancholia or Convivial Culture*, London: Routledge, 2004.
9 Paul Gilroy, *After Empire: Melancholia or Convivial Culture*, London: Routledge, 2004, p. 2.
10 Wiktoria Tuńska, 'Those Scary Migrants: Feanxiety and Brexit in Agnieszka Dale's Fox Season and Other Short Stories', *Textual Practice* (2023), 1–19. Web. p. 1.
11 Wiktoria Tuńska, 'Those Scary Migrants: Feanxiety and Brexit in Agnieszka Dale's Fox Season and Other Short Stories', *Textual Practice* (2023), 5.
12 Roger Hewitt, *White Backlash and the Politics of Multiculturalism*. Cambridge: Cambridge University Press, 2005, p. 3.
13 Roger Hewitt, *White Backlash and the Politics of Multiculturalism*. Cambridge: Cambridge University Press, 2005, p. 4. Hewitt goes on to discuss the parallel academic discussions around multiculturalism in the United States that were broadly critical of its potential to contribute to racial equality and the rise of the One Nation Party in the Australia, 'which attacked multiculturalism without ambiguity' (p. 4).
14 Roger Hewitt, *White Backlash and the Politics of Multiculturalism*. Cambridge: Cambridge University Press, 2005, p. 4.
15 Roger Hewitt, *White Backlash and the Politics of Multiculturalism*. Cambridge: Cambridge University Press, 2005, p. 15.
16 Roger Hewitt, *White Backlash and the Politics of Multiculturalism*. Cambridge: Cambridge University Press, 2005, p. 15.

17 Roger Hewitt, *White Backlash and the Politics of Multiculturalism*. Cambridge: Cambridge University Press, 2005, p. 15. Here, Hewitt, in detailing stream 2, makes specific reference to 'The Universal Declaration of Human Rights and the various later conventions on civil, political and economic rights including the United Nations Declaration on the Rights of Persons Belonging to National, Ethnic, Religious and Linguistic Minorities (1992)'.
18 Abdulrazak Gurnah, *By the Sea*, London: Bloomsbury, 2001. Subsequent references are given in the main text after *BTS*.
19 Lasse Thomassen, *British Multiculturalism and the Politics of Representation*, Edinburgh: Edinburgh University Press, 2017, p. 4.
20 Lasse Thomassen, *British Multiculturalism and the Politics of Representation*, Edinburgh: Edinburgh University Press, 2017, p. 4.
21 Richard T. Ashcroft and Mark Bevir, 'British Multiculturalism after Empire: Immigration, Nationality, and Citizenship', in *Multiculturalism in the British Commonwealth: Comparative Perspectives on Theory and Practice*, 1st edition, eds. Richard T. Ashcroft and Mark Bevir, California: University of California Press, 2019, pp. 25–45: 34.
22 Monica Ali, *Brick Lane*, London: Doubleday, 2003. Subsequent references are given in the main text after *BL*.
23 Monica Ali, *Brick Lane*, London: Doubleday, 2003, p. 34.
24 https://assets-global.website-files.com/61488f992b58e687f1108c7c/617bff8c9e95ea704015a8b0_ACommunityOfCommunitiesAndCitizens-2000.pdf.
25 https://assets-global.website-files.com/61488f992b58e687f1108c7c/617bff8c9e95ea704015a8b0_ACommunityOfCommunitiesAndCitizens-2000.pdf. The six tasks are to rethink the national story and national identity; to recognise that all communities are changing; to hold a balance between cohesion, difference, and equality; to address and remove all forms of racism; to reduce economic inequalities; to build a pluralist human rights culture.
26 https://assets-global.website-files.com/61488f992b58e687f1108c7c/617bff8c9e95ea704015a8b0_ACommunityOfCommunitiesAndCitizens-2000.pdf.
27 Kamila Shamsie, *Home Fire*, London: Bloomsbury, 2017. Subsequent references are given in the main text after *HF*.
28 www.theguardian.com/uk-news/2014/mar/04/author-kamila-shamsie-british-citizen-indefinite-leave-to-remain.
29 Ashcroft and Bevir, 'British Multiculturalism after Empire: Immigration, Nationality, and Citizenship', p. 35. Ashcroft and Bevir outline the 'similar views articulated by the nongovernment Left in David Goodhart's famous series of articles in Demos and Prospect. This shift can be seen in numerous statements by figures such as Communities Secretary Ruth Kelly, the various reports on the 2001 riots, David Blunkett's introduction to the 2002 White Paper *Secure Borders, Safe Haven*, the introduction of "ideological" criteria for community group funding, and in the fact and form of the new nationality test and citizenship ceremonies'. p. 35.
30 Ashcroft and Bevir, 'British Multiculturalism after Empire: Immigration, Nationality, and Citizenship', p. 35.
31 Giorgio Agamben, 'We Refugees', *Symposium (Syracuse)*, 49:2 (1995), 114–9: 114.
32 www.theguardian.com/books/2015/sep/12/the-turmoil-of-todays-world-leading-writers-respond-to-the-refugee-crisis?CMP=share_btn_url.
33 www.theguardian.com/books/2015/sep/12/the-turmoil-of-todays-world-leading-writers-respond-to-the-refugee-crisis?CMP=share_btn_url.
34 Kristian Shaw, 'Brexlit', in *Brexit and Literature*, ed. Robert Eaglestone, London: Routledge, 2018, pp. 15–30: 26.
35 Ashcroft and Bevir, 'British Multiculturalism after Empire: Immigration, Nationality, and Citizenship', p. 37 (emphasis added).
36 Anne-Marie Fortier, *Multicultural Horizons: Diversity and the Limits of the Civil Nation*, London: Routledge, 2008, p. 3.

37 Anne-Marie Fortier, *Multicultural Horizons: Diversity and the Limits of the Civil Nation*, London: Routledge, 2008, p. 3.
38 Susheila Nasta, *Home Truths*, London: Bloomsbury, 2017, p. 2.
39 Corinne Fowler, *Green Unpleasant Land: Creative Responses to Rural Britain's Colonial Connections*, Leeds: Peepal Tree Press Ltd, 2020.
40 Fortier, *Multicultural Horizons: Diversity and the Limits of the Civil Nation*, p. 3.
41 Petra Tournay-Theodotou, Eva Ulrike Pirker and Sofía Muñoz-Valdivieso, 'Britishness beyond the New Britain: British Identities and the Identity of Britain in Recent Black and Asian British Writing', *Journal of Postcolonial Writing*, 52(1) (2016), 1–5.
42 Simon Featherstone, *Postcolonial Cultures*, Edinburgh: Edinburgh University Press, 2005, p. 23.
43 John McLeod, 'Warning Signs: Postcolonial Writing and the Apprehension of Brexit', *Journal of Postcolonial Writing*, 56:5 (2020), 607–20: 607.
44 John McLeod, 'Warning Signs: Postcolonial Writing and the Apprehension of Brexit', *Journal of Postcolonial Writing*, 56:5 (2020), 608.
45 John McLeod, 'Warning Signs: Postcolonial Writing and the Apprehension of Brexit', *Journal of Postcolonial Writing*, 56:5 (2020), 611.
46 John McLeod, 'Warning Signs: Postcolonial Writing and the Apprehension of Brexit', *Journal of Postcolonial Writing*, 56:5 (2020), 611.
47 Nicole Weickgenannt Thiara, *Salman Rushdie and Indian Historiography: Writing the Nation into Being*, Basingstoke: Palgrave Macmillan, 2009, p. 23.
48 Fortier, *Multicultural Horizons: Diversity and the Limits of the Civil Nation*, p. 68.
49 Kenan Malik, *From Fatwa to Jihad: The Rushdie Affair and Its Legacy*, London: Atlantic Books, 2010, p. 4.
50 Jan Dobbernack, Nasar Meer and Tariq Modood, 'Muslim Political Agency in British Politics', in *British Muslims and Their Discourses*, ed. Laurens De Rooij, Cham: Springer, 2024, pp. 3–22: 7.
51 Jan Dobbernack, Nasar Meer and Tariq Modood, 'Muslim Political Agency in British Politics', in *British Muslims and Their Discourses*, ed. Laurens De Rooij, Cham: Springer, 2024, p. 10.
52 Jan Dobbernack, Nasar Meer and Tariq Modood, 'Muslim Political Agency in British Politics', in *British Muslims and Their Discourses*, ed. Laurens De Rooij, Cham: Springer, 2024, p. 10.
53 Claire Forbes, 'Politics, Public Relations and Islam in the UK Public Sphere', in *British Muslims and Their Discourses*, ed. Laurens De Rooij, Cham: Springer, 2024, pp. 55–75: 62.
54 Claire Forbes, 'Politics, Public Relations and Islam in the UK Public Sphere', in *British Muslims and Their Discourses*, ed. Laurens De Rooij, Cham: Springer, 2024, p. 62.
55 Claire Forbes, 'Politics, Public Relations and Islam in the UK Public Sphere', in *British Muslims and Their Discourses*, ed. Laurens De Rooij, Cham: Springer, 2024, p. 63.
56 Dominic Head, *The Cambridge Introduction to Modern British Fiction, 1950–2000*, Cambridge: Cambridge University Press, 2002, p. 156.
57 Beatriz Pérez Zapata, *Zadie Smith and Postcolonial Trauma: Decolonizing Trauma, Decolonizing Selves*, New York, NY: Routledge, 2021, p. 69.
58 Beatriz Pérez Zapata, *Zadie Smith and Postcolonial Trauma: Decolonizing Trauma, Decolonizing Selves*, New York, NY: Routledge, 2021, p. 69.
59 Beatriz Pérez Zapata, *Zadie Smith and Postcolonial Trauma: Decolonizing Trauma, Decolonizing Selves*, New York, NY: Routledge, 2021, pp. 69–70.
60 Beatriz Pérez Zapata, *Zadie Smith and Postcolonial Trauma: Decolonizing Trauma, Decolonizing Selves*, New York, NY: Routledge, 2021, p. 72.
61 Ulrike Tancke, '*White Teeth* Reconsidered: Narrative Deception and Uncomfortable Truth', in *Reading Zadie Smith: The First Decade and Beyond*, ed. Philip Tew, London: Bloomsbury Academic, 2013, pp. 27–38: 27.

62 Ulrike Tancke, '*White Teeth* Reconsidered: Narrative Deception and Uncomfortable Truth', in *Reading Zadie Smith: The First Decade and Beyond*, ed. Philip Tew, London: Bloomsbury Academic, 2013, p. 27.
63 Graham MacPhee, *Postwar British Literature and Postcolonial Writing*, Edinburgh: Edinburgh University Press, 2011, p. 163.
64 Fortier, *Multicultural Horizons: Diversity and the Limits of the Civil Nation*, p. 17.
65 Fortier, *Multicultural Horizons: Diversity and the Limits of the Civil Nation*, p. 17.
66 Fortier, *Multicultural Horizons: Diversity and the Limits of the Civil Nation*, p. 18 (original emphasis).
67 Tancke, '*White Teeth* Reconsidered: Narrative Deception and Uncomfortable Truth', p. 28.
68 Tancke, '*White Teeth* Reconsidered: Narrative Deception and Uncomfortable Truth', pp. 29–30.
69 Tancke, '*White Teeth* Reconsidered: Narrative Deception and Uncomfortable Truth', p. 33.
70 Zapata, *Zadie Smith and Postcolonial Trauma: Decolonizing Trauma, Decolonizing Selves*, p. 27.
71 Zapata, *Zadie Smith and Postcolonial Trauma: Decolonizing Trauma, Decolonizing Selves*, pp. 27–8.
72 Zapata, *Zadie Smith and Postcolonial Trauma: Decolonizing Trauma, Decolonizing Selves*, p. 28.
73 MacPhee, *Postwar British Literature and Postcolonial Writing*, p. 2.
74 Paul Gilroy, *Postcolonial Melancholia*, New York: Columbia University Press, 2005, p. 2.
75 See Peter Childs, *Contemporary Novelists: British Fiction since 1970*, Basingstoke: Palgrave Macmillan, 2005 for a fuller discussion on the element of chance and contingency in *White Teeth*.
76 Jonathan P. A. Sell, 'Chance and Gesture in Zadie Smith's White Teeth and The Autograph Man: A Model for Multicultural Identity?' *Journal of Commonwealth Literature*, 41:3 (2006), 27–44.
77 Rushdie, *Imaginary Homelands: Essays and Criticism, 1981–1991*, pp. 137–8.
78 Rushdie, *Imaginary Homelands: Essays and Criticism, 1981–1991*, pp. 137–8.
79 Dominic Head, 'Zadie Smith's *White Teeth*: Multiculturalism for the Millennium', in *Contemporary British Fiction*, eds. Richard J. Lane, Rod Mengham and Philip Tew, Cambridge; Oxford: Polity, 2003, pp. 106–19: 111.
80 Fortier, *Multicultural Horizons: Diversity and the Limits of the Civil Nation*, p. 18.
81 This can be seen in the recent debate at the National Trust. See also Corrine Fowler and Lucienne Loh on the role of complex imbrication of heritage scholarship in the context of decolonising agendas.
82 Tony Blair, speech at Downing St, 8/12/06.
83 Britta Timm Knudsen, John Oldfield, Elizabeth Buettner and Elvan Zabunyan, 'Introduction', in *Decolonizing Colonial Heritage: New Agendas, Actors and Practices in and beyond Europe*, eds. Britta Timm Knuden et al., Abingdon: Routledge, 2022, pp. 1–21: 7.
84 Tancke, 'White Teeth Reconsidered: Narrative Deception and Uncomfortable Truth', p. 36.
85 Magdalena Maczynska, '"That God Chip in the Brain": Religion in the Fiction of Zadie Smith', in *Reading Zadie Smith: The First Decade and Beyond*, ed. Philip Tew, London: Bloomsbury Academic, 2013, pp. 127–41: 129.
86 Magdalena Maczynska, '"That God Chip in the Brain": Religion in the Fiction of Zadie Smith', in *Reading Zadie Smith: The First Decade and Beyond*, ed. Philip Tew, London: Bloomsbury Academic, 2013, p. 129.
87 Magdalena Maczynska, '"That God Chip in the Brain": Religion in the Fiction of Zadie Smith', in *Reading Zadie Smith: The First Decade and Beyond*, ed. Philip Tew, London: Bloomsbury Academic, 2013, p. 130.

88 Arun Kundnani, 'Integrationism: The Politics of Anti-Muslim Racism', *Race and Class*, 48:4 (2007), 24–44: 26.
89 Arun Kundnani, 'Integrationism: The Politics of Anti-Muslim Racism', *Race and Class*, 48:4 (2007), 26.
90 Arun Kundnani, 'Integrationism: The Politics of Anti-Muslim Racism', *Race and Class*, 48:4 (2007), 27.
91 Arun Kundnani, 'Integrationism: The Politics of Anti-Muslim Racism', *Race and Class*, 48:4 (2007), 27.
92 Ali Rezaie, 'Cultural Dislocation in Monica Ali's *Brick Lane*: Freedom or Anomie?', *The Journal of Commonwealth Literature*, 51:1 (2016), 62–75. Rezaie provides a comprehensive view of these reactions from postcolonial scholars.
93 Ali Rezaie, 'Cultural Dislocation in Monica Ali's *Brick Lane*: Freedom or Anomie?', *The Journal of Commonwealth Literature*, 51:1 (2016), 62.
94 Ali Rezaie, 'Cultural Dislocation in Monica Ali's *Brick Lane*: Freedom or Anomie?', *The Journal of Commonwealth Literature*, 51:1 (2016), 63.
95 Ali Rezaie, 'Cultural Dislocation in Monica Ali's *Brick Lane*: Freedom or Anomie?', *The Journal of Commonwealth Literature*, 51:1 (2016), 66.
96 Nick Bentley, *Contemporary British Fiction*, Edinburgh: Edinburgh University Press, 2008, p. 88.
97 Stephen Morton, 'Multicultural Neoliberalism, Global Textiles, and the Making of the Indebted Female Entrepreneur in Monica Ali's Brick Lane', in *Muslims, Trust and Multiculturalism: New Directions*, eds. Amina Yaqin and Peter Morey, Cham: Springer International Publishing, 2018, pp. 171–92: 172.
98 Stephen Morton, 'Multicultural Neoliberalism, Global Textiles, and the Making of the Indebted Female Entrepreneur in Monica Ali's Brick Lane', in *Muslims, Trust and Multiculturalism: New Directions*, eds. Amina Yaqin and Peter Morey, Cham: Springer International Publishing, 2018, p. 172.
99 Nikita Lalwani, *Gifted*, London: Penguin, 2007. Subsequent references are given in the main text after *Gifted*.
100 Gauri Viswanathan, *Masks of Conquest: Literary Study and British Rule in India*, 25th anniversary edition, West Sussex, England: Columbia University Press, 2015. Viswanathan notes that 'although commerce was the means by which England expanded internationally into distant outposts, education was effectively the site on which its reach was consolidated' (xviii). Also, although Viswanathan, in making clear her argumentative remit, warns us against 'reading the history of nineteenth-century English studies as continuous with contemporary educational practice' (p. 168), her observations still give us a framework within which to place the role and legacy of English literature in colonial India.
101 Barbara Cassin, *Nostalgia: When Are We Ever at Home?*, New York: Fordham University Press, 2016.
102 Claire Chambers, *Making Sense of Contemporary British Muslim Novels*, London: Palgrave Macmillan, 2019, p. xxv.
103 Claire Chambers, *Making Sense of Contemporary British Muslim Novels*, London: Palgrave Macmillan, 2019, p. 72.
104 Claire Chambers, *Making Sense of Contemporary British Muslim Novels*, London: Palgrave Macmillan, 2019, p. 79.
105 Abdulrazak Gurnah, *By the Sea*, London: Bloomsbury, 2003, p. 13.
106 Chambers, *Making Sense of Contemporary British Muslim Novels*, p. 85.
107 Chambers, *Making Sense of Contemporary British Muslim Novels*, p. 86.
108 https://emergency.unhcr.org/protection/legal-framework/refugee-definition.
109 The United Kingdom has just passed a law firming up the process to transport 'illegal' asylum seekers to a third country after declaring Rwanda a 'safe' country in April 2024: www.gov.uk/government/publications/the-safety-of-rwanda-asylum-and-

immigration-bill-factsheets/safety-of-rwanda-asylum-and-immigration-bill-factsheet-accessible#what-are-we-going-to-do.
110 https://youtu.be/EDAhSqYLV6E.
111 Bill Ashcroft, *Postcolonial Transformations*, London: Routledge, 2001, pp. 47–8.
112 Ashcroft, *Postcolonial Transformations*, pp. 47–8.
113 Lucinda Newns, 'Homelessness and the Refugee: De-Valorizing Displacement in Abdulrazak Gurnah's *By the Sea*', *Journal of Postcolonial Writing*, 51:5 (2015), 506–18: 513.
114 Lucinda Newns, 'Homelessness and the Refugee: De-Valorizing Displacement in Abdulrazak Gurnah's *By the Sea*', *Journal of Postcolonial Writing*, 51:5 (2015), 513.
115 Sarah Gibson, 'Accommodating Strangers: British Hospitality and the Asylum Hotel Debate', *Journal for Cultural Research*, 7:4 (2003), 367–86: 370.
116 David Farrier, 'Terms of Hospitality: Abdulrazak Gurnah's By the Sea', *Journal of Commonwealth Literature*, 43:3 (2008), 121–39: 122.
117 David Farrier, 'Terms of Hospitality: Abdulrazak Gurnah's By the Sea', *Journal of Commonwealth Literature*, 43:3 (2008), 122.
118 David Farrier, 'Terms of Hospitality: Abdulrazak Gurnah's By the Sea', *Journal of Commonwealth Literature*, 43:3 (2008), 126 (my emphasis).
119 Edward Said, *Culture and Imperialism*, London: Chatto & Windus, 1993, p. 261.
120 Sissy Helff, 'Measuring Silence – Dialogic Contact Zones in Abdulrazak Gurnah's *By the Sea* and *Desertion*', *Matatu*, 46:46 (2015), 153–268.
121 Sissy Helff, 'Measuring Silence – Dialogic Contact Zones in Abdulrazak Gurnah's *By the Sea* and *Desertion*,' *Matatu*, 46:46 (2015), 157.
122 Giorgio Agamben, 'We Refugees', trans. Michael Rocke, *Symposium*, 49:2 (1995), 114–9.
123 Giorgio Agamben, 'We Refugees', trans. Michael Rocke, *Symposium*, 49:2 (1995), 117.
124 Ulla Rahbek, *British Multicultural Literature and Superdiversity*, Cham: Springer International Publishing, 2019, pp. 9–10.
125 Ulla Rahbek, *British Multicultural Literature and Superdiversity*, Cham: Springer International Publishing, 2019, pp. 209–10.
126 Ulla Rahbek, *British Multicultural Literature and Superdiversity*, Cham: Springer International Publishing, 2019, p. 143.
127 Sudesh Mishra, *Diaspora Criticism*. Edinburgh: Edinburgh University Press, 2006.
128 Sudesh Mishra, *Diaspora Criticism*. Edinburgh: Edinburgh University Press, 2006, p. 53.
129 Mishra here is alert to what he call's Zenner's sidestepping of 'the territorial presence of modern-day Israel', p. 53.
130 Sudesh Mishra, *Diaspora Criticism*. Edinburgh: Edinburgh University Press, 2006, p. 53.
131 Sudesh Mishra, *Diaspora Criticism*. Edinburgh: Edinburgh University Press, 2006, p. 55.
132 Sudesh Mishra, *Diaspora Criticism*. Edinburgh: Edinburgh University Press, 2006, p. 56.
133 Mishra goes on to also argue that he does not want to espouse a loss of specificity (what he calls archival specificity) but, rather, that he wants to dislodge the imagined immutable and stable connection to territory often afforded to diaspora imaginaries. p. 96.
134 Avtar Brah, *Cartographies of Diaspora: Contesting Identities*, London: Routledge, 1996, p. 183 (my emphasis).
135 Nasta, *Home Truths*.
136 www.nationalarchives.gov.uk/education/outreach/projects/migration-histories/marking-the-50th-anniversary-of-the-arrival-of-ugandan-asians-in-britain-2022/.
137 Brah, *Cartographies of Diaspora: Contesting Identities*, p. 182.

138 Anindya Raychaudhuri, *Homemaking: Radical Nostalgia and the Construction of a South Asian Diaspora*, London: Rowman and Littlefield International, 2018, p. 3.
139 Anindya Raychaudhuri, *Homemaking: Radical Nostalgia and the Construction of a South Asian Diaspora*, London: Rowman and Littlefield International, 2018, p. 4 (my emphasis).
140 Anindya Raychaudhuri, *Homemaking: Radical Nostalgia and the Construction of a South Asian Diaspora*, London: Rowman and Littlefield International, 2018, p. 12.
141 Anindya Raychaudhuri, *Homemaking: Radical Nostalgia and the Construction of a South Asian Diaspora*, London: Rowman and Littlefield International, 2018, p. 12.
142 Anindya Raychaudhuri, *Homemaking: Radical Nostalgia and the Construction of a South Asian Diaspora*, London: Rowman and Littlefield International, 2018, p. 12.
143 Anh Hua, 'Diaspora and Cultural Memory', in *Diaspora, Memory, and Identity: A Search for Home*, ed. Vijay Agnew, University of Toronto Press, 2005, pp. 191–208: 198.
144 Vijay Agnew, *Diaspora, Memory and Identity: A Search for Home*, University of Toronto Press, 2005, p. 14.
145 Brah, *Cartographies of Diaspora: Contesting Identities*, p. 193.
146 Brah, *Cartographies of Diaspora: Contesting Identities*, p. 194.
147 Hua, 'Diaspora and Cultural Memory', p. 196.
148 Hua, 'Diaspora and Cultural Memory', p. 197.
149 Rajinder Kumar Dudrah, *Bollywood Travels: Culture, Diaspora and Border Crossings in Popular Hindi Cinema*, London: Routledge, 2012, p. 66.
150 Rajinder Kumar Dudrah, *Bollywood Travels: Culture, Diaspora and Border Crossings in Popular Hindi Cinema*, London: Routledge, 2012, p. 67.
151 Salman Rushdie, *Imaginary Homelands: Essays and Criticism, 1981–1991*, London: Granta Books, 1992, p. 102.
152 Figures that Rushdie rightfully acknowledges as equally important to the narrative of Indian Independence.
153 Rushdie, *Imaginary Homelands: Essays and Criticism, 1981–1991*, p. 104.
154 'Interview with Kamila Shamsie', Robert Spencer and Anastasia Valassopoulos, April 29th, 2019, Manchester.
155 Rob Nixon, *Slow Violence and the Environmentalism of the Poor*, Cambridge, MA: Harvard University Press, 2011, p. 11. '"In these terms" Nixon argues, "we can recognize that the structural violence embodied by a neoliberal order of austerity measures, structural adjustment, rampant deregulation, corporate megamergers, and widening gulf between rich and poor is a form of covert violence in its own right that is often a catalyst for some recognizably overt violence."' pp. 10–1.
156 Robert Spencer and Anastasia Valassopoulos, *Postcolonial Locations: Issues and Directions in Postcolonial Studies*, Abingdon: Routledge, 2021, p. 61.
157 Shaw, 'Brexlit', p. 15.
158 Shaw, 'Brexlit', p. 17.
159 Rehana Ahmed, 'Towards an Ethics of Reading Muslims: Encountering Difference in Kamila Shamsie's *Home Fire*', *Textual Practice*, 35:7 (2021), 1145–61: 1153.
160 Nivedita Majumdar, 'The Terrorist Next Door: Kamila Shamsie's *Home Fire* and the Pitfalls of Terrorism Discourse', *Journal of Global Postcolonial Studies*, 9:1 (2022), 18–29: 19.
161 Nivedita Majumdar, 'The Terrorist Next Door: Kamila Shamsie's *Home Fire* and the Pitfalls of Terrorism Discourse', *Journal of Global Postcolonial Studies*, 9:1 (2022), 25.
162 Nivedita Majumdar, 'The Terrorist Next Door: Kamila Shamsie's *Home Fire* and the Pitfalls of Terrorism Discourse', *Journal of Global Postcolonial Studies*, 9:1 (2022), 26.

Conclusion

British Writing from Empire to Brexit has characterised Britain as an empire. Britain ought to be seen as a kind of Greater England, though the England that expanded during the eighteenth and nineteenth centuries and then began to contract in the twentieth was less the specific geographical territory South of the Tweed and East of the Marches than the economic interests of England's predominantly Southern ruling bloc. Britain was an imperial construction in short. Furthermore, it is less a nation state than a state nation. Power and wealth in Britain are unusually concentrated in a state that presides shakily over an increasingly disgruntled and fissiparous congeries of different groups, classes, regions, and nations. With the post-imperial British state now plainly disunited and dysfunctional, there is very little of the old British affluence and arrogance to force it together. In these circumstances, sullen English nationalists are among those who crave the break-up of Britain and England's own independence. Or like the modern Tory Party, English nationalists are prepared to go through the motions of British nationalism a little longer, parroting the phrases of archipelagic unity and 'levelling up' the regions while actually stoking the forces that are driving Britain's break-up: inequality, high-handed centralisation, regional under-investment, and the exorbitant privilege of the finance sector. Irish unity and Scottish and Welsh separation, plus meaningful devolution to England's regions, await the overdue expiry of a British nationalism that is now little more than a mask for the economic self-interest of England's ruling groups.

How might writers respond to the zombified continuation of a still-unbroken-up Britain? We expect that poems, plays, and novels will continue to reimagine the deep histories and broader geographical connections of these isles as well as their variegated localities. Novelists as different from one another in other respects as Abdulrazak Gurnah, Kamila Shamsie, Caryl Philips, Kazuo Ishiguro, and Bernardine Evaristo nonetheless share a determination to counter what the historian David Olusoga calls the newly brazen practice of 'historical forgetting' that is trying to simplify understandings of British history.[1] We wish we had the space to discuss the work of the Orcadian novelist and poet George McKay Brown in order to demonstrate that the tracing of local particularities, deep histories, and unexpected connections is frequently the business of writers from the outermost edges

DOI: 10.4324/9781003230816-5

of the archipelago. Brown's work places the wind-battered Orkney Islands at the confluence of a Northern European and even global geography of travel, trade, and connection. Brown styles himself as a beachcomber, a largely stationary but imaginatively itinerant figure, picturing the journey of a boy in the eleventh century (when Orkney was part of Norway) from Stromness to the Vikings' North American colony in *Vinland* (1992) or in the formally daring *Magnus* (1972) intertwining the deaths of two martyrs, the twelfth-century saint Magnus Erlendsson, Earl of Orkney, and the Lutheran pastor Dietrich Bonhoeffer in Flossenbürg concentration camp in 1945.

In the next few years, Scotland, Wales, and Northern Ireland might disentangle themselves from the lines tethering them to the listing vessel of British statehood. Writing from Scotland, Wales, and Ulster explores what sort of disruptions and connections that severing might enable in the works of writers like Deirdre Madden, Don Paterson, James Kelman, Liz Lochhead, Alys Conran, and Anna Burns. The poetry of place and of intimate experience will hopefully continue to make connections with global histories of migration, conquest, travel, and ecology in works by poets like Kathleen Jamie, Alice Oswald, Elizabeth-Jane Burnett, Daljit Nagra, Jackie Kay, and Jason Allen-Paisant. One of our hopes for the next few years is that writers will produce more nuanced and textured fictions of place. In our view, short story collections are already starting to compile these sorts of intricately layered and polyphonic portrayals of specific locations. We have in mind Lucy Wood's stories about Cornwall in *Diving Belles* (2012) and *The Sing of the Shore* (2018), Sarah Hall's more itinerant *The Beautiful Indifference* (2011), and Jon McGregor's *This Isn't the Sort of Thing That Happens to Someone Like You* (2012) about the friable fenlands, or even McGregor's *Reservoir 13* (2017), which is a kind of novel about place (the Peak District) brought closer to the collage effects of the short story collection. The point is to articulate oblique perspectives and possibilities. Works of literature will, as always, be a means of articulating the experiences and aspirations of groups excluded from or simply antagonistic to dominant definitions of nationhood. They help us reimagine the archipelago.

We want to end, therefore, by looking briefly at two novels that explore the future of these islands by rewriting their past: alternative Second World War fantasies of invasion and resistance. Owen Sheers' *Resistance* (2007) and C. J. Sansom's *Dominion* (2012) are explicitly anti-fascist texts. They belong to a genre of cautionary tales of fascist Britain that includes Katharine Burdekin's earnest *Swastika Night* (1937), Len Deighton's thriller *SS-GB* (1978), Humphrey Jennings' radical propaganda film *The Silent Village* (1943), and Kevin Brownlow and Andrew Mollo's unique, very-low-budget film *It Happened Here* (1964). We are not necessarily suggesting that Britain is going fascist, as it were. But we have certainly not been reassured by the speeches given at the National Conservatism conference in May 2023 or by the wildly inflammatory stories pushed for years in the right-wing press about 'cultural Marxism', the various threats posed to 'white society', and the dangers of 'wokeness'. That last term in particular has become not so much a dog whistle as an ear-splitting claxon to summon everyone who rejects the basic premises that citizens of Britain are all equal and that asylum seekers are human beings. There are very few firewalls in Britain's post-liberal polity, its aggressively conservative media, or its extremely undemocratic political institutions to keep authoritarian nationalism out.

Fintan O'Toole argues in his *Heroic Failure: Brexit and the Politics of Pain* (2018) that Brexit Britain's endless harping on World War II myths of heroic defiance and the ubiquitous kitsch Churchilliana (of which Boris Johnson is one of the chief hawkers) testify to a 'weird need to dream England into a state of awful oppression'.[2] Very real grievances about problems like wage stagnation and regional inequality are channelled into spurious grievances about foreign invasion. British people are told ceaselessly that they have been invaded by immigrants, that the European Union is the Fourth Reich, and that their real enemies are a fifth column of uppity minorities and 'metropolitan elites'. The defeat of the British military in Afghanistan and Iraq showed that it is not so much war that gives Britons their kicks and reassures them of the possibility of 'a meaningful collective existence' but 'the idea of invasion and submission'. Hence also, O'Toole contends, the perennial popularity, particularly in the last 20 years, of alternative-history versions of the Second World War in which Britain is invaded by Germany and made to submit. It is as if the English might weld themselves together, O'Toole continues, only with the aid of fantasies about resistance to foreign invasion. What is notable about *Resistance* and *Dominion*, however, is certainly not that they underwrite the war nostalgia or the Churchill cult that, in 2019, saw the nation dreaming of its past under the auspices of a bad Churchill impersonator. In fact, they are explicitly anti-fascist works. Moreover, they strike blows against the enduring, if not intensifying, appeal of what David Edgerton calls 'the central national myth'[3] that, in 1940, an 'island nation' stood heroically alone against the threat of invasion. In both novels, the real danger of an authoritarian takeover comes from within, not from without.

Sansom's *Dominion* was first published in 2012 towards the beginning of the long period of Tory hegemony that would issue in the Brexit vote. For Owen Hatherley, a culture of austerity at this time, from retro architectural trends and the flag-heavy 2012 Olympics to the ubiquitous 'Keep Calm and Carry On' merchandise, nostalgically conjured up the shared sacrifices of the Second World War and its immediate aftermath.[4] The supposed national mission this time, however, was not a 'people's war' or the socialist policies of reconstruction but a rearguard defence of class power. The Tory-Lib Dem coalition's programme of austerity inflicted belt-tightening measures mainly on the young, the disabled, and the very poor while lavishing tax cuts and asset price inflation on the wealthy.[5] All this took place in tandem with the paranoid nationalism of Theresa May's 'hostile environment' and creeping Europhobia. *Dominion* registers but certainly does not exalt this reactionary structure of feeling. The novel, in short, is much more than a conservative lament for 'majesty turned to subjection', as O'Toole's brief account unfairly alleges, not least because in the novel Britain has not been invaded at all but has gone fascist of its own accord.

Set in 1952, *Dominion* describes a Britain that has surrendered to Nazism without a fight after the retreat from Dunkirk, as indeed Foreign Secretary Lord Halifax and other Tory politicians at that time wished it to do. It is now an impoverished nation of thugs and cowards, its meagre resources drained by anti-colonial insurgencies in India and East Africa. One of the titillations of the 'What if Hitler won the war?' genre is seeing how familiar people and places fare in this very long book's richly imagined parallel dimension. *Dominion* treats us to the bizarre and comical, such as television shows in which Fanny Craddock demonstrates how to make sauerkraut, as well as the bizarre and sinister: the Isle of Wight as a German naval base, Marie Stopes advising the Department of Health on how to 'sterilise lunatics', the art deco massif of Senate House in Bloomsbury doubling as a swastika-draped headquarters for the Gestapo. The shady newspaper baron Lord Beaverbrook is the prime minister, at the head of a motley cast of proto- and actual fascists, like Enoch Powell (Secretary of State for India) and Oswald Moseley (Home Secretary). Powell's televised address about troop build-ups in India disturbingly echoes the language of his racist 'Rivers of Blood' speech.

The terrifically thrilling plot centres on the efforts of a pleasingly representative selection of heroic ordinary folk (a gay Glaswegian communist, a woman who leads the Slovakian resistance, a working-class Irish couple, and a bowler-hatted civil servant and his wife) to spring a scientist from an asylum and get him to an American submarine before he can spill the beans to the SS about how to make an atom bomb. One of the interesting things about this pitiably maladjusted figure of the scientist, we learn from a lengthy digression, is that his left hand was crippled by school bullies on a cross-country run at an austere Scottish boarding school. It is the damaged masculinity of the public school system in which an instantly recognisable and plausible British fascism is incubated. Sansom's Britain is not a colony oppressed by some foreign foe, as pre-Brexit Britain imagined itself under the heel of the EU. *Dominion* portrays a disarmingly familiar-sounding realm that 'had turned *itself* into a place where an authoritarian government in league with Fascist thugs thrived on nationalist dreams of Empire, on scapegoats and enemies'.[6] The italics are very much our emphasis; we'd put the insight in letters a hundred feet high if we could.

Dominion is not especially radical, we should stress. An elderly Churchill is, inevitably, the Resistance's heroic leader, though oddly enough, his headquarters have been set up in his own house, which is surely the first place where the Gestapo would look for him. Sansom's real ire (including in an odd 'Historical Note' at the end in which he urges his compatriots not to vote for independence) is reserved for a Nazi-collaborating Scottish National Party, whose members play the bagpipes as accompaniment to the breaking up of trade union meetings by street thugs! But whatever its hobby horses, *Dominion* depicts a horribly plausible and cautionary version of Britain. In fascist Britain, bureaucrats waiting for retirement turn a blind eye to disappearances and deportations. An authoritarian government is fronted by odious xenophobes, public school bullies, and unscrupulous newspaper hacks. The alternative to all this, the novel simply but quite movingly suggests, takes shape in revulsion towards sadism and chauvinistic flag-waving. 'They can't do this. Not here, not in England.'[7] It is this declaration, made by an outraged suburban housewife just before she heroically sits down in front of a line of mounted policemen who are frogmarching British Jews into detention along Tottenham Court Road, that the novel sets out to refute. The novel applauds the resistance and it wants us to ask who 'they' really are.

There is no exact Welsh equivalent to the second Scottish Renaissance after 1979, the assertive process of cultural self-representation that has both chronicled and quickened the simultaneous struggle for political autonomy in works by novelists like Alasdair Gray, James Kelman, Janice Galloway, and Irvine Welsh, or by poets such as Liz Lochhead and Tom Leonard.[8] There are no 'Indyref novels' in Wales, because there is no prospect yet of a referendum on independence there.[9] This process is both more nascent and more tentative in Wales. The Anglo-Welsh poet and novelist Owen Sheers's *Resistance*, published in 2007 in the years after the founding of the Welsh Assembly and in the midst of the increasingly chauvinistic atmosphere of English politics in that period, articulates devolutionary aspirations not so much for sovereignty or separatism but for cultural autonomy and a kind of civic and egalitarian ethos. The novel does so via an implicit critique of the self-serving war myths and invasion fantasies of English and Great British nationalism. Set in a secluded valley on the English–Welsh border country in 1944 in the months after a German invasion, *Resistance* is a searching meditation on the meaning of that word. Again, it is not so much a foreign foe that is being resisted by the sheep farmers, who, at the start of the novel, leave their homes in the middle of the night, to fight the invaders, or by their wives, who are obliged to accommodate an increasingly pacifistic band of German soldiers on a mystery mission to the Welsh hills. In fact, the soldiers are an impressively cultured and sympathetic group, helping to dig the ewes out of snowdrifts, train a foal, and generally wile away the time reading and thinking in this out-of-the-way hamlet until the fighting is over. If there is a nationalist element to the resistance, then the guerrilla campaign (about which we hear very little) actually recalls the myths of Welsh resistance to their immediate neighbour. It is a territory or a home that is being defended by the off-stage operations of these sheep-farming irregulars. But which territory, and what sort of home?

Before our heroine Sarah flees the village at the end of the novel, she stops to torch the Mappa Mundi to prevent it from falling into the hands of the advancing English volunteers of the SS Albion division. That beautiful thirteenth-century map of the world has been taken from Hereford Cathedral and hidden before the invasion in a nearby cave; Captain Wolfram's men have been tasked with spiriting it away to Himmler's castle in Wewelsburg, a sort of Nazi Camelot, to which Europe's looted medieval treasures are being taken. In short, it is Sarah's commitment to a certain ideal of culture, not in the sense of priceless artefacts, but in the great Welsh cultural theorist Raymond Williams's sense of a community's 'whole way of life', that is doing the resisting here.[10] The Mappa Mundi represents her culture's expressive power and its distinctive way of seeing and encountering the world. By burning it, she refuses to let that power be taken away by the approaching fascists, who intriguingly are English, not German. The novel is replete with allusions to rebellions and references to Welsh and Anglo-Welsh poetry, including an epigraph from Edward Thomas, the nearby ruins of the utopian schemes of

Walter Savage Landor, and especially Sarah's conversations as a child with the artist and poet David Jones as he painted by the valley streams near Eric Gill's artistic community at Capel-Y-Ffin. Sarah recollects Jones's stories about a Welsh king beaten by Edward Longshanks, whose entire army is sleeping in the hills, 'ready to wake and defend the country in its hour of need'.[11] Needlessly to say, it is fascism that is being resisted here, but it is definitely not Britain, let alone England, that is being defended.

These anti-fascist fictions work to dispel the neurotic fixation with foreign invasion in British nationalism. Earlier we compared the British state to the deathless Sibyl. On reflection, perhaps it is more like Dickens's Miss Havisham, a bitter nostalgic endlessly chewing over its memories and resentments in a battered bath chair, with the clock stopped forever at whenever it was in June 1940 that Churchill promised the House of Commons that 'we shall defend our island'. If the United States has 1776 and France has 1789, the British have 1940: the British nation's origin myth. In fact, the war mythology and the accompanying Churchill cult are of surprisingly recent vintage. The war itself was regularly mocked in post-war British culture, from the skits of the *Beyond the Fringe* comedy revue in the early 1960s to Joe Orton's 1969 farce *What the Butler Saw*, which stars Churchill's detachable penis. Howard Brenton's *The Churchill Play*, which opened at the Nottingham Playhouse in 1974, imagines a near-future Tory–Labour coalition government in thrall to the old ruling class warrior locking up trade unionists in a gulag that is oddly reminiscent of the detention camp at Long Kesh near Belfast. The play begins with a decomposing Churchill rising from his Union Jack–draped catafalque. This turns out to be a rehearsal for a scene in a subversive play that the inmates are putting on for a visiting parliamentary delegation. Here the incessant haunting of modern Britain by that 'bloody man' is an occasion for critique, not veneration: 'People won the war', as one of the detainees declares: 'He just got pissed with Stalin.'[12]

Most Second World War poetry is equally allergic to nationalist myth-making. The Welshman Alun Lewis had a knack for capturing telling details and for describing the longueurs of army life for working-class conscripts in poems like 'All Day it Has Rained . . .', which is, by the way, perhaps one of the few experiences that the extremely diverse inhabitants of the archipelago all share. Keith Douglas, on his departure for the Middle East in May 1941, likewise undercuts the rhetoric of heroic elegy:

Remember me when I am dead
and simplify me when I'm dead.[13]

Douglas is sceptical not so much about the war as about the way that rituals of public remembrance will misrepresent the lives and 'opinions' of those who fought in it. This aversion to the ritualised sanitisation of the Second World War can be heard in Dylan Thomas's ambivalent elegies 'A Refusal to Mourn the Death, by Fire, of a Child in London' and 'Among Those Killed in the Dawn Raid Was a Man Aged a Hundred', from his important collection *Deaths and Entrances* (1946).

These poems balk at the process by which violence is falsely translated into some complacent official narrative of redemption. Both Douglas and Thomas express an aversion to the official rituals of remembrance and commemoration whereby death is expediently covered over by national imaginings.

Angus Calder's study of *The Myth of the Blitz* (1992) illustrated the rapidly diminishing returns of the 'mythification' of 1940 in post-war British culture. Calder's aim was not so much to debunk the myth, in the way that Clive Ponting sets out to in *1940: Myth and Reality* (1990).[14] In some respects, the myth of 'their finest hour' is actually true, Calder acknowledges: Britain did resist fascism, and Hitler did not invade. Obviously, the myth is radically selective: inconvenient facts such as Churchill's responsibility for the disastrous Norway campaign, the British bombing of German cities, or the fact that Britain did not fight alone in 1940 but did so with the aid of American arms and money and with the practical assistance of an entire empire and of exiled Polish, Czechoslovakian, and French forces are 'unmythworthy'[15] and must therefore be forgotten or downplayed. '1940' is not a lie so much as a myth, in Roland Barthes's sense, a heroic narrative purged of its complexities that nonetheless shapes the experiences of its adherents.[16] It had right-wing versions of national and imperial renewal. There were left-wing versions that fed projects of anti-fascist struggle and socialist reconstruction. For example, the wartime propaganda films that Humphrey Jennings made with the Crown Film Unit, such as *Fires Were Started* (1943), *Listen to Britain* (1942), *A Diary for Timothy* (1945), and *The Silent Village* (1943), emerged from the English modernist milieu of the 1930s. The montage techniques that juxtapose their disparate images of England (or Wales) and their emphasis on cooperation and on the skill of ordinary workers and service people owe a lot to the GPO Film Unit's 1936 film *The Night Mail* (with words by Auden and music by Benjamin Britten). Calder's aim is to show how these struggles over the meaning of '1940' have been resolved by an outsized and simplified version of '1940' that has held subsequent generations in thrall.

Calder shows that, over time, this myth became more imperialist and nationalist in nature, though alas he was wrong that Margaret Thatcher's appropriation of the paradigm weakened it. It has actually been immeasurably strengthened in the years since and now looms oppressively, as we have been arguing, as a kind of origin myth of the modern British nation. Another text that anatomises this myth, one that deserves to be better known, is the socialist historian Patrick Wright's *The Village that Died for England*. Wright's study, first published in 1995 and recently reissued, tells the detailed story of the requisitioning by the army of a South Dorset village in 1943 and Tyneham's strange aftermath as a symbol of postwar Labour governments' supposed betrayal of the patriotic community in the shape of decolonisation, immigration, social equality, and European integration. 'Thanks to its posthumous cult, Tyneham became emblematic of the wider cultural syndrome, endemic in post-war Britain, that leaves its victims unable to grasp the modern world except through allegorical fables of malign encroachment.'[17] These paranoid fantasies of infiltration continue to imprison our political imaginations. But as we have seen, works of literature that interrogate these noxious oppositions between natives and invaders, contest reactionary definitions of 'the people' and their enemies, or simply deflate the complacent mythologising of the modern British nation's founding myth of heroic defiance might help us 'grasp the modern world' very differently. Then the peoples of Britain might stop daydreaming about the past and imagine a future, cease hunting for traitors and intruders, and look in the mirror for the source of the nation's many problems. They might recognise that diversity is not a threat but a source of strength and solidarity.

We do not think so-called Brexit novels, or what Kristian Shaw too glibly calls 'Brexlit', have yet managed to do these things.[18] We have not opted to read recent Brexit novels as such, that is, texts that explicitly address the vote to leave the European Union, such as Ali Smith's *Autumn* (2016), Jonathan Coe's *Middle England* (2018), or Ian McEwan's *The Cockroach* (2019). In our view, there is something rather jejune about these works. However well-intentioned their efforts to depict the 'two nations' of Brexit Britain, they tend to flatten out various complexities (social, economic, cultural, regional, etc.) in favour of liberal plaints about Leavers and Remainers not listening to each other. Even Coe's *Middle England*, with its veritably Dickensian host of characters and eccentric perspectives, sticks like glue to its middle-class milieu, though in fairness, it does not profess to be doing anything else. There is a brief walk-on role for a young Muslim woman and her daughter who use foodbanks. Socialists are represented by a surly millionaire's daughter, called Coriander, who is obsessed with imaginary transphobic microaggressions. This is a comic pre-history of the fateful year of 2016, when the Humpty Dumpty of national unity supposedly fell off the wall, a condition-of-middle-class-England novel that, like all the king's horses and all the king's men, desires in vain to put things back together again. But Coe's novel has no real understanding of Britain's deeper divisions and no better solution to them than its trite final image of the imminent 'Brexit baby' of reunited Remain-voting Sophie and her Leave-voting husband, Ian.[19] *Middle England* is at least candidly aware, like the young art historian Sophie when she visits Hartlepool for a friend's wedding, of a 'powerful feeling that she did not understand this place, that she had no sense of the life it contained'.[20]

Let us end, then, with a simple plea for literary works about Britain that convey *a sense of the life it contains*. We want to underline the forms of critique, resistance, and anticipation that literary texts engender even and perhaps especially when dominant national imaginings seem to be most unshakable. Nationalism is by no means on the retreat. To the contrary: across the globe, a form of militant nativism or national populism is the standard ideology of conservative movements. Escalating economic crises reinforce the grievances of the groups and classes that have something to lose, leading to rearguard assertions of exclusively defined national communities. Global warming is likely to intensify the tendency towards beggar-thy-neighbour nationalism, possibly including new forms of eco-fascism. The climate emergency will intensify the temptation to respond to large movements of populations with assertions of sovereignty, fantasies of ethnic purity and border walls, a possible future already explored by John Lanchester's *The Wall* (2019) and Mohsin Hamid's *Exit West* (2017). We stand in urgent need of the kind of alternative perspectives that, we hope to have demonstrated, are often opened up by literary texts: perspectives on more provisional and inclusive forms of national identity, on ethical and political connections across national boundaries, on forms of democratic localism, and on other kinds of identity and experience that complicate the certainties of group belonging.

Now might be the time to reveal that the three of us have, for nearly 20 years, been teaching a second-year undergraduate course at the University of Manchester called Writing, Identity, and Nation that looks at how British and Irish writing after around 1900 explores national identity. We have found that the most interesting and the most productive texts to teach have been those with the most loose ends, those that raise the most questions, or simply those that provoke the most extensive discussions. Many of those texts are discussed in these pages. We calculate that more than 2,000 students have taken this course in its various incarnations. No party line has ever been imposed on it, except to lay down the hypothesis that literary texts help, as we have said, to construct, deconstruct, and reconstruct national identity, particularly the vexed forms of national identity that have prevailed on these isles. Britain and Britishness are at once peculiarly persistent and oddly vacuous: projects and identities that came into being in the process of colonial expansion, with attendant forms of sexual, racial, gender, class, and regional partiality, that have survived and even been revived long after their hollowness and uselessness should have been apparent. The implicit task the texts discussed in this study set us is to dismantle those identities and projects or, as it were, to break them up like beached and rusty cargo ships. What emerge from those texts and what has always arisen from our discussions with students over the years is a new appreciation of the exciting complexity and diversity of these isles that deserve new forms of cultural and, we hope, ultimately, political expression.

Notes

1 David Olusoga, *Black and British: A Forgotten History*, London: Pan Books, 2016, p. 15.
2 Fintan O'Toole, *Heroic Failure: Brexit and the Politics of Pain*, London: Head of Zeus, 2018, p. 52. The most compelling recent rejoinder to the Churchill cult is Tariq Ali's *Winston Churchill: His Times, His Crimes*, London: Verso, 2022.
3 David Edgerton, *The Rise and Fall of the British Nation: A Twentieth-Century History*, Harmondsworth: Penguin, 2019, p. 26.
4 Owen Hatherley, *The Ministry of Nostalgia*, London: Verso, 2016.
5 Richard Seymour, *Against Austerity: How We Can Fix the Crisis They Made*, London: Pluto Press, 2014.
6 C. J. Sansom, *Dominion*, London: Pan Books, 2013, p. 379.
7 Sansom, *Dominion*, p. 238.
8 See Michael Gardiner, 'The 1980s and 1990s', in *The Edinburgh Companion to Twentieth-Century Scottish Literature*, eds. Ian Brown and Alian Riach, Edinburgh: Edinburgh University Press, 2009, pp. 181–92.
9 Scott Hames, 'Democracy and the Indyref Novel', in *Scottish Writing After Devolution: Edges of the New*, eds. Marie-Odile Pittin-Heddon, Camille Manfredi and Scott Hames, Edinburgh: Edinburgh University Press, 2022, pp. 81–103.
10 Raymond Williams, 'Culture is Ordinary', in *Resources of Hope: Culture, Democracy, Socialism*, London: Verso, 1989, pp. 3–18.
11 Owen Sheers, *Resistance*, London: Faber & Faber, 2007, p. 177.

12 Howard Brenton, *The Churchill Play: As it Will Be Performed in the Winter of 1984 by the Internees of Churchill Camp Somewhere in England*, London: Eyre Methuen, 1974, p. 12.
13 Keith Douglas, *Complete Poems*, ed. Desmond Graham, Oxford: Oxford University Press, 1978, p. 74.
14 Clive Ponting, *1940: Myth and Reality*, London: Ivan R. Dee, 1993.
15 Angus Calder, *The Myth of the Blitz*, London: Pimlico, 1992, p. 106.
16 Roland Barthes, *Mythologies*, trans. Annette Lavers, London: Vintage, 1993, p. 143.
17 Patrick Wright, *The Village that Died for England: Tyneham and the Legend of Churchill's Pledge*, London: Repeater, 2021 [1995], p. 77.
18 Kristian Shaw, *Brexlit: British Literature and the European Project*, London: Bloomsbury, 2021.
19 Jonathan Coe, *Middle England*, Harmondsworth: Penguin, 2018, p. 421.
20 Coe, *Middle England*, p. 368.

Index

Adorno, Theodor 33, 71
Agamben, Giorgio 142, 163
Agnew, Vijay 169
Akala 13
Ali, Monica 137, 139; *Brick Lane* 140–1, 148, 152–8
Allinson, Adrian 61
Amoko, Apollo 134
Anand, Mulk Raj 46
anarchism 49–50, 109
Anderson, Benedict 11, 19–20; *Imagined Communities* 13
Anderson, Perry 4, 6, 21n14, 22n23, 92; 'Nairn-Anderson thesis' 5–7
anti-colonialism 49–50
Arendt, Hannah 70, 133n45
Armstrong, Paul B. 35, 55
Arts Council 114
Ashcroft, Bill 160–1
Ashcroft, Richard T. 141, 143, 177n21
Aslam, Nadeem 158
asylum 135, 158–9, 162, 163
Attlee, Clement 75–6
Auden, W.H. 4, 62, 69; *Night Mail* 61, 189
Austen, Jane 4, 19
Azoulay, Ariella Aïsha 19

Baden Powell, Robert 29
Bangladesh 147, 154, 156–7
Bank of England 90
Banks, Aaron 9
Barker, Pat 46
Barthes, Roland 189
Battle of Cable Street 65
Beatles, The 108
Beckett, Samuel 11, 119
belonging 5, 13, 45, 99, 110, 113, 135–6, 138–40, 143–5, 148, 151, 157, 163, 166, 170, 172, 174–5, 191; unbelonging 147, 150, 162
Bengal/ Bengali 43, 150, 157
Bengal Famine 76
Benjamin, Walter 63
Bennett, Alan: *Alleluja!* 11–12; *Forty Years On* 28
Bentley, Nick 97–8, 139, 154
Bernard Shaw, George 27
Bevir, Mark 141, 143, 177
Bhabha, Homi: hybridity 137; *The Location of Culture* 137; mimicry 137, 156
bildungsroman 32, 60, 154, 156
Billington, Michael 119
Black Britons 5, 95, 97, 102–4, 108, 152
Blair, Tony 153–4
Blatchford, Robert 50
Blunt, Scawen Wilfred 49, 65
Boehmer, Elleke 27, 41, 43, 128–9
Boland, Eavan 113
borders 2, 13, 18, 45, 49, 70, 75, 90, 104, 111–13, 117, 135, 142, 159, 163, 174, 190
Bose, Subhas 171
Boyle, Danny 73
Bradshaw, David 37
Brah, Avtar 166, 169–70
Brannigan, John 14, 53
Brecht, Bertolt 122
Brennan, Timothy 34
Brenton, Howard 188
Brexit 5, 9–10, 12, 15, 60, 116, 135, 139, 142–5, 168, 172–4, 185–6; Brexit novels 189
Brittain, Vera 46
Britten, Benjamin 61, 118
Britishness 2–3, 13–14, 17–18, 91–2, 95–6, 104, 113, 128–31, 135–6, 144–5, 148, 151–3, 173, 191

Index

British Museum 41
British Nationality Act, 1948 95
British theatre 114–28
Brierly, Walter 64–5
Brockway Fenner 71, 88n215
Brontë, Charlotte 18
Brontë, Emily 18
Brooke, Rupert: 'The Old Vicarage, Grantchester' 31; 'Peace' 44; 'The Soldier' 44
Brown, George Mckay 183–4
Buchan, John 30
Buck, Clare 45
Bunting, Basil 13
Buchan, John 62
Burdekin, Katherine 69, 184
Burgess, Anthony 129
Burton, Richard 58
Butler, Judith 124–5
Byron, Robert 56–8, 73

Calder, Angus 189
Callaghan, James 93
Campaign for Nuclear Disarmament 117
capitalism 3, 6, 18, 31–4, 50, 59, 70, 91, 96, 117, 121–2, 126, 136; British capitalism 8–9, 21, 116; 'print capitalism' 13
Care Collective, The 20
Caribbean 3, 8, 9, 28, 60, 66, 69, 94, 99; Caribbean immigrants 15, 97, 100
Caribbean Voices 71
Carpenter, Edward 51, 65
Caswell, Catherine 62
Cassin, Barbara 158
Catholicism 67
Cavafy, C. P. 45
Césaire, Aimé 70
Chamberlain. Joseph 76
Chambers, Claire 158
Chaucer, Geoffrey 110, 156
Christie, Agatha 69
Churchill, Caryl 96, 114, 124–8
Churchill, Winston 28, 47, 120, 185–6, 188, 189, 191n2
citizenship 2, 12, 139, 142, 163, 170
Civil War, The English 6
Clark, T. J. 35, 63–4
Clays, Gregory 84
Clean Air Act, 1956 99
Coe, Jonathan 190
Colley, Linda 7, 21n20
Colls, Robert 15–16
Colston, Edward 10

Commonwealth 76–7
Commonwealth Immigration Acts *see* immigration
Communist Party of Great Britain 50, 58
Conan Doyle, Arthur 99
Condition-of-Empire Novels 31–40
Connor, John 45
Conrad, Joseph 18, 42; 'Amy Foster' 30; *Heart of Darkness* 39; *The Secret Agent* 30
Conservative Party 49, 60, 107; Tory-Lib Dem coalition 185; Tory Party Monday Club 107
Constantine, Learie 65
Compton Burnet, Ivy 69
coronavirus 1
Cottrell-Boyce, Frank 73
Crawford, Robert 61
Crinson, Mark 63
Cunard, Nancy 72; *Authors Take Sides on the Spanish Civil War* 69; *Negro Anthology* 70
Cundy, Cath 145

Darwin, John 8
Das, Santanu 46–7
Davies, Norman 4, 8, 21n8
Dawson, Graham 46
decolonisation 135
Defoe, Daniel 59, 101
Deighton, Len 184
democracy 112
Denning, Michael 14
Derbyshire, Delia 13
diaspora 166, 169
Dickens, Charles 18, 31, 99, 156, 188
Dilke, Charlies 4, 30
Documentary Film Movement 60
Dobbernack, Jan 146
Douglas, Keith 188–9
Du Bois, W. E. B. 28, 71
Dudrah, Rajinder 170–1
Du Maurier, Daphne 69
Dutt, Rajani Palme 50
Dyer, Rebecca 67
Dylan, Bob 163–4

Eagleton, Terry 42
Edgar, David 130
Edgerton, David 1, 9, 90, 113
Eliot, George 18
Eliot, T. S. 27, 66–7; 'The Hollow Men' 39; *The Waste Land* 28, 56, 99, 129

Index

Empire 28, 30, 33, 37, 40, 50, 70–1, 75, 158; British Empire 6, 10, 13, 15–19, 25–7, 29, 34, 44–5, 49, 52–3, 60–7, 71–8, 129, 141; British Empire Exhibition 51, 60; 'Empire Day' 60; Empire Marketing Board 60–1; end of British Empire 90–8, 105–6, 108–9, 114–28, 131, 145, 147
England/ English people 1, 3–4, 8, 11–16, 18, 24–5, 30, 31, 34, 37, 40, 42, 48, 51, 57, 63–9, 72, 75, 94, 96, 99, 104–30, 157, 184–90
Englishness 11, 15, 16, 18, 24–5, 30, 53, 64–6, 74, 139, 176
English Review, The 31
Esty, Jed 66, 75, 129–30
Etherington, Thomas 41
European Union 10–11
Evaristo, Bernadine 183

Farage, Nigel 9
Farrier, David 162
Faye, Shon 22n31
fascism 59, 70, 130–1; British Union of Fascists 65, 133n43 (*see also* Oswald Mosely); British fascism 107–8, 133n43; Francisco Franco 69 (*see also* Spanish Civil War); Nation Forward 130
Featherstone, Simon 144
Feminism 93, 125
First World War 44–7; Gallipoli 45; post-war period 47–9, 69
Fletcher, C. R. L. *A History of England* 29
Fleming, Ian 14–15
Foot, Paul 94–5
Forbes, Claire 146
Fordham, John 64–5
Forster, E. M. 15–16, 42, 45, 49, 61, 68, 73, 77; 'The Abinger Pageant' 68; *Howards End* 16, 31, 35–8; *Letter to Timothy* 73; 'The Machine Stops' 35; *Maurice* 16, 35; *A Passage To India* 54–6, 59, 87n195
Fortier, Anne Marie 143, 146, 148, 151
Fowler, Corinne 66, 144
Freud, Sigmund 126
Fry, Michael 122
Fryer, Peter 48, 95
Fabianism 27, 29, 52
Fine Romanow, Rebecca 3
Flanagan and Allen 73
Fussell, Paul 56

Galsworthy, John 29
Gandhi, Mohandas 46, 62, 65, 166, 170–1
Gandhi 170–1
Garvey, Amy 71
Gasiorek, Andrzej 77
Gaugin, Paul 59
Georgians 31
General Post Office Film Unit 61, 72, 189
General Strike of 1926 65, 110–11
Germany 91
Gibson, Sarah 162
Gilroy, Paul 94, 139, 150–1, 165
Gissing, George 33
Glendinning, Victoria 52
Glorious Revolution 7
Glover, David 30
Golding, William 129
Gollancz, Victor 64
Goodfellow, Maya 95
Gopal, Priyamvada 21n21, 27, 71
Gowan, Peter 8–9
Grahame, Kenneth 29
Grassic Gibbon, Lewis 62
Great Depression 63, 73
Green, J. R. 29–30
Greene, Graham 67, 129
Greenslade, William 68
Grierson, John 61
Griffiths, Peter 110, 132
Gurnah, Abdulrazak 137, 142, 183; *Afterlives* 46; *By the Sea* 140–2, 152, 157–63; *Paradise* 46

Haggard, H. Rider 162
Hall, Catherine 25
Hall, Stuart 109–10, 130
Hamid, Mohsin 142, 190
Harding, J. M. 128
Hardy, Thomas 18, 30–1, 156
Harlem Renaissance 48
Harman, Claire 60
Hartley, Anthony 90–1
Harvey, David 121, 132
Hatherley, Owen 168
Hazeldine, Tom 8
Head, Dominic 147, 151
Helff, Sissy 162
Hennessey, Peter 90
Henty, G. A. 161
Heritage 152, 153, 154
Hess, Myra 73
Hewit, Roger 139–40, 176n12–7n17
Hicks, Dan 21
Hitler, Adolf 131

Hilton, Jack 64
Hobson, J. A. 33
Hoggart, Richard 129
Høgsbjerg, Christian 72
Holtby, Winifred 66
Horkheimer, Max 71
'Hostile environment' 100, 103, 144, 153, 185
Housing 105, 158
Housman, A. E. 30–1
Howe, Stephen 84
Hua, Anh 169

immigration 3, 5, 92, 94–5, 106, 116, 135, 138, 141, 147, 153, 128, 175, 185; anti-immigration 1, 9, 107, 109, 116, 120–1, 129, 130, 173–4; Commonwealth Immigration Acts 95, 107, 107; *see also* asylum and refugee
imperialism 3, 26, 60, 76, 92, 130, 145, 148
India 8, 53, 57, 62, 165, 167–8; 1857 Uprising 54; Indian National Congress 65; partition 76; colonial 104; post-First World War 106
Industrial Workers of the World union 79n15
integration 135, 138, 153
Iran 58
Ireland: Republic of 4, 5; Irish writing 184; Northern 93
Irish Home Rule Bill 49
Ishiguro, Kazuo 183
Islam: Islamic art 57; British Muslims 146–7, 153, 174; mediatisation 146–7, 175–6
It Happened Here 184

James, C. L. R. 65–7, 72, 144; *The Black Jacobins* 71; *Toussaint Louverture* 70–1
James, Henry 31, 42, 99
James, Winston 50
Jameson, Fredric 37, 42
Jameson, Storm 65, 69
Jenkins, Roy 153
Jennings, Humphrey 184; *Fires Were Started* 73, 189; *Letter to Timothy* 73, 189; *Listen to Britain* 72–3, 189
Jones, David 44
Jones, Lewis 28
Joyce, James 28, 56

Kerr, Douglas 73–4
Keynesian economics 130

Kipling, Rudyard 25, 27–8, 42, 66, 76–7, 130, 161; *Actions and Reactions* 25; 'The Destroyers' 34; *A Diversity of Creatures* 44; *A History of England* 29; 'The Lesson' 29; *Jungle Books* 29; *Puck of Pook's Hill* 29; 'The Return' 24–5, 29; 'The Recall' 25; *Rewards and Fairies* 29; 'Sun of the Suburbs' 43–4
Klaesson, Carin 159–60
Knudsen, Britta Timm 152
Koestler, Arthur 91
Kritzer, Amelia 125
Kumar, Krishnan 98
Kundnani, Arun 153
Kureshi, Hanif 77

Labour Party 49–51, 53, 65, 71, 95, 100, 116, 141
Ladoo, Harold Sonny 100
Lalwani, Nikita 137; *Gifted* 140–1, 152, 155, 159, 163–72
Lamming, George 130
Lanchester, John 144, 190
Lawrence, D.H. 40, 46; *The Daughter-in-Law* 29; 'England, my England' 43; *The Rainbow* 5, 18, 38–40; *Women in Love* 43
Lawrence, Stephen 139
Lawrence, T. E. 45
League of Nations 45, 56, 70
Leavis, F. R. 38
Le Carré, John 129
Lefebvre, Henri 32
Lenin, Vladimir 50, 84n112
Lessing, Doris 130
Levy, Andrea 60, 148
Lewis, Alun 188
Liberal Party 49, 140, 185
Light, Alison 69
Lindsay, Jack 65
Lodge, David 32
London 63; City of London 1, 3, 8–9, 91, 93; postcolonial London 104
Love Thy Neighbour 102
Lowry, L. S. 63–4
Luckhurst, Mary 128
Lukács, Georg 32
Lynn, Vera 117

MacDiarmid, Hugh 62
MacDonald, Graeme 121–2
MacDonald, Ramsay 53
MacInnes, Colin 129

MacKenzie, John M. 60
MacPhee, Graham 15, 75, 100–1, 148, 150
Macpherson Inquiry Report 139
Maczynska, Magdalena 153
Madox Ford, Ford 31
Major, John 74
Majumdar, Nivedita 175
Malaya 76
Malik, Kenan 146
Manchester Museum 41
Mao, Douglas 26–7, 78n6
Masterman, Charles 34
Markandaya, Kamala 5, 96; *The Nowhere Man* 101–10
Marshall, H. E. 29–30
Mason, Una 71
May, Theresa: 'citizens of nowhere' 108; 'hostile environment' 100, 185
McEwan, Ian 190
McKay, Claude 47–9, 71; 'England' 48–9
Meer, Nasar 146
Meiksins Wood, Ellen 8
Melville, Herman 160–1
Mendez, Paul 100
McClintock, Anne 3
McGrath, John: *The Cheviot, The Stag, and the Black, Black Oil* 96, 121–4
McGregor, Jon 184
McLeod, John 100, 136, 144–5
Miliband, Ralph 21n15, 96
Milligan, Spike 102
Mishra, Pankaj 10
Mishra, Sudesh 165, 169–70
Mitchell, Peter 10
Mitchinson, Naomi 69
Mitford, Unity 57
Mittelholzer, Edgar 100
modernism 26–7, 28, 34, 63; Scottish modernism 62
Modood, Tariq 146
monarchy 2
Montague, C. E. 47
Moore, Jason W. 19
Morel, E. D. 47–8
Morris, William 51, 65, 115
Morton, A. L. 65, 84
Morton, H. M. 64
Morton, Stephen 154–5
Mosely, Oswald 57, 65, 106
Muir, Edwin 62, 64
Muir, Willa 62
multiculturalism 100, 130, 135, 138, 140, 148–9, 151–5

Nairn, Tom 2, 4, 6; *The Break-Up of Britain* 1, 5, 6, 13, 113–4, 131; 'Nairn-Anderson thesis' 5–7
Nasta, Susheila 143, 166
nationalism 10–12, 15, 17, 57, 61–2, 94–6, 114, 117, 131, 136, 172; British nationalism 7, 18, 121, 183; Scottish nationalism 6, 62; Welsh nationalism 93
National Council for Civil Liberties 73
National Front 107
National Parks 66
Nazism 59, 69–70, 72, 185–6
Nehru, Jawaharlal 46, 62
Newns, Lucinda 161–2
neoliberalism 95–6, 155; *see also* Thatcherism
New Left Review 5–6
New Statesman, The 117
Niven, Alex 11–13, 119
Nixon, Rob 173, 182n155
Noble, Denise 132

Okri, Ben 141
Olivier, Laurence 72, 119
Olusoga, David 93–4, 183
Orwell, George 25, 61, 64, 69, 72–3, 78n1, 117
Osbourne, John: *Déjàvu* 118; *The Entertainer* 5, 96, 118–21; *Look Back in Anger* 96, 118–21
O'Toole, Fintan 22n35, 116, 185
Owen, Nicholas 84
Owen, Wilfred 44

Padmore, George 52, 70–2
Pan-Africanism 70
Pan-African Congress 28, 72
Pan-African Federation 72
Pankhurst, Sylvia 48, 49
Parry, Benita 34
Patel, Raj 19
Patel, Ian Sanjay 95
Phillips, Caryl 144, 183
Pincus, Steven 6
Pinter, Harold 114
Pittock, Murray 62
Ponting, Clive 189
Pound, Ezra 49
Powell, Enoch 93–5, 102, 103, 109, 114, 117, 132n19; 'Rivers of Blood' speech 93, 104–6, 167, 186
Powell, Michael 72
Powys, Cowper John 68
Powys, T. F. 68

Prebble, John 124
Pressburger, Emeric 72
Priestly, J. B. 114, 117; *English Journey* 11, 64; *Summer Day's Dream* 5, 96, 114–5
primitivism 40–3
Pratt, Marie Louise 137, 162

queer 3, 4, 16, 18, 35–6, 56, 59, 67–9, 75, 92, 100; kinship 127; liberation 15, 51, 93

racism 26, 69, 92, 94, 95, 100, 108–9, 131, 148, 153, 166–7, 173; anti-racism 49–50, 93
Rahbek, Ulla 163–4
Raychaudhuri, Anindya 168–9
Reader, Luke 53
realism 99; socialist realism 58
refugee 135, 142, 158–9, 162–3, 167
Reid, Jimmy 93
Reynolds, Reginald 71
Rezaie, Ali 154
Rickword, Edgell 65
Riley, Charlotte Lydia 3
'Rivers of Blood' speech *see* Powell, Enoch
Roediger, David 128
Roberts, Kate: *The Awakening* 96, 113–4
Roberts, Michael
Robeson, Paul 65, 70
Rose, Sonya 25
Rosenberg, Isaac 44
Ross, Alex 133–4n59
Rothman, Benny 65
Roy, Arundhati 130
Royle, Nicholas 36–7
Rushdie, Salman 10, 135, 137, 151; *Imaginary Homelands* 138, 171; *Midnight's Children* 145–6; the Rushdie affair 146; *The Satanic Verses* 137, 146

Said, Edward W. 162; *Orientalism* 18–19, 40, 74
Salkey, Andrew 100
Samuel, Raphael 65, 76
Sampson, Anthony 90–1
Sanson, C. J.: *Dominion* 184–6
Sartre, Jean-Paul 63
Schreiner, Olive 43, 65
Schwarz, Bill 75–6
Schofield, Camilla 94–5, 132
Scott, Paul 55
Scott, Walter 124
Scottish Arts Council 123
Scottish history 121–3

Scottish independence 22
Scottish National Party 11, 22n34, 186
Second South African War 29–30, 43, 76
Second World War 141, 150; poetry 188; reconstruction 90
Seeley, John 25
Sellar, W. C. 65
Selvon, Sam 5; *The Lonely Londoners* 97–103; *Moses Ascending* 101–3, 116; *Moses Migrating* 103–4
sexuality 28, 42, 68, 75, 77, 91, 100; Britishness and sexuality 96, 128; heterosexuality 36, 128; homosexuality 48, 69, 126, 174; imperialism 125–6; performance of 35, 126; sexual liberation 126
Shaffer, Brian W. 15
Shakespeare, William 19, 101, 114–16
Shamsie, Kamila 137, 183; *Home Fire* 140–3, 146–7, 152, 172–6
Shanks, Michael 90, 131n6
Shaw, Kristin 142, 173–4, 189
Sheers, Owen 184, 187–8
Sherry, Vincent 27
Shiel, M. P. 30, 79
Shklovsky, Viktor 96, 132
Sinfield, Alan 91
slavery 3, 8, 10, 59, 75, 94
Slobodian, Quinn 96
Smith, Ali 190
Smith, Zadie 77, 108, 137, 144; *White Teeth* 138–41, 147–50, 153, 176
Snaith, Anna 42, 52
Snow, C. P. 91
Sommerfield, David 65
Sophocles 172
Soviet Union 50
Spanish Civil War 69
Spencer, Robert 173
Stevenson, Robert Louis 59
Stone Roses, The 13
Streit, Clarence K. 72
Suez Canal Crisis 118–21
Sykes, Christopher 56
Sykes-Picot Agreement 45, 56

Tancke, Ulrike 148–9, 152
Tanzania 158–9
Taylor, A. J. P. 17, 90
Tagore, Rabindranath 42–3, 61–2, 170
terrorism 135, 153, 174, 175; 7/7 143, 153; 9/11 142, 146; War on Terror 142
Thatcher, Margaret 74, 93, 141, 189
Thatcherism 94, 95–6

Thomas, Dylan 61, 188–9
Thomas, Edward 44
Thomassen, Lasse 140
Thompson, E.P. 8, 53
Tolkien, J. R. R. 117
Torrance, David 51
transgender 22, 128
transport 64
Tressell, Robert 29
Trinidad 99, 103
Tuńska, Wiktoria 139
Tynan, Kenneth 118
Tyndall, John 107

Uganda 167
United Kingdom 4, 9
United Nations 140; UHCR 159

Vertovec, Steven 163
Vaughan Williams, Ralph 35, 41, 80n40, 101, 116
Viswanathan, Gauri 33, 156, 180n100

Wales 184, 187
Walkowitz, Rebecca L. 26–7
Ward, Stuart 75
Warner, George Townsend 33
Warner, Sylvia Townsend 46, 58–60; *The Flint Anchor* 59–60; *The Kingdom of Elfin* 58; *Lolly Willowes* 58, 68; *Mr Fortune's Maggot* 59; 'My Shirt is in Mexico' 59
war on terror *see* terrorism
Waugh, Evelyn 66, 69; *Brideshead Revisited* 66

Webb, Beatrice 52, 66
Webb, Sidney 51–2, 66
Welch, Denton 68
Wells, H.G. 27–8; *Ann Veronica* 32; *Experiment in Autobiography* 31; *A London Symphony* 34; *Tono-Bungay* 31–4, 36, 38
West, Alick 64
whiteness 125, 128
Whittle, Matt 129–30
Windrush 97–8
Wilde, Oscar 115
Wilkinson, Ellen 65
Williams, Raymond 4, 17–18, 26, 66, 73, 130, 133, 187; *Border Country* 96, 110–3
Wilson, Edmund 27
Wilson, Peter 52
women's suffrage 46
Wood, Lucy 184
Woolf, Leonard 52, 73
Woolf, Virginia: *Between the Acts* 52, 68; *Mrs Dalloway* 46, 65, 129; *The Voyage Out* 52; *Women and Labour* 43
Worrell, Rodney 52
Wright, Patrick 189

Yeatman, R. J. 65
Yeats, W. B. 43

Zapata, Perez 147, 150
Zenner, Walter P. 165
Zola, Émile 33
Zornado, Joseph L. 29